The Historian's Heart
of Darkness

Recent Titles in The Historian's Annotated Classics

The Historian's Huck Finn: Reading Mark Twain's Masterpiece as Social and Economic History
Annotated by Ranjit S. Dighe

The Historian's Narrative of Frederick Douglass: Reading Douglass's Autobiography as Social and Cultural History
Edited by Robert Felgar

The Historian's Heart of Darkness

Reading Conrad's Masterpiece as Social and Cultural History

ଓଃ୫ଠ

EDITED BY
MARK D. LARABEE

The Historian's Annotated Classics
Ranjit S. Dighe, Series Editor

 PRAEGER™

An Imprint of ABC-CLIO, LLC
Santa Barbara, California • Denver, Colorado

Library of Congress Cataloging-in-Publication Data

Names: Larabee, Mark Douglas, 1964- author. | Conrad, Joseph, 1857-1924.
   Heart of darkness. | Conrad, Joseph, 1857-1924. Congo diary.
Title: The historian's Heart of darkness : reading Conrad's masterpiece as social
   and cultural history / edited by Mark D. Larabee.
Description: Santa Barbara : Praeger, 2018. | Series: The historian's annotated
   classics | Includes bibliographical references and index.
Identifiers: LCCN 2017028292 (print) | LCCN 2017038429 (ebook) |
   ISBN 9781440851070 (ebook) | ISBN 9781440851063 (hardcover : alk. paper) |
   ISBN 9781440851087 (pbk. : alk. paper)
Subjects: LCSH: Conrad, Joseph, 1857-1924. Heart of darkness. | Psychological
   fiction, English—History and criticism. | Africa—In literature. | Colonies in literature.
Classification: LCC PR6005.O4 (ebook) | LCC PR6005.O4 H4776 2018 (print) |
   DDC 823/.912—dc23
LC record available at https://lccn.loc.gov/2017028292

ISBN: 978-1-4408-5106-3 (hardcover)
      978-1-4408-5108-7 (paperback)
      978-1-4408-5107-0 (ebook)

22 21 20 19 18   1 2 3 4 5

This book is also available as an eBook.

Praeger
An Imprint of ABC-CLIO, LLC

ABC-CLIO, LLC
130 Cremona Drive, P.O. Box 1911
Santa Barbara, California 93116-1911
www.abc-clio.com

This book is printed on acid-free paper ∞
Manufactured in the United States of America

ೞ೩ಐ
Contents

Series Foreword   vii

Preface   ix

Chronology   xv

Chapter 1. Joseph Conrad: Observer of Empire   1

Chapter 2. *Heart of Darkness* as Witness to History   13

Heart of Darkness (with "Author's Note")   43
by Joseph Conrad, with Annotations by Mark D. Larabee

"The Congo Diary"   151
by Joseph Conrad, with Annotations by Mark D. Larabee

Bibliography   163

Index   169

⊂ℜ⋈

Series Foreword

Most if not all literature is historical, in the sense of reflecting its time and place and the history behind them. Even science fiction and fantasy literature tends to extrapolate from the present, which, like a patient, has a history of its own. Works from previous eras take on an additional historical dimension, as they were written in a time with which we are personally unfamiliar.

While great works of literature are timeless, we can often enjoy them more by knowing more about their historical setting and the by-now-obscure references they sometimes make. This is where Praeger's Historian's Annotated Classics series comes in. The literary classics selected for this series are accompanied by annotations and new essays that highlight their historical context and continuing relevance.

Ultimately, this series is about connecting each book to crucial historical issues of its time. Novels, biographies, and other literature of a time are indispensable markers of what people of that time said and thought. Thus this series should be ideal for people with a strong interest in history—students, history teachers, history buffs. The books in this series can also be valuable supplementary texts that add spice to college and advanced high school classes. The history often becomes more vivid when seen through the lens of an enduring literary work from that era.

The Historian's Heart of Darkness is a stellar addition to this series. Joseph Conrad's novella is already compelling, even to readers oblivious to its historical context. Coupled with Mark Larabee's comprehensive annotations, it offers a splendid introduction to late-19th-century African and European history, colonialism, imperialism, and myriad other topics. Re-reading the novella with Larabee's annotations is an eye-opening experience. Larabee's introductory chapters tell engaging stories of their own. The first presents Conrad's remarkable life, notably his merchant marine career that gave him firsthand exposure to Belgium's brutal colonization of the Congo Free State. The second augments the history lesson with a balanced, insightful treatment of the controversial subject of European imperialism in the tropics. Period photographs, lithographs, and drawings make the book more expansive still.

Ranjit S. Dighe
Professor of Economics
State University of New York at Oswego

❧
Preface

The words "heart of darkness" seem to be everywhere: the phrase has appeared in thousands of newspaper articles alone in the last few decades. Early readers of Joseph Conrad's *Heart of Darkness* (first published in 1899) could see in its pages a devastating indictment of European exploitation in Africa. Since then, these words have been used to describe not only the Congo that Conrad saw on his 1890 river journey, but also the Congo after independence; the 1999–2003 civil war in Liberia; and terrorism in Iraq, Afghanistan, and Syria today.[1] Yet "heart of darkness" has also appeared in articles on drug violence in Mexico, the 1977 New York City power blackout, and college basketball rivalry.[2] The widespread use of the story's title suggests how striking these words are to many people who may have only heard of *Heart of Darkness* and have not yet read it. How did this phrase become so evocative? The answer lies in the richness and acute insight of Conrad's tale. Moreover, the fame of its title indicates how much this masterpiece deserves to be studied for its specific historical and cultural value.

Within *Heart of Darkness* intersect many crucial themes of European and world history that run through the last two centuries: civilization, exploration, colonialism, imperialism, great-power rivalry, racial difference, trade and globalization, commercial exploitation, the impact of changing technology, European dependence on foreign raw materials, and expanding networks of communication and transport. Most vividly, the book records the deeds of a government whose mass murders and other atrocities ultimately claimed some 10 million African lives, foreshadowing the later

---

1. *Wall Street Journal,* 18 January 2001; *New York Times,* 21 January 1996; *Wall Street Journal,* 28 September 2005; *The Christian Science Monitor,* 8 February 2010; *Wall Street Journal (Online),* 5 February 2014.

2. *Wall Street Journal (Online),* 16 March 2017; *Wall Street Journal,* 18 August 2003; *New York Times Book Review,* 2 April 2006.

deaths of tens of millions more in wars and under totalitarian regimes around the globe. Furthermore, Conrad's story brings these themes to life by illuminating their human consequences—their individual impact on the minds, bodies, and morals of the people who lived through what he portrayed. This edition is consequently designed to make students more knowledgeable not only of 19th- and 20th-century history but also of the vital—if perhaps paradoxical—role of the imagination in reconstructing and understanding reality.

Reading fiction can work wonders in a history class, as experienced teachers already know. Fiction can help give students a feel for the environment as it was lived by historical figures. Fiction fills in factual background and makes historical settings and episodes come alive in exciting, memorable ways. Fiction shows us what gets talked about, or not talked about, in the author's world. Moreover, fiction is especially good for illustrating the significance of point of view: identifying who is recording and sending historical information, and understanding how limitations and values are involved in that point of view. Yet literary scholars may justifiably claim that fiction goes beyond its historical circumstances. In this assessment, reading fiction merely as documentary evidence limits what it says. One can add, though, that the characteristics of fiction can also make it especially valuable as a vehicle for truth telling, as *Heart of Darkness* reveals in particular.

Given the literary qualities of *Heart of Darkness,* it is no wonder that it is perhaps the most frequently assigned modern short novel in college English classes. I have taught it with success in a wide array of such courses. However, just as *Heart of Darkness* lends itself well to many different English classes, it can enrich a range of history classes too—from introductory surveys to advanced seminars, such as ones on:

- British history
- European history
- African history
- 19th- and 20th-century world history
- Western civilization
- Colonialism and imperialism
- Exploration
- World trade and economics
- Globalization
- Trauma studies
- Slavery
- Genocide
- The philosophy of history

Because the story incorporates so many social and cultural themes and fits into so many courses, there can be no one-size-fits-all method for

ෆ෨ൟ
Preface

teaching it as history. Accordingly, I would offer a flexible approach based on six levels of reading, listed below in generally increasing order of complexity. Instructors can choose from (or combine) these levels depending on the amount of time available for *Heart of Darkness,* what other books are assigned, and the overall goals of the course. History students can read *Heart of Darkness* as:

(1) an embedding of historical facts about European colonialism in Africa;

(2) an interpretation of what one part of Africa looked like to one European visitor in 1890 in particular;

(3) a document that has a history of its own, in how it was read over time;

(4) a record of the lived experience of individuals and their mentalities—the set of values held by the author and his contemporary readers;

(5) a linguistic structure whose literary features play an important role in presenting reality; and

(6) an artifact of witnessing.

On each level, instructors can craft correspondingly suitable questions for study, discussion, or writing, such as:

(1) What facts about European and African history does the story bring to life? How does it illustrate the level of advances in transportation, medicine, and other technologies at the time? What does the story show us about such things as the behavior of Europeans in Africa, the conditions of the ivory trade, and daily life for Europeans and the natives? What are the social habits of the characters? What are the dilemmas that they face?

(2) In what ways is Conrad's background significant to his writing the story? How do the story's details concur with or differ from what we know of Congolese history? What does Conrad's fictional account omit from, add to, or change what he recorded in his "Congo Diary"? What characteristics of his Congo experience are thereby emphasized? Why might he have made such changes? What are the various points of view that the story presents?

(3) What does the history of the story's writing, publishing, and reception tell us about the social and cultural context of Conrad's time? What is it about this book that would lead to its connection to the movement that ended Leopold's rule? What can be gleaned from how this story fits into the rest of Conrad's life and writing? What do later controversies and responses to the story indicate about how history is remembered and interpreted?

(4) What do the story's details show us about Conrad's intended audience? Judging by what is included and left out, what would Conrad's

original readers have to know in order to make sense of the story? What can we infer about the assumptions and values of Conrad's intended readers, and what assumptions and values does Marlow or Conrad share with them? What do the reactions of Conrad's readers tell us about their own concerns and biases and their understanding of current events, politics, culture, and history?

(5) What particular words and images recur in the story, and what becomes emphasized by the patterns formed? What does the story show us about the limits of spoken and written language in understanding and describing historical truth? How do allusions to such things as dreams, the passage of historical time, and the unreal reflect the experience of reality? What do the story's mood and descriptions of the setting illustrate about the historical Congo and Europe? What might Kurtz's appearance, actions, and dying words signify? How does he represent all of Europe? Why does Marlow lie to Kurtz's fiancée?

(6) How is our understanding of Marlow's experience shaped by the fact that he is telling us a survival story? How have Marlow and Conrad been shaped or changed by what Conrad underwent? What morals and values of Marlow's and Conrad's are revealed or challenged by Conrad's experience? Conrad and Marlow are not identical; how are they different? What do the similarities and differences between them tell us about the nature of survival, witnessing, and memory?

The scholarship on *Heart of Darkness* is vast; there is far too much to offer a survey of it here. As a start, instructors preparing courses and students doing supplementary reading can benefit from the following resources:

1. Biography: Zdzisław Najder, *Joseph Conrad: A Life*.
2. General introduction to Conrad's life and works: John G. Peters, *The Cambridge Introduction to Joseph Conrad*.
3. Colonial African history: Thomas Pakenham, *The Scramble for Africa*.
4. Leopold's rule over the Congo: Adam Hochschild, *King Leopold's Ghost*.
5. Conrad in his historical context: Norman Sherry, *Conrad's Western World;* Allan H. Simmons, "Africa" and "Nationalism and Empire."
6. Conrad and colonial history: Christopher GoGwilt, "Joseph Conrad as Guide to Colonial History."
7. Dates of events in Conrad's life: Owen Knowles, *A Conrad Chronology*.
8. Reference encyclopedia on Conrad's life and works: Owen Knowles and Gene Moore, *Oxford Reader's Companion to Conrad*.

However, this edition is designed to be a stand-alone text. Readers will find in this book the background necessary to see how *Heart of Darkness* both sprang from its historical and cultural contexts and shaped those contexts in turn. Chapter 1 surveys Conrad's life and outlines his Congo River journey of 1890. I focus on how his upbringing, his career in the British merchant service, and his powers of observation and writing combined to make him a uniquely qualified chronicler of the social and cultural history of colonialism and imperialism.

Chapter 2 begins with the exploration and partitioning of Africa and the founding and running of the Congo Free State under King Leopold II of Belgium. I describe the ivory and rubber trades, how Conrad came to write *Heart of Darkness* as news of atrocities began to seep out, and the role that the story played in awakening European awareness of conditions in the Congo. I discuss Conrad's thinking about race and empire, as well as ensuing controversies surrounding the book. The chapter goes on to discuss the relations between fact and fiction in the story, the problems of representing atrocity, and how the literary qualities of *Heart of Darkness* form an essential part of its historical meaning.

The text of *Heart of Darkness* includes extensive annotations that illuminate the links between the story and its contexts, discuss how Conrad shaped historical facts for his fictional portrayal, and explain special terms. Throughout this chapter and the previous ones, images depict the Congo as Conrad saw it, and as his readers would have understood it, along with maps and portraits. Conrad's "Author's Note," added in 1917 to a collected edition that included his fictional tale, appears at the end of *Heart of Darkness*.

"The Congo Diary" is a transcription of the diary that Conrad kept on the overland part of his journey, also annotated. This document is important and useful in a number of ways. First, comparing "The Congo Diary" with historical records highlights what Conrad considered worth noting and omitting when writing his diary. What this European observer found significant about the historical Congo tells us key things about both the observer and his particular circumstances. Second, the dated entries of Conrad's diary give us his observations with unvarnished immediacy, while *Heart of Darkness* was begun eight years later and presents an image of Africa filtered by Conrad's memory. He wrote the diary for his private reference, while he shaped the fictional story for a public audience. Thus, how the two accounts overlap and differ can help illustrate the nature of witnessing and memory under extraordinary conditions, as well as the uses of storytelling in portraying historical truth.

Conrad's imaginative vision of Africa came out of a historically specific place and time, as this edition is designed to illustrate. However, as the ubiquity of the phrase "heart of darkness" amply proves, this story also goes far beyond that place and time. Readers will see how *Heart of Darkness* is also increasingly relevant for understanding such features of our own world as contemporary globalization, how colonialism led to enduring conflicts, and how cruelty and suffering persist in the 21st century— right up to today's headlines.

Chronology

Date	Key Events in European and Central African History	Key Events in Joseph Conrad's Life
1482	Portuguese explorer Diogo Cão discovers mouth of the Congo River	
1807	Slave trade abolished in British Empire	
1834	Slavery abolished in British Empire	
1848	Slavery abolished in French colonies	
1853–1856	British missionary and explorer David Livingstone crosses Central Africa and discovers Victoria Falls	
1857		Józef Teodor Konrad Korzeniowski born in Berdyczów, western Ukraine (3 Dec), only child of Apollo Korzeniowski and Ewa Korzeniowska (*née* Bobrowska)

Date	Key Events in European and Central African History	Key Events in Joseph Conrad's Life
1858	British explorers Richard Burton and John Speke discover Lake Tanganyika; Speke discovers Lake Victoria	
1861		Korzeniowskis move to Warsaw
early 1860s	Leopold begins searching for colonies for Belgium	
1862		Parents sentenced to exile in Vologda, Russia, and take their son with them
1863		Family transferred to Chernikhiv, northeastern Ukraine
1865	Accession of Leopold II, King of the Belgians	Ewa Korzeniowska dies
1866	Livingstone sets out on his third African expedition, searching for the source of the Nile	
1868		Apollo Korzeniowski and son move to Lwów
1869	Henry Morton Stanley commissioned by the *New York Herald* to find Livingstone	Apollo Korzeniowski and son move to Cracow
		Apollo Korzeniowski dies; Ewa's brother Tadeusz Bobrowski becomes Józef Korzeniowski's unofficial guardian
1871	Livingstone discovers the Lualaba River, to the west of Lake Tanganyika	
	Stanley begins search for Livingstone in Zanzibar and finds him at Ujiji, on Lake Tanganyika	

Date	Key Events in European and Central African History	Key Events in Joseph Conrad's Life
1873	Livingstone dies in what is now Zambia	
1874		Leaves Poland for Marseilles for training in the French merchant service
1874–1875		Makes voyages to the Caribbean as passenger, and then ship's boy, on the *Mont-Blanc*
1876	Leopold hosts Geographical Conference in Brussels	
	Leopold forms the International African Association	
1876–1877		Sails to the Caribbean as steward on the *Saint-Antoine*
1877	Stanley descends the Lualaba, discovering the course of the Congo River and arriving at Boma on the Atlantic Coast	
late 1870s	Dutch, German, and Portuguese traders have trading posts established on the Lower Congo near the Atlantic Coast	
1878	Leopold forms the Committee for Studies of the Upper Congo	Decides to join the British Merchant Marine; Sails from Marseilles to the Sea of Azov and finally Lowestoft, England, as unofficial apprentice on the British steamer *Mavis*

Date	Key Events in European and Central African History	Key Events in Joseph Conrad's Life
		Makes three voyages between Lowestoft and Newcastle as ordinary seaman on the coasting schooner *Skimmer of the Sea*
1878–1879		Sails from London to Sydney and back as ordinary seaman on the wool clipper *Duke of Sutherland*
1879	Leopold forms the International Association of the Congo	
1879–1880		Voyages from London to the Mediterranean and back as ordinary seaman on the steamship *Europa*
1879–1884	Stanley explores the then-unclaimed Congo River basin for Leopold	
1880–1881		Sails from London to Sydney and back as third mate on the sailing ship *Loch Etive*
1881–1882	Stanley founds Léopoldville	Sails from London for Bangkok as second mate on the sailing ship *Palestine* (which catches fire and sinks off Sumatra); reaches Singapore and returns to London as a passenger
1883–1884		Sails from London to Madras as second mate on the sailing ship *Riversdale*
1884	USA, France, and Germany recognize Leopold's claim to establish "independent States" in the Congo	Sails from Bombay to Dunkirk as second mate on the sailing ship *Narcissus*

Date	Key Events in European and Central African History	Key Events in Joseph Conrad's Life
1884–1885	West Africa Conference held in Berlin	
1885	Leopold establishes the Congo Free State Stanley publishes *The Congo and the Founding of Its Free State*	
1885–1886		Sails from Hull to Singapore, returning via Calcutta to Dundee, as second mate on the sailing ship *Tilkhurst*
1886	Force Publique formally constituted	Becomes naturalized British subject
1886–1887		Sails from London to Penarth as second mate on the sailing ship *Falconhurst*
1887	Stanley begins expedition in Africa for the relief of Emin Pasha Surveying for Matadi-Léopoldville railway begins	Sails from Amsterdam to Java as first mate on the sailing ship *Highland Forest;* injured on the voyage and recuperates in Singapore
1887–1888		First mate on the iron steamer *Vidar;* makes four trips between Singapore and ports in the Netherlands East Indies
1888–1889	Société Anonyme Belge pour le Commerce du Haut-Congo formed	As master of the sailing ship *Otago,* his only permanent command, sails from Bangkok to Sydney; makes round-trip voyage from Australia to Mauritius before resigning command and returning to England

Date	Key Events in European and Central African History	Key Events in Joseph Conrad's Life
1889	Leopold convenes Anti-Slavery Conference at Brussels	Begins writing his first novel, *Almayer's Folly* (Nov) Meets with Albert Thys in Brussels
1890	(Mar) Construction of Matadi-Léopoldville railway begins (Apr) Stanley given hero's welcome in Brussels on his return from Africa George Washington Williams's letter to Leopold on Congo atrocities distributed in Europe and the United States	(Feb) Returns to Brussels and visits his cousin Aleksander Poradowski and wife, Marguerite Poradowska (Feb–Apr) Visits relatives in Poland and Ukraine (Apr) Passes through Brussels on the way back to England; learns that he is appointed to command the SAB steamer *Florida* in the Congo (10 May) Departs from Bordeaux for Africa on the steamer SS *Ville de Maceio* (12–13 June) Arrives at Boma, then Matadi; in Matadi, he meets Roger Casement (28 June–2 Aug) Overland journey from Matadi to Kinshasa; in Kinshasa, learns that the *Florida* has been damaged (3 Aug–1 Sep) Upriver journey from Kinshasa to Stanley Falls on the steamer *Roi des Belges* (7 or 8 Sep) Departs downriver from Stanley Falls on the *Roi des Belges,* with sick Company agent Georges Antoine Klein aboard (21 Sep) Klein dies and is buried ashore at Tchumbiri

Date	Key Events in European and Central African History	Key Events in Joseph Conrad's Life
		(24 Sep) Arrives at Kinshasa and leaves the *Roi des Belges*
		(Nov–Dec) In Matadi
		(Dec) Leaves Africa
1891		(by 1 Feb) Arrives in London
		(Feb–Apr) Convalesces at German Hospital, Dalston, London
		(May–June) Convalesces at spa in Champel-les-Bains (on the outskirts of Geneva)
		(Summer) Makes two trips in Thames Estuary in G. F. W. Hope's yawl *Nellie*
1891–1893		Makes two round-trips from London to Adelaide as first mate on the sailing ship *Torrens*
1893–1894		Sails from London to Rouen and back as second mate on the steamer *Adowa*
1894		Uncle Tadeusz Bobrowski dies
		Completes *Almayer's Folly*
		(Aug–Sep) In poor health, returns to Champel-les-Bains for hydrotherapy
1895	Mutiny of Force Publique soldiers at Luluabourg	Publishes *Almayer's Folly* under the pen name Joseph Conrad
1896	Leopold appoints Commission for the Protection of the Natives	Writes "An Outpost of Progress" and publishes *An Outcast of the Islands*
		Marries Jessie George; settles in Stanford-le-Hope, Essex

Date	Key Events in European and Central African History	Key Events in Joseph Conrad's Life
1897	Mutiny of Force Publique soldiers in northeast Congo World's Fair in Brussels includes living display of 267 Congolese natives	Meets Henry James Sails again with G. F. W. Hope on the *Nellie* "An Outpost of Progress" published Meets Stephen Crane *The Nigger of the "Narcissus"* published
1898	Matadi-Léopoldville railway completed	Son Borys born *Tales of Unrest* published Meets Ford Madox Ford, with whom he collaborates on writing *The Inheritors* Conrads move to Pent Farm, Kent; H. G. Wells lives nearby (Dec) Begins writing *Heart of Darkness*
1899	Boer War begins	Receives literary prize for *Tales of Unrest* (Feb–Apr) "The Heart of Darkness" published in magazine form
1900	Edmund Morel publishes articles exposing conditions in West Africa	*Lord Jim* published
1901	Morel quits work at Elder Dempster	*The Inheritors* published Collaborates with Ford on *Romance*
1902	Boer War ends	(Nov) *Heart of Darkness* published in Britain in a volume with "Youth" and *The End of the Tether*

Date	Key Events in European and Central African History	Key Events in Joseph Conrad's Life
1903	(May) British Parliament passes Congo protest resolution; Foreign Office directs the British Consul in the Congo Free State, Roger Casement, to investigate the interior and send a report on conditions there	(Feb) *Heart of Darkness* published in USA in a volume with "Youth" and *The End of the Tether* *Typhoon and Other Stories* and *Romance* published
1904	(Feb) Casement report reveals atrocities in the Congo Free State Morel and Casement found the Congo Reform Association in Britain Morel helps found the American Congo Reform Association (June) Congo atrocities debated in British House of Commons Morel publishes *King Leopold's Rule in Africa*	Jessie Conrad injures her legs in a fall; she will become permanently disabled *Nostromo* published
1906	Morel publishes *Red Rubber* President Roosevelt announces cooperation with Britain in pressuring the Belgian government to take control of the Congo Free State	Son John born *The Mirror of the Sea* published
1907		*The Secret Agent* published Moves to Someries, a farmhouse in Bedfordshire

Date	Key Events in European and Central African History	Key Events in Joseph Conrad's Life
1908	Congo Free State officially transferred to Belgium and made a state colony	*A Set of Six* published
1909	Leopold II dies	
1910		(Jan–May) After finishing *Under Western Eyes,* suffers mental and physical breakdown; confined to bed for two months
		Moves to Capel House, a farmhouse in Kent
1911		*Under Western Eyes* published
1912		*A Personal Record* and *'Twixt Land and Sea* published
1913	Britain recognizes the Congo as a Belgian colony	
	Congo Reform Association holds final meeting	
1914	World War I begins	*Chance* published in book form: his first popular success
1915		*Within the Tides* and *Victory* published
		Son Borys joins the British Army
1917		*The Shadow-Line* published
1918	World War I ends	
1919		*The Arrow of Gold* published
		Moves to Oswalds, a house near Canterbury, his final home
1920		*The Rescue* published

Date	Key Events in European and Central African History	Key Events in Joseph Conrad's Life
1921		*Notes on Life and Letters* published
		Collected editions of his works begin publication in Britain and America
1923		(May–June) Makes promotional tour in America, visiting New York and New England and giving a public reading from *Victory*
		The Rover published
1924		(May) Declines offer of knighthood
		(3 Aug) Dies of a heart attack
		(7 Aug) Buried at Canterbury, England
		The Nature of a Crime and *Laughing Anne & One Day More* published
1925		*Tales of Hearsay* and *Suspense* published
		"The Congo Diary" first published
1926		*Last Essays* published

CHAPTER 1

❦

Joseph Conrad:
Observer of Empire

The facts of Joseph Conrad's birth did not foretell a life that would produce the most powerful critique of Europeans in Africa ever written in English. Józef Teodor Konrad Korzeniowski was born in 1857 to minor Polish gentry in what is now Ukraine. Berdyczów, his birthplace, is in a landlocked province, hundreds of miles from the nearest open water (the Black Sea). In that year, most of Africa was under native rule, and the center of the continent was still a forbidding mystery. English would not be his first or even his second language. Yet the unexpected twists and turns of his future would carry him around the globe and eventually into the deepest interior of the "Dark Continent." What he saw there would become, through the alchemy of his artistic imagination, the world's most vivid, enduring, and even controversial portrayal of European colonialism and imperialism. When he turned from sailing to writing, he published his fiction as Joseph Conrad. Conrad's life was a remarkable journey from relative obscurity to fame, replete with worldwide travel, exotic ethnic encounters, and dramatic personal transformation. By the time he came to write about the Congo, his upbringing and careers as a sailor and writer had combined to make him a uniquely perceptive, eloquent recorder of social and cultural history in the age of empire.

To begin with, his youth was shaped by the problems of a people living under foreign occupation. Poland had ceased to exist as an independent country in the late 1700s, when it was partitioned and annexed by Russia, Prussia, and Austria. A series of 19th-century Polish insurrections against Russian rule culminated in the January Uprising of 1863–1865. His father, Apollo Korzeniowski, was a devoted nationalist involved in secret plans for the insurrection. Arrested in 1861 for criminal activity against Russian rule, Apollo spent seven months imprisoned in the Warsaw Citadel. Then, convicted of seditious activity, he was sentenced to internal exile. Apollo, along with his wife and son, were sent first to Vologda, northeast of Moscow and nearly 800 miles away.

Adding to Conrad's memories of oppressive imperial rule, his lonely life of exile became marked by personal tragedy. After seven months in Vologda, the family was transferred to Chernikhiv (in northeastern Ukraine). In Chernikhiv, the family was beset by financial difficulties, and the health of both parents declined. Conrad's mother, Ewa, died in 1865 when he was seven years old. Apollo, suffering from tuberculosis, was allowed to resettle. Father and son moved next to Lwów and then Cracow, where Apollo died in 1869.

During his short but intense years with his father, Conrad absorbed and developed language skills that would prove crucially important in his future. His father translated Shakespeare, Hugo, and Dickens; wrote patriotic and religious poetry, and comedies in verse (Knowles and Moore 2000, 192); contributed social and political articles to newspapers; served as secretary of a company publishing educational books; and founded a biweekly literary and cultural journal (Najder 2007, 17). The young Conrad, an avid reader, burrowed into the classics. His reading included Victor Hugo and Shakespeare, Polish Romantic poetry, and travel literature and sea stories (Najder 2007, 27). At age eleven, he wrote plays on patriotic themes and had memorized long stretches of works by Adam Mickiewicz, Poland's national poet (Najder 2007, 33). Conrad's childhood exposure to the riches of language went beyond his native Polish. In his youth he also heard other languages being spoken, such as Russian, Ukrainian, Yiddish, and possibly also Ruthenian dialects (Knowles and Moore 2000, 196). His schooling included Latin, German, and Greek (Najder 2007, 46–47). He later claimed to be able to read French at the age of five and to have read a great deal of French literature by the age of ten (Knowles and Moore 2000, 196–97).

Exploration and geography sparked his imagination and became a lifelong interest. Many years later, he wrote in *A Personal Record* (1912), "It was in 1868, when nine years old or thereabouts, that while looking at a map of Africa of the time and putting my finger on the blank space then representing the unsolved mystery of that continent, I said to myself with absolute assurance and an amazing audacity which are no longer in my character now: 'When I grow up I will go *there*'" (Conrad 2008b, 26). In 1923 Conrad again looked back at how he had been captivated in his childhood by tales of African explorers—such as Mungo Park and James Bruce, who had explored Sudan and Ethiopia, respectively, in the 18th century. Conrad described how, in the late 1860s, he "laboriously" drew the outline of Lake Tanganyika into his "beloved old atlas." Published in 1852, the book had only a blank space where Richard Burton and John Speke found the Great Lakes of Africa in 1858. "The heart of its Africa was white and big," Conrad reflected, as he recalled his boyhood dreams of filling in that space by making his own geographical discoveries (Conrad 2010a, 12).

In the meantime, Conrad continued to explore languages and cultures in the first years after his parents' deaths. Left in the care of his family and friends in 1869, he had a surrogate father and unofficial guardian in Tadeusz Bobrowski, his maternal uncle. Conrad was sent to Switzerland for medical care in 1873, in what turned out to be a 12-week excursion including Northern Italy, Munich, and Vienna (Najder 2007, 43). Having for some time read sea literature by such authors as Frederick Marryat and James Fenimore Cooper, and expressing a desire to follow a life at sea, he received permission from Bobrowski to go to Marseilles for maritime training in 1874, leaving at age 17 (Najder 2007, 42, 44–45). Over the next three years, he sailed in two French ships on three voyages to the Caribbean, first as a passenger and then as a ship's boy and a steward (Knowles and Moore 2000, 346, 348). Thanks to these experiences, as an adult he spoke and wrote French fluently, skills that would later serve him well among French-speaking Europeans in the Congo Free State.

At this point, the circumstances of Russian imperialism intervened to change his life, dramatically extending his multicultural experiences. The matter of his citizenship was a special concern now that he was entering his adult years. He could not work in the French Merchant Marine service without a valid passport, but Russian authorities would not give him one. Also, he was liable to be drafted into the Russian army as a consequence of his father's involvement in revolutionary activities. On Bobrowski's advice, he sought a different naturalization route, ultimately joining the British Merchant Service even though he spoke no English then (Peters 2006, 2).

He learned this new language—his third—from the crews of over a dozen British merchant ships in which he sailed from 1878 to 1894. Furthermore, he heard a variety of other languages, both from foreigners among his shipmates and in the parts of the world he visited. At the same time, he encountered a wide range of foreign cultures. As an unofficial apprentice on the steamer *Mavis* (1878), he sailed from Marseilles and called at Malta, Constantinople, Kerch (in the Crimea), and Yeysk (on the Sea of Azov) before returning to England at Lowestoft. As an ordinary seaman on his next ship, the schooner *Skimmer of the Sea* (1878), he followed a coastal route between Lowestoft and Newcastle. On the clipper *Duke of Sutherland,* he embarked on a one-year round-trip from London to Sydney (1878–1879). The *Europa,* an iron steamer, showed him Italian and Greek ports on a Mediterranean voyage (1879–1880). As third mate on the square-rigged sailing vessel *Loch Etive,* he made another round-trip between London and Sydney (1880–1881). His next voyage, as second mate on the wooden bark *Palestine* (1881–1882), proved an ordeal. After departing from London and loading coal at Newcastle, she stopped at Falmouth for repairs and then left for Bangkok. Along the way, the cargo caught fire from spontaneous combustion, resulting in an explosion that forced the crew to abandon ship off Sumatra. He was brought to Singapore and made his way home as a passenger via the Suez Canal (Knowles and Moore 2000, 346, 348–49).

His succeeding ships showed him more of the East, and in the company of non-British shipmates. (In his time, foreign sailors—many from the Scandinavian countries—made up about 15 percent of the crews of British merchant ships, the proportion being higher on the long-distance routes [Najder 2007, 99; Cornewall-Jones 1898, 269–73; Brassey 1877, 37].) On the *Riversdale,* a full-rigged sailing ship, he traveled from London via South Africa to Madras, India, where he disembarked and then joined the *Narcissus* in Bombay (1883–1884). On the *Narcissus,* another full-rigged sailing ship, he returned to Europe among a crew that included seven Scandinavians (1884) (Najder 2007, 99). A succession of Eastern voyages ensued: on the *Tilkhurst,* Conrad saw Penarth, Singapore, Calcutta, St. Helena, and Dundee (1885–1886). After five days on the *Falconhurst* from London to Penarth he joined the *Highland Forest* as first mate in Amsterdam for a voyage to Java, winding up in Singapore to recover from an injury (1887). On the steamer *Vidar,* he called at Singapore and ports in Borneo and Celebes during four voyages in the Netherlands East Indies (1887–1888). From Singapore, he sailed to Bangkok as a passenger to take command of the *Otago,* whose master had died at sea. Returning to Singapore on that ship, he subsequently voyaged to ports in Australia and Mauritius (1888). The *Otago* would be his only permanent command and his last ship before leaving for the Congo, having accumulated a decade of experience sailing among the most distant ports and peoples a Briton could know, let alone a naturalized Polish former subject of Russia. (He became a British subject in 1886.) Hearing these foreign voices and seeing these non-European peoples enhanced Conrad's cosmopolitanism, whose seeds were already sown by his unusual upbringing.

During these voyages, Conrad also became exposed to the raw materials and global distribution systems of colonialism and imperialism, which would later underpin his understanding of the ivory trade in Africa. In the two decades of Conrad's sea career (1874–1894), Britain's share of worldwide maritime commerce, and the absolute quantity of various kinds of merchandise, both grew at a rapid pace. The portion of world cargo carried by British ships to the United Kingdom rose from 59 percent in 1855 to a peak of 73 percent in 1890. Meanwhile, in roughly the same period the worth of British foreign trade increased nearly 500 percent, while the tonnage cleared in homeports rose by more than 700 percent (Kirkaldy 1914, 337–39, app. 2, app. 17).

Ships on the routes that Conrad followed carried a rich variety of cargos, through which Conrad learned firsthand about networks of imperial ties and colonial goods. From India to England, raw materials such as rice, wheat, tea, coffee, cotton, silk, jute, and ores flowed from that colony to the imperial center. In return, iron, coal, steel, salt, cement, textiles, machinery, and manufactured goods went to the subcontinent and to the Cape Colony. Wool, wheat, metals, ores, timber, and cattle products came to Britain from Australia. Indian Ocean routes, such as the one Conrad sailed between Mauritius and Melbourne, brought sugar, vanilla, rum, coconut oil, and aloe fiber into the Australian colony. British ships carried metals, textiles, and opium on long-distance routes to China. On local routes, such as within the Netherlands East Indies, ships circulated raw materials, foodstuffs, textiles, manufactured goods, tin, and general cargo (Larabee 2010, 51–52). Furthermore, the opening of the Suez Canal in 1869 and the replacement over time of steam ships for sailing vessels combined to reduce transit times and increase the reliability, safety, and flexibility of trade routes and practices. These advances helped make the global patterns of maritime trade a surer foundation for the colonial network and imperial control.

After 16 years of his seagoing career, a single journey up the Congo River in 1890 became the pivotal experience of his lifetime. The cause of this voyage was his need for a new seagoing billet. He had resigned his position as master of the *Otago* in the spring of 1889 at Port Adelaide, Australia, for reasons that are still unclear. He returned to London in May as a passenger via the Suez Canal, living on savings, some income from his share in the shipping firm Barr, Moering & Co., and possibly also pay for working at the firm's office (Najder 2007, 134). By that fall he was looking for a job. First he sought command of a ship in an Antwerp-based firm, on their trading line with New Orleans and the West Indies. He was then recommended to a ship broker in Ghent named Baerdemaecker, who then turned to Albert Thys, managing director of a Belgian trading company, the Société Anonyme Belge (SAB) pour le Commerce du Haut-Congo (the Belgian Limited Company for Trade in the Upper Congo) (Najder 2007, 138). The SAB had been founded the year before, in 1888, for the purpose of organizing and administering a trade monopoly in the Congo Free State—a European dependency, established in 1885, that for all practical purposes was a private colony under the direct rule of King Leopold II of Belgium (Najder 2007, 145–46).

Baerdemaecker asked Thys: could Conrad be given a job in Africa? It seems to have been a matter of chance that Africa should be Conrad's destination, and anyway he had no other prospects at the time. However, he could very well have had his interest piqued not only by his childhood wish to go to Africa, but also by the dramatic news from that continent regarding the exploits of the famous explorer Henry Morton Stanley (Najder 2007, 138). Stanley was then leading an expedition to come to the aid of Emin Pasha, the German-born governor of equatorial Egyptian Sudan, who was threatened by the Mahdist uprising. Based on the introduction that Baerdemaecker gave him, Conrad traveled to Brussels in the first half of November 1889 to meet Thys, who drew a favorable impression of him (Najder 2007, 138). However, weeks went by without a decision.

While Conrad was waiting for word on this job prospect, in early 1890 he left England to visit his uncle Tadeusz Bobrowski and other relatives in Poland and Ukraine. Along the way, he stopped at Brussels on 5 February to see some distant relatives, his cousin Aleksander Poradowski and his wife, Marguerite. Aleksander died two days after Conrad's arrival, and the relationship that Conrad established with Marguerite would become a crucial element in his becoming a writer and in preserving factual details about his trip to the Congo. Marguerite Poradowska was herself an accomplished author, having written her own fiction and translated literature from Polish (Najder 2007, 139). Conrad addressed her as his "aunt"; the two became correspondents, and the letters that have survived record a good deal of what we know about Conrad's African journey.

While in Brussels, Conrad learned from the Company that he would have to report there, in Brussels, at the end of April 1890 for the forthcoming job (Najder 2007, 140). He continued on to Poland and Ukraine for his extended visit to relatives. After a 10-week visit, he passed again through Brussels in late April on his return home, seeing Albert Thys there once more. He learned the grisly news that Johannes Freiesleben, the master of one of the Company's steamships (the *Florida*), had been killed by natives, and Conrad would take his place. Suddenly, the long waiting for word from the Company turned into haste, as Conrad rushed between London and Brussels in preparation. He left London for Brussels on 6 May and continued to Bordeaux by train. There, he embarked on the steamer S.S. *Ville de Maceio,* which departed on 10 May bound for the Congo Free State (Sherry 1971, 12–13, 17; Najder 2007, 143–44).

The *Ville de Maceio* stopped at several ports on the African coast before arriving at the mouth of the Congo River the following month. On 12 June Conrad disembarked at Boma, the seat of the Congo Free State government, about 50 miles up the Congo River from the Atlantic. The next day he arrived at Matadi, the major port on the Lower Congo and the highest navigable point. From there he left on 28 June by the 230-mile overland route to Kinshasa, as the cataracts on the lower part of the river made it impassable. He arrived at Kinshasa on 2 August. In the meantime, the *Florida* had gone aground and been damaged, so Conrad instead continued upriver to Stanley Falls on a different steamboat, the *Roi des Belges* (*King of the Belgians*), under the command of another master (a Dane named Ludwig Rasmus Koch). They left Kinshasa on 3 August and arrived at Stanley Falls (now Kisangani) on 1 September—a passage of 1,000 miles. On probably 7 or 8 September they left Stanley Falls to return to Kinshasa (Knowles 2014, 20–21; Najder 2007, 159).

Conrad may have been in temporary command of the steamer on the return downriver, as Koch was sick. Another sick man aboard was a Company agent, Georges Antoine Klein, who died along the way on 21 September. Conrad arrived back in Kinshasa on 24 September and left the *Roi des Belges* there, having no prospects for a command of his own after all. He was ill himself, having suffered several bouts of fever while ascending the river and five days of dysentery in Stanley Falls. He was even more seriously ill after leaving the *Roi des Belges* in Kinshasa and continuing to the coast, evidently coming close to death from dysentery (Najder 2007, 162). There are gaps in his chronology at the end of 1890, but he was in Kinshasa on 19 October, in Matadi on 16 November and 4 December, and from there left for Europe by steamer (Knowles 2014, 22; Najder 2007, 161–62). He was in London by 1 February 1891, having returned from Africa via Brussels and another visit to Marguerite Poradowska (on whom he would model Marlow's aunt in *Heart of Darkness*) (Knowles 2014, 22).

He again sought a job, although he was still recovering from his African journey. One leg was swollen, and he found it difficult to walk. He spent the time from the end of February 1891 to the middle of April in a London hospital, undergoing treatment for neuralgia in one arm, gout, and recurrent malaria. He felt that his nerves were shattered, and he may well have been suffering from acute depression (Najder 2007, 166–68). To try a water cure in Switzerland, he left in mid-May for a spa near Geneva, where a stay of nearly a month was largely successful in restoring his health and spirits—if only temporarily so (Najder 2007, 170). After a summer of further recuperating in England, including sailing on a friend's yacht (the *Nellie,* owned by G. F. W. Hope), he accepted a new seagoing billet in November 1891. As first mate of the *Torrens,* a passenger clipper, he made two voyages between London and Adelaide via Capetown and St. Helena (1891–1893). Again as first mate on the *Adowa,* an iron steamer, he sailed from London to Rouen on a single round-trip (1893–1894). When he left the *Adowa,* he left his sea career entirely and turned full-time to writing fiction.

His move from sailor to writer had already begun a few years before, however, and Conrad's time in the Congo came during a crucial period of inner change. According to two close friends, "Conrad's Congo experiences were the turning-point in his mental life," something whose "effects determined his transformation from a sailor to a writer" (Garnett 1928, 8). The key project in this overlap period was his composition of *Almayer's Folly* (1895), begun before his trip to the Congo and finished afterward in 1894. He based the novel on four voyages to Borneo he had made in 1887, and he began writing it while on shore leave in London in 1889. While continuing to work on the manuscript intermittently, he carried it with him on his voyages, including up and down the Congo River. (He almost lost it in the river, in fact, on the return trip between Kinshasa and Léopoldville when the canoe he was traveling in overturned [Conrad 2008b, 27].)

During that time in the Congo, he also kept a private factual account of this trip in two leather-bound notebooks. The first, reproduced in this volume as "The Congo Diary," covers the period from 13 June to 1 August 1890, or from before his overland journey from Matadi, below the impassible Lower Congo River rapids, to his arrival at Stanley Pool, back on the river. In "The Congo Diary," Conrad describes the weather, terrain, and hardships of the caravan trip, along with his impressions of seeing wounded and dead natives in an otherwise depopulated countryside. He gave the label "Up-river book" to the second notebook, a river navigation guide that he clearly wrote for himself, with dated entries from 3 to 16 August 1890. During this time, the *Roi des Belges* traveled from Stanley Pool to Bangala (halfway to Stanley Falls), arriving on 19 August 1890. Thus his trip as a sailor was also as a writer, of both fiction and nonfiction, and on this voyage his powers of observation as a seaman and as an author mutually reinforced each other. As time went by, such details as those that he recorded in his "Congo Diary" would combine with other memories to produce *Heart of Darkness* at the end of the 1890s.

In the meantime, however, his fiction sprang from different geographical locations. First, it was his experiences in the East in the 1880s that furnished him with a storehouse of memories for fictional accounts based on his time at sea. He finished *Almayer's Folly* in 1894 and published it in 1895. In 1894 he began his second novel, *An Outcast of the Islands,* like *Almayer's Folly* set in the East Indies; it was published in 1896. The same year he began his novel *The Nigger of the "Narcissus,"* inspired by his 1884 voyage home from India on the ship of that name; this book appeared in 1897. That year, he also first published his story "An Outpost of Progress," which showed that his time in the Congo was working on his imagination. "An Outpost of Progress" is a satirical tale of two European ivory traders who meet disaster on the African coast, presenting skeptical themes about European colonialism that would reappear in *Heart of Darkness*.

Now permanently ashore, Conrad started a family. In 1894 he met Jessie George (1873–1936), who was working as a typist in London. Jessie was 16 years younger than Conrad and one of nine children of a deceased bookseller's assistant. The two married in 1896 and had two sons: Borys (1898–1978) and John (1906–1982). Conrad and his wife were devoted to each other, and Jessie was serious about playing a role as an author's wife. She served as Conrad's typist during their early years together, kept track of finished manuscripts, and ran the household as homemaker and cook. She also took care of Conrad, who tended toward nervous anxiety, capricious moods, depression, and hypochondria (Knowles and Moore 2000, 74).

The newlywed Conrads settled first in Stanford-le-Hope, a village in Essex near the Thames estuary, in 1896. From here Conrad continued his oldest friendship, that with G. F. W. Hope, and returned to boating with him on Hope's yacht the *Nellie*. (This is the boat that would reappear, under its own name, in the Thames estuary at the start of *Heart of Darkness*.) In 1897 the Conrads relocated nearby to Ivy Walls Farm, also in Essex. In October 1898, the family—now three with Borys—moved to Pent Farm, a farmhouse in Kent, which Conrad rented until 1907 (Knowles and Moore 2000, 160). Here he would write many of his most famous works. He also cultivated ties to other authors in a literary circle of friendships and collaborations, which included Stephen Crane, H. G. Wells, Ford Madox Ford, and Henry James.

Conrad began writing *Heart of Darkness* in December 1898, while working on his next novel (*Lord Jim,* based on his time in the East Indies). He finished the new African story quickly, by February 1899. It appeared in three parts in the monthly *Blackwood's Edinburgh Magazine* from February to April 1899. Soon it appeared in book form, along with "Youth" and *The End of the Tether,* in Britain in 1902 and the United States in 1903. Reviews at the time were generally positive if somewhat mixed, and in any case the story did not initially attract wide public attention (Knowles and Moore 2000, 154).

Likewise, Conrad's passage from seaman to storyteller was not easy. In 1899 his short story collection *Tales of Unrest* earned Conrad a literary prize (his only one), but many of his books did not sell well even if they attracted critical praise. He did not achieve commercial success as an author until much later, after publishing his novel *Chance* in 1914. This book was extraordinarily popular in the United States (selling 10,000 copies in the first week), and in England the novel garnered positive reviews and sold relatively well (Knowles and Moore 2000, 58). Yet both financial and medical problems plagued him throughout his writing life. He worried about his income from writing, which was his family's only means of support. His time in the Congo had traumatized his health; later, he suffered from gout, and he had a mental and physical breakdown in 1910. Despite these personal challenges, he published well over 100 novels, stories, essays, reviews, and other pieces before his death in 1924.

Throughout Conrad's writing, history forms the basis of much of his most important works. Real historical forces big and small, and their effects on people from many different walks of life, filled his fictional worlds. For example, *Lord Jim* (published in 1900, nearly simultaneously with *Heart of Darkness*) draws on a range of historical sources: from an English adventurer who became the first Rajah of Sarawak in 1841, to an 1880 maritime scandal involving a prematurely abandoned ship. Conrad's political novels followed a similar pattern of historical reworking. For the setting of his novel *Nostromo* (1904), Conrad created an imaginary country—an elaborately detailed, mythical South American republic named Costaguana—largely out of his historical reading of Spanish colonization. In *The Secret Agent* (1907), Conrad turned an attempted bombing

Joseph Conrad in 1916. (Reproduced by permission from the George Eastman Museum. Image is a digital positive from an original negative.)

of Greenwich Observatory in 1894 into a spy novel about anarchists set in a grittily realized London. Another political fiction, *Under Western Eyes* (1911), placed Russian exiles in Geneva, a city setting that Conrad meticulously recreated from his visits (Kirschner 1988; Knowles and Moore 2000, 134). There are many other examples of such fictional retellings of fact in his novels and stories.

Furthermore, his sea experiences had sharpened his tools of observation. Periodically during his first career, he underwent a series of exams in order to qualify for promotion to the next officer level in the merchant service. These exams involved memorizing detailed knowledge about seamanship, navigation, and cargo stowage and passing oral and written tests. To this list we can add the necessary sensitivity of any good seaman to the observable phenomena of winds and seas. In short, Conrad's time at sea gave him the tools and habits of careful observation that would stand him in good stead in the Congo—both as an observer of the world through which he traveled, and as a careful and deliberate chronicler of what he had seen, in both the nonfiction and fictional accounts that he would write.

Conrad's travels to distant parts of the world also heightened his sensitivity to racial, ethnic, and national differences. He was already attuned to such differences, having been raised as a Pole under Russian occupation, in a land of mixed Slavic and Russian ethnicity. To the end of his days, he carried "unforgettable" memories of one of the first Englishmen he saw (a pale-skinned hiker in Switzerland in 1873) (Conrad 2008b, 45) and a black man he encountered in Haiti not long after (Conrad 2016, 11). Not only did his ships' crews include sailors from different European countries, but also in his travels to Southeast Asia he encountered a mix of

Chinese, Malays, Indians, and peoples of native tribes under British and Dutch colonial rule.

As a result, a range of ethnic differences and colonial encounters filled his fiction. To cite just a few early examples, his trilogy of novels *Almayer's Folly* (1895), *An Outcast of the Islands* (1896), and *The Rescue* (begun 1896) are set in the East Indies and highlight the competition between British and Dutch imperialism there. *Lord Jim* features European characters among Arabs, Malays, Chinese, and Javanese. The plot of this novel moves among colonial ports in the Middle East, Indian Ocean region, and Southeast Asia: from British-held Aden on the Red Sea, at one end, to the Spanish colony of the Philippines at the other (Simmons 2014b, 190–92).

Even as a British subject settled in England, though, Conrad seemed somewhat out of place. While he became one of the greatest modern writers in our language, his spoken English was marked by grammatical errors and a strong foreign accent that lasted his whole life (Najder 2007, 256–57, 281). Many people in England thought that he was peculiar looking and that in his appearance and mannerisms he was foreign—even "Oriental" (Najder 2007, 207, 202, 543). He supported his adopted country nonetheless. Yet apart from that support, his attitudes about all of these national, racial, and ethnic differences are difficult to identify precisely, especially if we use his fiction as a guide—partly because it is not entirely clear to what extent his fictional characters and narrators reflect his own views.

Of all Conrad's works, *Heart of Darkness* has arguably had the furthest reach and influence in literature and culture around the world. It has inspired countless literary works, translations, and adaptations into other art forms. (*Apocalypse Now,* Francis Ford Coppola's 1979 film set in the Vietnam War, is only the most famous.) Its central story of a hero's harrowing journey into mystery, danger, and self-discovery has a timeless and placeless universal quality that is surely part of its enduring popularity. Yet this fictional tale also speaks to us eloquently about an undeniably specific time and place—even if through a kind of disguise, or under layers of doubt and uncertainty. *Heart of Darkness* shows us colonial Africa from the inside—or, perhaps more accurately, from an outsider's inside perspective. Such may be the most illuminating point of view that any of us can reach when we try to understand strange and alienating experiences.

Literary scholars may justifiably resist treating fiction as merely documentary evidence. Certainly, to read *Heart of Darkness* as a masterpiece of fiction involves a set of assumptions, procedures, and aims that necessarily differ from those used in this edition. However, the overlap of historical recounting and fictional storytelling in *Heart of Darkness* practically demands our attention. And for good reason: as the 20th and 21st centuries have worn on, bringing us greater horrors of war and genocide (eerily prefigured by Kurtz's dying words), readers have increasingly come to recognize how subtle and perceptive Conrad was as an observer of historical forces and human nature. *Heart of Darkness* stands as a signal example of how reading his fiction can be a surprisingly ideal way to enter the minds and hearts of people living through historical change. Conrad's early life and time in Africa positioned him to witness momentous changes affecting an entire continent, whose secret history—an appalling one— *Heart of Darkness* would bring to light.

CHAPTER 2

❦

Heart of Darkness
as Witness to History

"Before the Congo," Conrad once told one of his closest friends, "I was just a mere animal" (Jean-Aubry 1927, 1:141). To this day, the meaning of that statement remains something of a mystery. The man who heard it, Edward Garnett, concluded years later that his friend's youthful "generous illusions" had been "swept away" by the "sinister voice of the Congo with its murmuring undertone of human fatuity, baseness and greed," which "left him gazing into the heart of an immense darkness" (Garnett 1928, 8). Yet Conrad's first biographer, who also recorded the comment, interpreted it to mean that Conrad had never really thought about the meaning of his life, let alone the lives of others, up to that point (Jean-Aubry 1927, 1:141–42). Was it disillusionment, then, or enlightenment that he had undergone—or some enigmatic combination of the two? Even if Conrad exaggerated, something that he had encountered on his journey into the heart of Africa in 1890 had clearly awakened his consciousness, changing his self-understanding and sense of reality. He had witnessed something profound.

Heart of Darkness was the result of Conrad's witnessing. In his "Author's Note" (written two decades afterward) Conrad called the story, in his words, part of "the spoil I brought out from the centre of Africa, where, really, I had no sort of business." In this instance, "spoil" is a loaded and ambiguous term, for Conrad had based his charges against Belgian rule in the Congo on what he had described as Leopold's looting of the colony. Conrad's subtle, ironic use of this word exemplifies how, for many reasons, *Heart of Darkness* is a complex work that can be interpreted in many different ways, sometimes contradictory ones. Furthermore, the history of the Congo Free State is itself complicated as well as lengthy.

Consequently, the novella and its historical circumstances have sparked a huge amount of scholarly research—so in order to approach the topic, we must be selective. As a way in, this chapter treats reading *Heart of Darkness* as history by focusing on three dimensions: introducing the historical context that created Conrad's experience in the Congo; tracing how the story was read and how it influenced the history of Leopold's colony; and outlining specific techniques to read this fictional tale for its historical value today. For Conrad, the most melancholy aspect of his experience in the Congo was arguably how it dashed his boyhood dream of exploring the world's last blank space. First, then, we should step back in time to the Africa that Europeans knew in the years leading up to his momentous voyage.

1. "CURIOUS MEN GO PRYING INTO ALL SORTS OF PLACES": EARLY EXPLORATION OF THE "DARK CONTINENT"

As late as the middle of the 19th century, European knowledge of sub-Saharan Africa was still mostly limited to the coast. In 1482, the Portuguese explorer Diogo Cão had made landfall at the mouth of an immense river on the Atlantic coast, which would be named after the Kingdom of the Kongo, an African nation in present-day Angola. The wide estuary of the Congo River seemed promising as a route into the interior and whatever riches might be there, but the river remained largely unexplored for most of the next four centuries. First, impassable rapids blocked the way upstream. This huge river, second only to the Amazon in water flow, descends 1,000 feet in its last 220 miles to the sea, passing through narrow gorges and over 30 cataracts. Second, a rocky, broken terrain of ravines and cliffs surrounds the lower river. In this forbidding land, malaria, yellow fever, and other tropical diseases lay in wait for any European explorers hardy enough to try to get around the waterfalls. Eventually, Portugal, Spain, Britain, and France established a scattered presence around the African coast, but repeated attempts to find the source of the Congo by ascending it all met with failure.

Yet explorers continued to push into unknown territories elsewhere on the continent. In 1858–1859, Richard Burton and John Speke were the first Europeans to reach Lake Tanganyika (the world's longest freshwater lake) and Lake Victoria (the continent's largest lake) in East Africa. A decade later, fascinated Britons began to read sensational news from Africa about the colorful explorer Henry Morton Stanley, who was commissioned in 1869 by the *New York Herald* to find the Scottish missionary and explorer Dr. David Livingstone. Livingstone had been almost unheard of since 1866, when he had set out into the African interior in search of the source of the Nile. Stanley started from Zanzibar in early 1871. That fall he reached Lake Tanganyika, finding Livingstone and supposedly greeting him with the question, "Dr. Livingstone, I presume?" The two men were soon friends, and Stanley became famous. After Livingstone died in 1873,

"Stanley Cutting His Way Through the Dark Continent": ca. 1889 lithograph depicting Henry Morton Stanley on one of his African expeditions. (Library of Congress)

Stanley continued Livingstone's project of finding the source of the Nile and understanding the geographical nature of the Central African lakes. Stanley's epic travels there, from 1874 to 1877, won him further fame as he determined that Lake Tanganyika had no connection to the Nile. As he also discovered, the headwaters of a river to the west of the lake, the Lualaba, led not to the Nile but to the Congo. Finally, the river's source had been found, which Stanley proved when he descended the Congo and arrived at the Atlantic Ocean in 1877, to the wide acclaim of Europe.

Despite this dramatic series of discoveries, Stanley could not attract official British interest in further exploration and colonization of Africa. (The British were busy at the time with a crisis in the Middle East.) King Leopold II of Belgium, on the other hand, saw an opportunity; this monarch hungered after a colonial empire for his diminutive country. As a teenager in the 1850s, Leopold had demonstrated an obsession with the minutiae of commerce, to the bafflement of those around him (Hochschild 1999, 35). As a student, he was indifferent to most of his studies but was fascinated by the profits that Spain extracted from her colonies (Hochschild 1999, 37), and he took a notable interest in geography. Spurred on by an acquisitiveness that would mark his entire reign, Leopold cast about for a colony of his own.

2. "THE VILEST SCRAMBLE FOR LOOT": LEOPOLD II AND THE SCRAMBLE FOR AFRICA

Leopold had inherited great personal wealth, which he was willing to pour into creating a colonial empire. Yet he found to his dismay that most of the world had already been taken. Consequently, at one point he proposed buying a kingdom in Abyssinia; he also sought to buy lakes at the mouth of the Nile River, in order to drain them and make a colony out of the newly dry land (Hochschild 1999, 36). In the early 1860s, searching the world for land to take, he inquired about various other schemes: buying part of Argentina, claiming an island where the Uruguay and Paraná Rivers meet, acquiring Fiji, building railways in Brazil, and leasing land on Formosa (Hochschild 1999, 38). By the mid-1870s, with Africa clearly the last continent left with any available territory that could be practicably colonized, Leopold studied the British *Proceedings of the Royal Geographical Society* and carefully followed their accounts of European explorers in Africa (Hochschild 1999, 42).

Central Africa offered a tantalizing opportunity, for even by this time, while the African coasts were claimed by European powers, 80 percent of the continent was still under native rule (Hochschild 1999, 17, 42). European countries were already making inroads through trade, however. Dutch, German, and Portuguese traders were running trading posts along the Lower Congo near the coast, dealing in tropical crops such as groundnuts and palm oil (Gann and Duignan 1979, 51). These materials reached the outside world through commerce networks, in place since the 18th century, that linked Central Africa to the continent's Atlantic and Indian Ocean coasts. In exchange for ivory, slaves, and copper, natives received a variety of imported merchandise including cloth, ornaments, and muskets (Gann and Duignan 1979, 48). Along the Lower Congo, the main product delivered to what is now northern Angola was ivory, along with palm oil and kernels, raw cotton, rubber, and beeswax (Gann and Duignan 1979, 49).

Although the Congolese lived in a land that was rich with natural resources, they were in a poor position either to make the most use of those resources or to resist foreign conquerors. River transport on the Upper Congo was solely by canoe, while goods had to be carried around the cataracts on the lower river, limiting economic development of the region. Natives struggled against numerous incurable tropical diseases, and they made do with such simple hunting and farming tools as the bow, axe, and hoe. There was considerable diversity in societies, cultures, economies, and power factions throughout the region (which would require a separate book to describe fully). In general, though, most Congolese natives were farmers. They grew such crops as cassava, sorghum, and millet, along with imported plants that would survive local conditions: rice, tobacco, and maize, for example (Gann and Duignan 1979, 44). These natives were technologically unable to tap the land's mineral resources or hydroelectric power, transport bulky materials over long distances, or maintain robust food supply systems and networks as a safeguard against local famines (Gann and Duignan 1979, 43).

On the other hand, the Congolese peoples were rich in artistic production. They were skilled in carving, pottery, ironwork, and basket weaving. Furthermore, they had extensive traditions in oral literature, dramatic performance, and dance. Theological principles varied, although most Congolese generally believed in a supreme being and the immortality of the soul, as well as the guiding influence of ancestral spirits. Natives in about two-thirds of the Congo region spoke Bantu, a language group (part of the Niger-Congo language family) with a variety of idioms spoken by different ethnic groups (Gann and Duignan 1979, 44–45). However, the natives had no written language, making them vulnerable to being manipulated through the written treaties devised by Europeans.

Leopold took note of Stanley's 1874 expedition across the little-known equatorial center of the continent. The reports by Stanley and Livingstone of Africans being led in chains in slave caravans to the East Coast gave Leopold the inspiration for a way to acquire a colonial empire under publicly acceptable pretenses (Hochschild 1999, 42). A thriving slave market then existed in East Africa, where traders (mostly Africans) sold slaves from the interior to Arab plantation owners on the island of Zanzibar, and to other buyers on Madagascar, the Arabian Peninsula, and in Persia (Hochschild 1999, 28). The African slave trade came to be described as run by "Arabs" due to the slavers' Arab attire and Islamic faith, though only a minority were even partly of Arab descent. As a result, the slave trade fueled European indignation at the idea of Africa's being colonized and enslaved by non-Europeans (Hochschild 1999, 28).

This set of circumstances presented Leopold with the opportunity he was looking for. Livingstone's belief that Africa could be liberated by commerce, Christianity, and civilization—what became known as the "three Cs"—would provide cover for Leopold's aims. He could conceal his personal hunger for colonies beneath a cover of humanitarian impulses: to advance science, uplift the morals of natives, and suppress the "Arab" slave trade. Otherwise, his subjects would resist his attempts to enrich his country and himself, for his subjects had little appetite of their own for an empire. "The Belgian doesn't exploit the world," he explained to an advisor; "it's a taste to be created in him" (Lefebve de Vivy 1955, 23, my translation). While cultivating an image of himself as a disinterested philanthropist, in 1876 he began laying the groundwork for colonization by planning an international conference of geographers and explorers (Hochschild 1999, 42–43).

The Geographical Conference convened in September 1876 with Leopold as its host. Among the 13 Belgians and 24 foreigners attending were

Slavery and atrocities in Central Africa predated the Belgian administration. Henry Morton Stanley recorded this 1884 scene near the Equator Station. According to Stanley, the native Bakuti tribesmen were massacring slaves to accompany their recently deceased chief into the afterlife. (From Henry M. Stanley, *The Congo and the Founding of Its Free State*. New York, Harper & Brothers, 1885, opposite 2:182.)

the world's leading explorers, as well as military officers and leaders of humanitarian, business, and missionary organizations. The ostensible purpose of the conference was to coordinate exploration work and create international bodies that would oversee the opening of Africa. These goals the delegates accomplished, while the conference was a great success for Leopold personally as well. His welcoming speech had laid out humanitarian goals that would cloak his long-term plan for acquiring a vast African colony. To this end, the conference would determine the routes into the interior and the location of bases from which to abolish the slave trade. Conveniently, the chain of bases that the attendees marked out across unclaimed Central Africa laid a path through the part of the continent that Leopold coveted.

Leopold denied any personal stake in the proceedings (Pakenham 2003, 21). However, he maneuvered the attendees into voting to establish an International African Association, a philanthropic body of European explorers and royals, which would be headquartered (conveniently for Leopold) in Brussels. National committees in each country would be coordinated by an international committee—with him as its first chair. In return for Leopold's efforts, others would see him as nobly coordinating "the greatest humanitarian work of this time," in the admiring words of

"Feeding Slaves." The slave trade gave Leopold a humanitarian pretext for founding his colony: slaves being brought from Central Africa to the east coast in 1887. (From Hermann von Wissmann, *My Second Journey through Equatorial Africa*. London: Chatto & Windus, 1891, opposite 246.)

Ferdinand de Lesseps, the renowned builder of the Suez Canal (quoted in Pakenham 2003, 22).

3. "A TAINT OF IMBECILE RAPACITY BLEW THROUGH IT ALL": LEOPOLD FOUNDS A COLONY

Most of those national committees never got going, while the following year, the international coordinating committee met once; it reelected Leopold as its chairman and then disbanded (Hochschild 1999, 46). Meanwhile, beneath the altruistic veneer Leopold laid over his designs, he continued his plan to acquire a vast personal colony in Central Africa. Leopold employed Stanley in exploring the then-unclaimed Congo River basin for the purpose of annexing it to Belgium. Stanley spent 1879 to 1884 in the region on this mission. At the same time, Leopold played European and American leaders and diplomats against one another in order to pave the way toward his own goals. He explained to the other powers that his purpose was to open the region to free trade, to suppress slavery, and to extend the blessings of civilization and Christianity to the natives.

Beginning in 1876, Leopold created a series of cover organizations to help maintain the disguise: first the International African Association and then the Committee for Studies of the Upper Congo (Hochschild 1999, 45, 64–65, 174). By 1884, the United States, France, and Germany recognized his claim to establish "independent States" in the Congo (in Leopold's words to U.S. President Chester A. Arthur, later modified to a single "State" in public pronouncements) (Hochschild 1999, 82). Ostensibly, international organizations would administer the states or state. However, Leopold kept the public confused to conceal his real aims. The International African Association quietly became defunct, while Leopold transferred its flag (a gold star on a blue field) to a newly formed International Association of the Congo. In contrast to the International African Association, formed under the auspices of international supervision, the International Association of the Congo was under his complete control. The potentially misleading outward similarity of the two organizations was part of Leopold's design—and he instructed aides to take steps so that the public would not realize that the names of the two governing bodies were in fact different (Hochschild 1999, 65).

The crowning achievement of Leopold's efforts was accomplished at the West Africa Conference of 1884–1885, held at Berlin. Prince Bismarck, who hosted the conference, began by describing the aim of European involvement in Africa in terms of bringing commerce, Christianity, and civilization to the continent. Specifically, the conference had the objective of international agreement on three points: free navigation on the Niger River, free trade in the Congo, and a set of rules for future territorial annexation (Pakenham 2003, 241). The conference did not in fact partition Africa at that time (despite subsequent myth). The continent was just too big, and it would take a succession of later treaties to continue the division of spoils. Nevertheless, the result of this conference and related international agreements touched off what would later be described as "The Scramble for Africa," in the title of an article in the *London Times* on 15 September 1884. By 1914, all of Africa was under European rule, with the exceptions of Liberia and Ethiopia. The Scramble would ultimately create 30 colonies and protectorates, containing 110 million people spread out over 10 million square miles, under British, French, German, Portuguese, Italian, and Belgian rule (Pakenham 2003, xxi).

Although Leopold did not attend this conference, he won significant prizes at it. While he, Portugal, and France obtained land near the mouth of the Congo, Leopold received rights to the seaport at Matadi, on the lower river. Also, he controlled land necessary to build a railway from that port around the river's lower rapids to Stanley Pool, above which the Congo was navigable (Hochschild 1999, 86). Furthermore, a huge portion of Central Africa was designated a free-trade zone (Hochschild 1999, 86)—although Leopold had already secretly arranged treaties with hundreds of African tribes for trading monopolies in the Congo basin, as well as ownership of the land (Hochschild 1999, 71). As a result of Leopold's chesslike strategies, Britain and Germany had joined to give him 1 million square miles of the continent—most of Central Africa—primarily to keep the land out of French control.

Leopold was essentially named the trustee of a large part of Africa on behalf of all of Europe, to organize it in the spirit of Livingstone and the "three Cs." In the end, his humanitarian reputation was intact, as he garnered praise from Bismarck and the British press (Pakenham 2003, 255). British diplomats could rest easy that French colonial ambitions were in check, while the public could look forward to a huge new market for exported British goods in the Congo free-trade zone.

4. "THEIR ADMINISTRATION WAS MERELY A SQUEEZE": RUNNING THE CONGO FREE STATE

On 29 May 1885, Leopold officially established his private colony by royal decree. Characteristically, he superseded the previous names of the governing entity (the International African Association and the International Association of the Congo). In their place, he gave his vast fiefdom the new name of the État Indépendant du Congo, or the Congo Free State (although it was essentially under his one-man rule) (Hochschild 1999, 86–87, 115). Its capital would be Boma, near the mouth of the Congo River. Effectively, though, it would be administered from Brussels in offices on or adjacent to the Royal Palace grounds (Hochschild 1999, 115). In December 1888 the Société Anonyme Belge pour le Commerce du Haut-Congo (SAB) was formed. This organization (in English, the Belgian Limited Company for Trade in the Upper Congo) came into being to enhance the development of the region while dividing the cost of the colony among shareholders (Najder 2007, 145–46).

Despite these financial arrangements, the project consumed a fortune of Leopold's personal funds at the beginning. He spent much of the time between 1885 and 1890 seeking to raise more money through loans from bankers and the Belgian Parliament, the sale of bonds, and funds from private investors (Hochschild 1999, 91–92). While the colony made some individuals wealthy, it was not until 1899 that the colony became financially self-supporting (Najder 2007, 145–46). Until then, expenditures on the colony vastly outweighed incomes from there: in 1890, for instance, by a factor of ten to one (Pakenham 2003, 320, 397).

While Leopold sought to boost the colony's finances, he burnished his humanitarian image by sponsoring Christian missionaries in his African state and denouncing the slave trade then thriving in Central and East Africa. Because predominantly Muslim slavers carried out the slave trade, Europeans supporting the scramble for Africa could ease their consciences by opposing slavery while seeking colonial lands (Hochschild 1999, 92). Antislavery committees formed in Belgium, Holland, France, Spain, and Italy (Pakenham 2003, 397). The major powers convened an Anti-Slavery Conference at the end of 1889, selecting Brussels for its meeting site—to the great pleasure of Leopold, who offered the Congo Free State as a base to pursue the slavers, exploiting this opportunity to further his control of the Congo under a humanitarian guise (Hochschild 1999, 93).

Establishing the Congo Free State benefited from crucial advances in technology and medicine. One important development was the transition from sail to steam-powered merchant ships. Steam propulsion made it possible to move goods between Europe and Africa more reliably and faster, with less regard for bad weather and without dependence on the wind. Steam power also made it much easier to navigate the Congo and other African rivers than would have been possible under sail. This change came just in time for the opening of the vast waterway of the Congo and its tributaries—7,200 miles in all—to European trade (Gann and Duignan 1979, 41).

Meanwhile, developments in weaponry and medicine helped Europeans survive and control the native populations they found. The advent of breech-loading rifles in the late 1860s, and the use of waterproof brass cartridges, enabled Europeans to carry their firepower deep into the jungle. Without rain and dampness spoiling their ammunition, and able to shoot farther and more accurately than possible with muzzle-loaders and loose gunpowder, Europeans were more than a match for Africans. Natives were typically armed with spears, bows and arrows, and hand weapons; the best weapons generally available to the Congolese were muzzle-loaders (Hochschild 1999, 89).

Belgian settlers in the Congo were confronted, as were the natives, by serious illnesses. Diseases indigenous to the region included malaria, yellow fever, elephantiasis, sleeping sickness, and other insect-borne diseases. Water-borne diseases included river blindness, Guinea threadworm, and schistosomiasis (Gann and Duignan 1979, 43). Central Africa was hardly considered a healthy place for Europeans then. However, advances in medicine—especially the use of quinine to treat malaria—went a long way to mitigate the effects of tropical diseases that had made the Congo virtually impenetrable for outsiders in the centuries before.

To build up the colonial infrastructure and transportation network, first, a stream of experts and functionaries started moving to the Congo. Soldiers, traders, missionaries, and administrators arrived, along with Leopold's agents (almost all of whom were officers on leave from Europe's armies). At the end of 1889, 430 whites were working in the Congo for Leopold's colony. This was an international effort: fewer than half of these workers were Belgian, as the project attracted little interest among Leopold's subjects (Hochschild 1999, 90–91). They brought with them a flotilla of steamboats, which had to be carried in pieces around the lower river cataracts and assembled upstream. By 1890, there were seven steamers at Léopoldville,

"The Agents of the Modern African Slave Trade." Members of the Force Publique in a photograph published in 1904. Formally created in 1886, this multipurpose military organization was used to overcome widespread native resistance in the Congo Free State (Gann and Duignan 1979, 55, 65). (From Edmund D. Morel, *King Leopold's Rule in Africa*. London: William Heinemann, 1904, opposite 304.)

near Kinshasa on Stanley Pool, along with about 25 Europeans to support operations—such as administration officials, ship captains, engineers, and carpenters (Glave 1890, 619–20). Surveying for the railway around the cataracts had begun in 1887. However, because of the climate, diseases and insects, and rocky terrain, track laying would not start until 1890, and the route between Matadi and Stanley Pool would not be completed until 1898 (Gann and Duignan 1979, 71; Goffin 1907, 25, 37, 72–73).

Controlling the native inhabitants required establishing a military and police force. When Leopold declared the founding of the Congo Free State, the only coercive power he had in the colony consisted of a few hundred mercenary soldiers, recruited from Zanzibar and the West Coast of Africa for seven-year tours of duty. This army, formally constituted as the Force Publique in 1886, would by 1913 number over 44,000 men, led by over 3,500 white officers, or roughly one-quarter of the entire Belgian military strength with the home army included. Initially composed of Hausa tribesmen of West Africa, as it grew the Force Publique would also include natives from Zanzibar, Somalia, the Gold Coast, Dahomey, and Sierra Leone. Congo Free State authorities additionally recruited local Congolese, resorting to impressment as well as taking volunteers (Gann and Duignan 1979, 65, 73, 66, 225n10).

5. "THE WORD 'IVORY' RANG IN THE AIR": RESOURCES AND LABOR

Congo Free State income came from a 15 percent duty on exports of such products as ivory, rubber, and palm oil. Of all the resources in the Congo, ivory was the one that most sparked Leopold's interest as he planned his personal colony. Before the creation of the Congo Free State, an existing ivory market brought the product from the interior of the continent to the markets of Zanzibar, on the southeast coast of Africa, for sale to American and European merchants. Ivory—lightweight, easy to carve, and durable—was a material as useful to the 19th-century world as plastic is to us today. A typical pair of tusks from an African elephant contained 100 pounds of ivory, which could be made into piano keys (in the hundreds) or false teeth (in the thousands), as well as a wide range of household products such as fans, combs, billiard balls, knife handles, napkin rings, and more. Tusks from African elephants were preferred over those from Indian elephants, and tusks from elephants from Central Africa, including the Congo River basin, were the largest of all. Ivory was so widely available there that Stanley found Africans using tusks as doorposts for their homes (Hochschild 1999, 64).

As a consequence of African supply and European demand, in the years leading up to Conrad's arrival in the Congo, ivory was already one of the continent's major exports. In 1870, for instance, about 85 percent of the world's ivory consumption came from Africa (Gann and Duignan 1979, 117). French, British, and Dutch trading companies with posts at the mouth of the Congo were already buying ivory brought by African caravans from the interior (Gann and Duignan 1979, 117). Leopold's control of the center of the continent would help him capture this trade by monopoly. By the time Conrad arrived in the Congo in 1890, the Belgian ivory trade had already dramatically expanded since the founding of the SAB just two years before. In 1888, not quite 13,000 pounds of ivory was exported from the colony; in 1890, that amount had grown to 189,000 pounds—13 times as much (Büchler 1912, 1:233).

In the middle of 1890, Leopold's colony contained a number of stations on the Congo River that functioned as both military bases and ivory-collection points (Hochschild 1999, 101), and the amount of ivory gathered continued to expand. Antwerp became the most important center of ivory imports into Europe in the 1890s, surpassing Liverpool and London (Gann and Duignan 1979, 120), and by 1900, almost 730,000 pounds of ivory were collected (Büchler 1912, 1:233). Yet the ivory market could not be sustained in the long run. The Belgians took no measures to ensure the long-term survival of the elephant herds that provided the commodity. By the last years of the decade, so few elephants were left that much of the exported ivory consisted of old tusks that had long been in storage (referred

Store of ivory at Stanley Falls in 1887 belonging to Tippu Tip, an Afro-Arab trader from Zanzibar who was a notorious slave trader, ivory merchant, and governor of the Falls district from 1887 to April 1890 (Pakenham 318, 320). (©Illustrated London News Ltd/Mary Evans)

to inexactly as "fossil" in *Heart of Darkness*). In 1897, for example, over two-thirds of the tusks sold in Antwerp were of this kind (Gann and Duignan 1979, 120–21).

Against this background, Leopold's administration established draconian methods for sweeping up all the available ivory in the Congo, which was still, in 1890 when Conrad arrived, the most valuable commodity there (Hochschild 1999, 114). Congo Free State agents and African auxiliaries conducted sweeping raids during which they bought tusks at low prices, or just confiscated them, and they shot elephants themselves. Natives, who had been hunting elephants for centuries to sell the tusks in East African markets, could now provide ivory only to Leopold's agents. In 1890, the king established a sliding scale for the commission agents received, giving them a higher percentage of the European market price if the price they paid for the ivory in Africa was lower. Given this incentive, agents were encouraged to keep payments low and use force if necessary. In return for the ivory, natives were given small amounts of such goods as beads or cloth, or they were paid in the brass rods that had been decreed the Congo Free State's currency. For Africans to receive actual cash was forbidden (Hochschild 1999, 118).

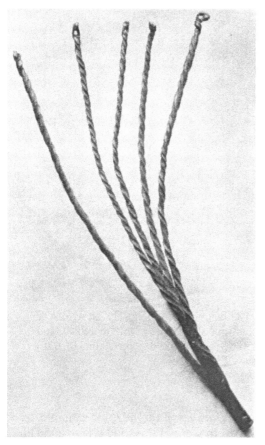

The *chicotte.* (From Sir Harry Johnston, *George Grenfell and the Congo*. London: Hutchinson, 1908, 1:467.)

Establishing this trade network was labor intensive. Settlers in Leopold's Congo found that horses could not be kept alive due to the climate, and the natives had no preexisting skills or incentives for training oxen, so all labor had to be done manually (Gann and Duignan 1979, 42–43). Drafting porters to transport cargo was a main concern in the early years of the Congo Free State. As a result, tens of thousands of Africans were conscripted to this service, during which they were chained and punished, even if they were usually paid. Essentially, they were slaves. The most crucial need for porters was on the three-week journey between Matadi and Stanley Pool, where the Congo River rapids had to be circumvented on foot until the railway was completed. In this effort, carrying sections of riverboat steamer was the most labor-intensive work, as one steamer alone could require a number of loads equivalent to what 3,000 porters would carry (Hochschild 1999, 119).

Eyewitnesses reported the misery endured by the exhausted, underfed, and sickly porters, and the death toll among natives undertaking long-range journeys was high. On one forced march carried out in 1891 for over 600 miles, for example, all 300 porters died (Hochschild 1999, 120). The primary means of disciplining the natives under Leopold's rule was the *chicotte,* a whip made out of dried hippopotamus hide and fashioned into a sharp strip. Usually used on the victim's buttocks, the *chicotte* caused permanent scars. Twenty-five blows could render the recipient unconscious, while the not-uncommon punishment of a hundred or more often meant death (Hochschild 1999, 120).

6. "THE MERRY DANCE OF DEATH AND TRADE": RED RUBBER

While it was the ivory trade that Conrad saw in the Congo, by the time he wrote his story, ivory had been surpassed in production and value by a different substance: rubber. Europeans had known about rubber for centuries, but it was during Conrad's lifetime that it became a widely used, vital commodity. Made by coagulating latex, a milky saplike fluid tapped from rubber trees or vines, natural rubber is a viscous, waterproof material that could be applied to cloth to make it impermeable. The American inventor Charles Goodyear discovered in 1839 that adding sulfur—in a process called vulcanization—made it adaptable to a much wider range of uses. John Dunlop in Ireland later found that rubber could be fashioned into an inflatable tire for bicycles. These advances, combined with new methods in mass production, revolutionized the use of rubber, such as when the Dunlop Company began producing tires in 1890. Soon, factories began churning out not only pneumatic tires for bicycles and automobiles but also a variety of products including tubing and hoses; waterproof clothing; and rubber insulation for the expanding worldwide electricity, telegraph, and telephone networks (Hochschild 1999, 159).

By the late 1890s, rubber had overtaken ivory as the most profitable resource in the Congo, but for Leopold, the beginning of the rubber boom also marked the start of a race against time (Hochschild 1999, 159–60). Rubber can be made from the latex of both the rubber vine and the rubber tree, and while wild rubber vines were plentiful in the Congo, rubber from cultivated rubber trees threatened his new fortune. It took years of careful tending before rubber trees were big enough to be tapped, during which time producing rubber from wild vines in the Congo promised Leopold a long period of market dominance. Eventually, though, rubber from plantations of trees elsewhere in the tropics would introduce major competition and inevitably cause a drop in the price worldwide.

Wild rubber, like ivory, required only manual labor to find and gather it. However, unlike finding and transporting ivory, which could be done by natives chained together, harvesting wild rubber was a grueling job that also required harvesters to climb trees and spread out in the jungle away from their European overseers. Rubber vines snaked their way through the limbs of multiple trees into the sunlight 100 or more feet above the ground. Tapping into the vine, harvesters gathered the dripping latex into buckets. As lower sections of the vine were tapped, natives had to go higher up for fresh latex, and as vines near villages became exhausted, harvesters had to venture farther into the jungle to find new vines. Then the latex had to be coagulated, which the natives accomplished by spreading it on their bodies—pulling off their hair in the process of removing it (Hochschild 1999, 160–63).

Natives disliked this work and had to be forced into doing it, so Europeans responded by drafting them into a vast labor army. At the turn of the century, this labor pool was gathering 11 million tons of rubber a year, all by hand (Gann and Duignan 1979, 123). However, these natives were essentially slaves, for while a flood of rubber and ivory was coming out of the Congo, virtually nothing that could be considered trade goods in return was going in (Morel 1968, 36; Hochschild 1999, 180). To keep this system going, agents resorted to ever more gruesome and barbaric techniques as they coerced natives to gather rubber, punishing those who failed to produce their quota. Such techniques included whipping with the *chicotte,* hostage-taking and imprisonment, plundering and burning villages, paying chiefs with human beings, forcing native men to kill and rape their own sisters and mothers, drowning natives, shooting them, cutting off their heads, and—most vividly in the news that would leak out into the world—severing hands, which became the deliberate policy of the Belgian rubber system in the Congo Free State (Hochschild 1999, 165).

7. "COME AND FIND OUT": NEWS OF ATROCITIES

Between 1890, when Conrad arrived in the Congo, and 1898, when he began writing *Heart of Darkness,* firsthand reports of conditions in the Congo Free State had already begun to seep into public awareness in Britain and the United States. Some early reporting of this kind arrived from George Washington Williams, a black American minister and author. In July 1890, he was at Stanley Falls on an investigative trip. There, Williams began writing a letter to Leopold, describing in vivid detail the live burials; decapitations; "piratical" raids; beatings with the *chicotte;* sexual enslavement; mass murder; toleration of cannibalism; and overall "the deceit, fraud, robberies, arson, murder, slave-raiding, and general policy of cruelty" of Leopold's administration in the Congo Free State (Williams 1890a, 2, 6, 8, 10, 11, 13, 15). By the end of the year, this letter was published as a pamphlet, excerpted and commented on in the European and American presses (Hochschild 1999, 112–13).

Due to the publicizing work of Protestant missionaries (mostly from the United States, Britain, and Sweden), news of severed hands and murdered natives began to circulate more widely, even if Leopold was initially successful in suppressing the news and counteracting it though public relations campaigns in the press (Hochschild 1999, 172–73). When a State officer killed an Irish trader in the Congo in 1895, though, Leopold was forced to act. He formed the Commission for the Protection of the Natives in 1896. By creating this commission, which was really an attempt to conceal the truth and manipulate public opinion, Leopold satisfied critics for the time being. The outbreak of the Boer War in 1899 distracted Britons, furthermore, and criticism of Leopold subsided in the popular press (Hochschild 1999, 174–75). In any case, during the latter half of the 1890s popular opinion tended to celebrate Leopold's rule rather than condemn it. Many Europeans who returned from the Congo shared little of what they knew. Furthermore, because the missionaries lacked political power and media talents, their accusations could not shake Leopold's brutal rule on their own (Hochschild 1999, 185).

The Congo Free State had been receding from public view in Britain when Conrad turned to his African experience to plan a new short story. In July 1896 he had already written one story set in Africa, "An Outpost of Progress" (published June–July 1897).

Leopold II, King of Belgium, 1897. (©Mary Evans / SZ Photo / Scherl)

This earlier tale portrays the downfall of two agents of a European trading company at an isolated trading post. After the men fail to adjust to their conditions and end up participating in slave-dealing, one agent accidentally kills the other in an argument and then commits suicide. Conrad explained to his publisher in a letter on 22 July 1896, relating the story to his past, "All the bitterness of those days [in the Congo], all my puzzled wonder as to the meaning of all I saw—all my indignation at masquerading philanthropy—have been with me again, while I wrote" (Conrad 1983, 294). In its irony, satirical view of "progress," critique of imperialism, and account of the moral degeneration of whites in the African wilderness, "An Outpost of Progress" shares significant characteristics with the much longer and more complex tale that he soon told in *Heart of Darkness.*

Conrad began writing *Heart of Darkness* around 15 December 1898, at a relative low point in news about outrages in the Congo. Only three articles mentioning the Congo Free State appeared in the *London Times,* for example, in the period from October to December 1898. However, public interest in the Congo started a new upswing as Conrad finished the story. In January 1899, five in-depth reports appeared in the *Times,* while Conrad completed the manuscript early the following month (Najder 2007, 286).

Originally titled "The Heart of Darkness," it was first published serially in *Blackwood's Edinburgh Magazine,* in three consecutive monthly issues from February to April 1899. The story later appeared in book form, with the revised title *Heart of Darkness,* in *Youth: A Narrative and Two Other Stories* (published in Edinburgh and London in November 1902) and in *Youth and Two Other Stories* (published in New York in February 1903).

Not long after the first magazine publication of the story, a decisive new campaign against Leopold began. This campaign was launched by someone with inside knowledge of the Congo Free State operations at the European end. Edmund Dene Morel, a staff member of the Liverpool-based shipping company Elder Dempster, had begun to suspect what was going on in Leopold's colony. Employed as the company's liaison to Congo Free State officials, he was in a position to examine the records of goods shipped by Elder Dempster to and from the Congo—records that did not accord with statistics announced to the public by the Congo Free State (Hochschild 1999, 179). As he discovered by 1900, public trade figures, doctored at

"Expert Opinion." Leopold II depicted consulting with "Abdul" about "so-called atrocities" in the satirical British magazine *Punch* in 1905, at a time when the efforts of the Congo Reform Association in Britain were taking hold and abuses in the Congo were increasingly condemned. In 1904, Congo Reform Association founder Edmund Dene Morel had praised *Heart of Darkness* for its "powerful picture of Congo Life" (Morel 1904, 173-74). (From *Punch* 31 May 1905, 381.)

Leopold's orders, concealed that Congo exports arriving in Europe consisted of thousands of tons of materials, primarily rubber, while virtually no trade goods were sent from Europe to the Congo. There was, however, a steady supply of armaments for the Congo Free State's army (Pakenham 2003, 591). Morel concluded that Leopold's philanthropic mission in the Congo was a fraud.

Morel resigned from Elder Dempster and turned to writing full time about West Africa. He published a number of articles in *The Speaker* in the summer of 1900, exposing what he had learned (Pakenham 2003, 591). In 1903 he founded his own journal devoted to conditions in Africa, *West African Mail.* He also published a series of books elaborating his

"In the Rubber Coils." Shortly after this illustration appeared in *Punch*, growing outrage in America led to President Theodore Roosevelt announcing on 11 December 1906 that America would join Britain in pressuring the Belgian government to take control of the Congo Free State from Leopold (Pakenham 1991, 659). (From *Punch* 28 November 1906, 389.)

condemnation of Leopold's rule: *Affairs of West Africa* (1903), *King Leopold's Rule in Africa* (1904), and *Red Rubber* (1906). Through a prolific and tireless humanitarian campaign of publications and speeches, Morel revived public interest in the Congo, resulting in the passing of a Congo protest resolution in Parliament in May 1903.

As a consequence of Parliament's resolution, the Foreign Office directed the British consul in the Congo to investigate into the interior of the country and report back on conditions there. This man was Irishman Roger Casement, whom Conrad had met at Matadi in June 1890. Casement had at the time been a supervisor for the Compagnie du Chemin de Fer du Congo, working on building the Matadi-to-Léopoldville railway line (Najder 2007, 149). Casement, now Britain's first consul in the Congo Free State, published his report in February 1904. He joined forces with Morel, the two forming the Congo Reform Association in early 1904. As a result of increasing international pressure on Leopold and the bringing to light of his regime's misdeeds in governing the Congo, ultimately the region passed out of his hands in November 1908 and became a colony of the Belgian state. (It is now the independent Democratic Republic of the Congo.)

8. "THE SUBJECT IS OF OUR TIME DISTINCTLY": REACTIONS AND CONTROVERSIES

The publication of *Heart of Darkness* sparked a number of books published in Belgium or elsewhere in Europe that portrayed travels to the Congo (Gann and Duignan 1979, 194). In Britain, however, the story's first reviewers—literary critics—disregarded the historical Congo as they evaluated the novella as a work of fiction. Conrad himself evidently thought of the story in primarily this way at the time. In a letter to his publisher describing it, he wrote on 31 December 1898, "The criminality of inefficiency and pure selfishness when tackling the civilizing work in Africa is a justifiable idea. The subject is of our time distinc[t]ly—though not topically treated" (Conrad 1986, 139–40). Morel saw the value of *Heart of Darkness* as history, though. In *King Leopold's Rule in Africa* (1904), Morel credited Conrad's story with providing a "powerful picture of Congo life" (Morel 1904, 173–74). In a 7 October 1909 letter to Sir Arthur Conan Doyle, Morel described *Heart of Darkness* as "the most powerful thing written on the subject" (quoted in Morel 1968, 205n1). The political scientist and philosopher Hannah Arendt likewise praised this "powerful" quality of *Heart of Darkness* in *The Origins of Totalitarianism* (1951). According to Arendt, race and bureaucracy were the two new and necessary ingredients in the imperialist expansion of European power—which she dated to "no sooner than around 1884" (Arendt 1968, 185, xvii), the year that the Berlin Conference convened. She claimed furthermore that *Heart of Darkness* "is the most illuminating work on actual race experience in Africa" (Arendt 1968, 185). She quoted at length from Conrad's novella to compare whites to Kurtz, and to make Marlow's vision of "prehistoric man" emblematic of the Western encounter with the natives of the Dark Continent (Arendt 1968, 189–90).

However, Conrad's portrayal of racial difference became controversial. Chinua Achebe, a prominent Nigerian novelist, asserted in 1977 that *Heart of Darkness* demonstrates an ignorance of the actual Africa, records its author's racist attitudes, and effectively dehumanizes African natives. Achebe famously called Conrad a "bloody racist" (Achebe 1977, 788) (a charge later revised to "thoroughgoing racist" [Achebe 1988, 257]). Against Achebe's claims, a number of literary critics have offered rebuttals and other explanations of Conrad's position on Africa and Africans (Hawkins 1979; Watts 1983; Brantlinger 1985a; Firchow 2000); there is far more on this topic than room here allows. We can certainly think about *Heart of Darkness* as a window into what people thought about race in Conrad's time, although one complication is that while the idea of racism existed then, the word itself did not yet exist. Consequently, when reading *Heart of Darkness* today we face a problem of definitions—complicated still further by what we know of what Conrad and others in his time meant by "race." This word comes up only once in *Heart of Darkness:* Marlow uses it to describe the English peoples, and it is in this sense (a sense since transferred to "ethnicity" and "nation") that "race" then had its primary meaning (Firchow 2000, 5).

Conrad's language is nevertheless jarring, especially Marlow's use of the word "nigger." Clearly, the term was known at the time to be derogatory. However,

"The Guilt of Delay." While the Congo Free State came under Belgian government control in 1908, the Belgian Parliament did not announce plans for reform until October 1909. Morel chafed at the delays and believed the promised reforms to be a sham (Pakenham 1991, 668). The same month, he called *Heart of Darkness* "the most powerful thing written on the subject" of Leopold's rule in the Congo (quoted in Morel 1968, 205n1). (From *Punch* 24 December 1909, 363.)

Marlow may simply be reflecting the typical worldview, if not just the terminology, of the British merchant seamen of which both he and Conrad were a part. After all, English was Conrad's third language (after Polish and French), and he learned colloquial English from his merchant navy shipmates. Conrad may also have given this language to Marlow as a marketing strategy to help sell the book: to make Marlow seem more authentically British, out of Conrad's concern that British readers might not identify with a narrator who seemed foreign—as Conrad himself was potentially seen. ("Foreigner" could be a term of abuse as well at that time.) In *Heart of Darkness,* "nigger" appears along with the more neutral "Negro" and most neutral "black," all at various times, indicating that

Conrad's thinking along these lines was fluid (Firchow 2000, 38–39, 200n12).

Perhaps most important, Conrad saw bonds of humanity between people regardless of race. In a letter written on 16 December 1903 to Kazimierz Waliszewski (a Polish author and historian), Conrad wrote, "As to the 'inferiority of the races,' I mean to protest—although if I gave you the wrong idea of my purpose, the fault is obviously mine. It's the *difference* between the races that I wanted to point out" (Conrad 1988a, 94). Conrad clearly meant to discuss difference rather than superiority, and moreover the bonds between humans—despite racial differences—were paramount in Conrad's mind and art.

As Conrad explained in a letter to Casement written on 21 December 1903, if he abused his horse through overwork, he would be liable to the law, and "it seems to me," he went on, "that the black man—say of Upoto [on the Congo River]—is deserving of as much humanitarian regard as any animal [because of his faculties of sense . . .]. But as a matter of fact his happiness and misery are much more complex than the misery or happiness of animals and deserving of greater regard. He shares with us the consciousness of the universe in which we live—no small burden. Barbarism per se is no crime deserving of a heavy visitation; and the Belgians are worse than the seven plagues of Egypt" (Conrad 1988a, 96). While "race" appears only once in *Heart of Darkness,* "kinship" and "brother" figure several times, indicating the significance of these other ideas to Conrad's thinking about Marlow's situation.

A second point of controversy surrounding the book involves deciding on its attitude toward imperialism and colonialism. Conrad was conflicted in his attitudes about empire, having been born in a Poland colonized by the Russian Empire but later serving the British Empire in one of the most important instruments of imperial power: a merchant navy. He opposed the Boer War (1899–1902), a conflict of imperial control in British South Africa—but because he believed that it was a distraction from the dangers of Russian and German imperial expansion in East Asia (Simmons 2014b, 190). While Conrad's positioning with regard to empire might seem contradictory to a certain extent, it may be because his background made him attuned to the complexities of the imperial age, as well as its inescapable scope. As Allan H. Simmons has observed, "Empire was *the* fact of British life in the late nineteenth century. ('Empire Day' was established in 1902.)"—coincidentally, the year that *Heart of Darkness* appeared in book form (Simmons 2014b, 190).

Critics have, therefore, been divided on whether Conrad supports or attacks imperialism in *Heart of Darkness,* resulting in many articles and books on the question. As we see with the word "race," one of the problems we face is that the words "colonialism" and "imperialism" have meanings for us today that differ from what Conrad and his contemporaries would have understood. First, Conrad never actually uses those two words in *Heart of Darkness*. However, he does apparently draw a distinction between colonialism and imperialism that J. A. Hobson would also make at almost the same time in his influential book *Imperialism: A Study* (1902).

In the words of one Conrad critic, the key difference is one that Hobson draws "between 'colonialism,' or emigration to relatively unpopulated areas and the establishment of a culture attempting to reproduce that of the home country (e.g., Australia, New Zealand, Canada), and 'imperialism,' in which the settlers form a ruling caste among an overwhelmingly native population" (Fleishman 1967, 98). Yet even Hobson found that imperialism seemed to defy easy definition, noting furthermore, "Nationalism, internationalism, colonialism, [imperialism's] three closest congeners, are equally elusive, equally shifty." Nevertheless, he settled on "investigat[ing] the theory and the practice of Imperialism regarded as a 'mission of civilisation,'" along with its "effects upon 'lower' or alien peoples." Hobson claimed that imperialism was a word "on everybody's lips and . . . used to denote the most powerful movement in the current politics of the Western world" (Hobson 1902, 1, v; Firchow 2000, 14–15). As a result, imperialism and what Conrad called "the civilizing work in Africa" practically demanded such studies and illustrations as those that Conrad and Hobson provided, even if the terms used to describe imperialism seemed slippery.

9. "IT IS EXPERIENCE PUSHED A LITTLE (AND ONLY VERY LITTLE) BEYOND THE ACTUAL FACTS OF THE CASE": COMPARING FACT AND FICTION

How valid is it to look for an understanding of history in reading a work of fiction? Because authors of fiction are not bound by historical fact, a novel might not be the best source of reliable information about dates, names, and specific events. In the case of *Heart of Darkness,* Conrad made many alterations of historical fact. For example, the seat of the Congo Free State government, Boma, was more developed than the story indicates; so too was Stanley Falls. Also, Kurtz has little in common with Klein, the dying agent Conrad brought downriver. Two larger potential alterations are that Conrad made the Congo River seem more isolated than it really was, and that he made the Belgian administration more of a shambles than it really was. Conrad's biographers have debated the extent to which these conclusions are accurate. It is possible that the river journey was routine and well organized, and that it proceeded along a waterway fairly well frequented by steamboats that passed by a series of factories and trading posts (Sherry 1971, 51, 61). On the other hand, the boats that the *Roi des Belges* encountered may have seemed few and far between, and in any case the river is miles wide in places—so the isolated atmosphere in the story may be true to fact after all (Najder 2007, 156–57).

Accordingly, the relation between fact and fiction in this story has proven to be another point of controversy over the years. According to Conrad's "Author's Note" (written in 1917), the story "is experience pushed a little (and only very little) beyond the actual facts of the case." Ever since, scholars have debated this claim. Some have asserted that the story is remarkably accurate in depicting the details of life in the Congo Free State (Hochschild 1999, 143; Hawkins 1981–1982, 68). According to a contrasting argument, rather than directly representing reality, the story expresses essential cultural and historical truths as reshaped through Conrad's imagination (Watt 1980, 138). Yet, as some have argued, the story's literary qualities indicate that the story asks to be read only as fiction; therefore, Conrad cannot be held accountable to historical truth as though he had written a documentary account (Miller 2002, 24–29).

Other readers have made the point that the story is not mainly or only about Marlow's colonial surroundings anyway, or about Kurtz or other Belgian officials, but about Marlow himself (Guerard 1958, 37). The story does avoid historical specificity, after all; consequently, according to still other scholars, to try to place the action in the historical Congo places limits on the statement that Conrad makes through the tale, which has to do with the destruction of the self (Simmons 2007, 40). One way around this impasse is to note that making direct comparisons between Conrad's and Marlow's experiences may not be the most important task at hand. Instead, as Conrad's foremost modern biographer has proposed, one ought to ask such questions as "In what categories did [Conrad] perceive what he observed? How did he understand it?" (Najder 2007, 149). According to this logic, to find and evaluate factual correspondences in search of the "real Congo" misses the point.

However, the fact remains that while such deliberately documentary efforts as Casement's consular report and Morel's many books and pamphlets directly led to the end of Leopold's personal rule of his colony, that material is largely forgotten today. On the other hand, *Heart of Darkness* is the most widely read piece of writing about the Congo under Leopold, the one that most shapes our thinking today about the historical Congo (Firchow 2000, x). It evidently insists to be read not only as fiction but also, and at the same time, as something dealing powerfully with history— or else such acutely minded responses as Achebe's, and those he touched off, would not have appeared. Postcolonial Indonesian author Pramoedya Ananta Toer remarked in 1995, "In Conrad's works there are historical facts which have not been recorded elsewhere," indicating how important Conrad's stories are to the recovery of colonial histories everywhere (GoGwilt 1996, 156).

How then should we understand the "historical facts" that Conrad incorporates, especially when he has changed so much? As we have seen, one way is to glean the story's details about the historical Congo—but thinking about what Conrad changed and why he might have made those changes. In this effort, comparing the novella and "The Congo Diary" can be instructive. In that diary, Conrad explicitly set out to record a factual account of what exactly happened to him on part of his journey. By matching Conrad's experiences as he recorded them in "The Congo Diary" and how he transmuted those details in placing them in *Heart of Darkness*— what he added, left out, emphasized, or refocused—we can discover what Conrad found most striking or memorable about what he had seen in the Congo.

10. "THAT SOMBRE THEME HAD TO BE GIVEN A SINISTER RESONANCE": IMPRESSIONS, VISIONS, AND VALUES

In this light, we can profitably turn to Conrad's own explanations about the relation between fact and fiction. He claimed in 1924, "I do not write history, but fiction, and I am therefore entitled to choose as I please what is most suitable in regard to characters and particulars to help me in the general impression I wish to produce" (Jean-Aubry 1927, 1:77). This statement helps us, if we take Conrad at his word. We can look for historical truth in the overall combination of episodes in a fictional work of his; there is in fact a truth, as Conrad sees it, inside his narratives despite their changes of historical details; and the "general impression" that a fictional work gives is a key part of what Conrad wants to present to his readers.

In the specific case of *Heart of Darkness,* Conrad left additional indications. In his "Author's Note," after claiming that the story "is experience pushed a little (and only very little) beyond the actual facts of the case," he goes on to give his reason for altering the facts: "for the perfectly legitimate, I believe, purpose of bringing it home to the minds and bosoms of the readers. There it was no longer a matter of sincere colouring. It was like another art altogether. That sombre theme had to be given a sinister resonance, a tonality of its own, a continued vibration that, I hoped, would hang in the air and dwell on the ear after the last note had been struck." Consequently, we can think about part of the historical truth in *Heart of Darkness* as residing not in the factual details that the story incorporates but in the impression it creates.

As one critic has noted, "In reading Conrad's *Heart of Darkness . . .* we are not seeking to determine what the 'real' Africa was like, assuming that such a determination is or was ever possible; instead, we want to know how (and why) Conrad *envisioned* Africa as he did, and what that *vision* meant to him and to his readers" (Firchow 2000, 21). Thus, we would look for what the story tells us about such things as the author's intended audience and his assumptions about his readers, the values that the author shares with that audience, the cultural world they both inhabit, and the vision of reality that the author seems to want to induce in the reader's imagination.

Specifically, fiction helps us see the "mentalities"—attitudes, world-views, and values—shared by the author and the audience. To reach these mentalities, a historian might ask such questions as "What does the author say through the novel? How does what he says resemble or differ from what is already known about his world? What were the social, political, and economic constraints on the author's vision expressed in the novel? What is the text's place in history?" (Allen 1983, 241). Further questions are "What did the novel mean to readers within a specific historical mi-lieu? What does the novel itself say about those readers and their time?" (Allen 1983, 245). Also, "Who are the readers assumed by the narrator in the text? What are the social values and attitudes he expects his audience to share? How does the novel help to define a community of readers and their shared preconceptions?" (Allen 1983, 247, 249). A fictional book creates a mental world that the audience helps to build; thus the details of that world tell us about that audience and its worldview, beyond whether or not they correspond to the actual Africa that Conrad saw, in this case (Allen 1983, 247, 249).

A more philosophical way of looking at such truth claims in fiction has to do with the idea that there are multiple kinds of truth. One is the scien-tific kind—statements about observable facts that can be declared true or false based on empirical evidence. This truth is correspondence between reality and what is said about reality. Obviously, there is much historical truth that operates according to this model. However, there is also a lot that scientific truth leaves out: in the words of another literary critic, "visions of how the world was, is and ought to be, things that are core for people's personal and communal identity, feelings and judgements" (Eaglestone 2003, 152). How this works, according to this more deeply philosophical model, is through "uncovering" or "revealing," as opposed to the model of corresponding. According to some critics, following the lead of philoso-pher Martin Heidegger, literature tells us the truth of the world not by presenting facts but by opening our eyes to something we had not before seen or recognized for what it is—through "'defamiliarising' what we take for granted in the world, and so drawing attention to it" (Eaglestone 2003, 153). In this way, technical accuracy is less important than the act of un-veiling the truth for the reader.

11. "THE MEANING OF AN EPISODE WAS NOT INSIDE LIKE A KERNEL BUT OUTSIDE": THE ROLE OF THE READER

Conrad went further to explain how the reader cooperates in creating the truth in fiction. In an 8 January 1902 letter to his agent, Conrad wrote, "One writes only half the book; the other half is with the reader" (Conrad

1986, 370). Because the reader brings a psychological response to the story—such things as emotional reactions, memories, and associations—part of the historical truth of the episodes on which the story is based lies in the effects of historical details on the people who perceive them. However, while studying the story in this way can tell us about the readers in Conrad's world, we can also learn about our own world too. The psychological responses that we bring to the story through our experience of reading it are part of the historical truth about the Congo that it presents: what the Congo means to us today is part of the social and cultural history of the Congo.

Furthermore, through our engagement with the story we can learn about ourselves as observers of history. *Heart of Darkness* does still more than give us images of colonialism. It makes its readers—us—participate in Marlow's fascination with what he sees, and how he interprets it, through the acts of imagination provoked in our minds while reading the story (Simmons 2007, 41). We too are implicated in the events that the story describes.

We can end up searching our own motives and reactions to suffering and exploitation, and we can bring up all sorts of questions: about how we would respond in such a situation, for instance, and where our obligations to other people lie. Furthermore, if we find it hard to follow the story, Conrad makes us like Marlow, who at various points finds it difficult to understand what is happening to him. In this way, if the story seems evasive about facts, it also shows us the more general problems of recording and interpreting historical facts—making us aware of the inherent difficulties in understanding the world we live in (GoGwilt 2010, 138–39).

12. "DO YOU SEE ANYTHING?": THE PROBLEM OF REPRESENTING ATROCITY

It is worth remembering that the novella seemed to have an influence on the Congo reform movement all out of proportion to its status as a fictional story that does not ever actually name the Congo and was not a bestseller in its time. Yet, as Allan Simmons has argued, the "relationship between the facts of the Congo atrocities and the fictional form in which Conrad presents them seems to me to be the essence of the novel's contribution to the debate" (Simmons 2002, 101). Furthermore, he writes, by providing a "(fictionalised) context," Conrad "enabled the subsequent transmission of uncomfortable facts" (Simmons 2002, 101). Because the facts of the atrocities made people so uncomfortable, only through reading a fictionalized account could they come to grips with the reality of Leopold's Congo.

If conditions in the Congo were so bad that it took a work of fiction for Europeans to face historical reality and demand change, then part of what *Heart of Darkness* shows us about history is the difficulty of using language to represent atrocity. For example, there are things in *Heart of Darkness* that Marlow finds impossible to describe or even to name out loud—such as the "unspeakable rites" that Kurtz attended. When Marlow asks his listeners, "Do you see the story? Do you see anything? It seems to me I am trying to tell you a dream—making a vain attempt," he seems to despair of being able to say anything convincing about what he has witnessed.

A significant problem involved in reporting atrocity is that the report may not be trusted, no matter how accurate it is and how factually it is conveyed. Some things are simply too terrible to contemplate. In the early 1890s, Morel's attempts to move the British government to action by factually describing conditions in the Congo "fell on deaf ears," in his words (Morel 1904, xi). Later, when an American engineer described similar atrocities carried out during rubber harvesting in the Amazon basin, his series of articles published in *Truth* magazine in 1909 were likewise disbelieved (Simmons 2002, 98). Facts and statistics may not get us closer to historical truth, for reasons that they may seem preposterous or exaggerated. Fictional stories can get us closer, however, despite Marlow's despairing claim—for the reason that we hold fiction to a different standard of historical accuracy.

13. "A FORM OF IMAGINED LIFE CLEARER THAN REALITY"

Paradoxically, then, it is because *Heart of Darkness* is a work of fiction that it allowed Conrad to express historical truths of the kind that Marlow could not even say out loud. But this is only part of how fiction can be more truthful than fact. Ten years after writing *Heart of Darkness,* Conrad asked a question defining novels: "what is a novel if not a conviction of our fellow men's existence, strong enough to take upon itself a form of imagined life clearer than reality and whose accumulated verisimilitude of selected episodes puts to shame the pride of documentary history?" (Conrad 2008b, 27–28). Here Conrad makes his strongest claim for the truth-value of fiction, which invites us to consider how fiction creates an imagined life in the first place—fiction's specifically literary techniques.

Some of the literary techniques in *Heart of Darkness* that allow a story to operate this way include the novella's indirectness, its episodes of delayed decoding, its atmosphere and mood, and its first-person narrative point of view (Simmons 2015, 19–25). In its indirectness, the story hints at more than it describes outright, inviting us to imagine what those horrors are (or were), thereby implicating us in establishing the truth of what happened—because we can already think we see it in our mind's eye. "Delayed decoding" is a term first used by Ian Watt to describe how Conrad's narratives give us details that seem at first not to make sense, but later they do: such as when Marlow sees "sticks" flying through the air, and they turn out to be arrows; or when the helmsman seems to have grabbed a cane from someone on shore, but it turns out to be a spear thrust into him. That Marlow undergoes this mental process, and we see it, shows us that our understanding of things (such as atrocities) takes time and dawns on us slowly (Watt 1980, 176–78).

Likewise, the novella's atmosphere of gloom and tension, of ever-present but undefined danger, tells us something historically accurate about Leopold's Congo, even if it is through the impressions and feelings of one person—because impressions and feelings are part of what it was like to be in the Congo. Finally, Marlow's account comes to us from the story's frame narrator, who seems to us to have written down the yarn that Marlow speaks out loud to his audience on the *Nellie*. Marlow gives his account an arresting immediacy, drawing us into his world, by telling his story through speaking it and by making it his own report of something he saw. He also gives his story an authenticity that somehow goes beyond what gets delivered through a deliberately more objective report, such as an anonymous, purportedly factual and emotionless newspaper article.

However, we should remember that Conrad cherished nonfiction stories too, as he revealed when he studied atlases and learned about explorers so excitedly in his youth. Toward the end of his life, he looked back again at his time in the Congo. In his essay "Geography and Some Explorers" (1924), Conrad recalled how a boyhood boast of exploring in Africa had surprisingly resulted in the sordid reality of what he saw there in 1890. While moored in his steamboat on the bank of the Congo River, he later remembered, the "idealised realities of a boy's day-dreams" had been dashed by "the unholy recollection of a prosaic newspaper stunt and the distasteful knowledge of the vilest scramble for loot that ever disfigured the history of human conscience and geographical exploration" (Conrad 2010a, 14). In the words of this recollection of his, we see several of the themes of Congo history, as Conrad experienced it, that this chapter organizes. From the "prosaic newspaper stunt" (Stanley's search for Livingstone) to the "Scramble for Africa" and Leopold's looting of his personal colony, what Conrad witnessed in the Congo irreparably marred his ideals of exploration and morality. By reading his story, we too can share in that witnessing.

❦

Heart of Darkness

By Joseph Conrad

With Annotations
by Mark D. Larabee

I

The *Nellie*,[1] a cruising yawl,[2] swung to her anchor[3] without a flutter of the sails, and was at rest. The flood had made, the wind was nearly calm, and being bound down the river, the only thing for it was to come to and wait for the turn of the tide.[4]

The sea-reach[5] of the Thames stretched before us like the beginning of an interminable waterway. In the offing[6] the sea and the sky were welded together without a joint, and in the luminous space the tanned sails of the barges[7] drifting up with the tide seemed to stand still in red clusters of canvas sharply peaked, with gleams of varnished sprits.[8] A haze rested on the low shores that ran out to sea in vanishing flatness. The air was dark above Gravesend,[9] and farther back still seemed condensed into a mournful gloom, brooding motionless over the biggest, and the greatest, town on earth.[10]

---

1. Conrad ties the fictional *Heart of Darkness* to his historical experience of the Congo through the very first words of the story. *Nellie* was the name of a 33-foot-long, 9-ton yacht that was owned by G. F. W. Hope, a friend of Conrad's, from 1889 to 1892 (during the time of Conrad's trip) (*Lloyd's Register of Yachts,* 1889–1893; cited in Stape and Knowles 2006, 106). Conrad went sailing twice as he recovered his health in the summer after returning from Africa, from 18 to 22 June 1891 and 3 to 6 July 1891 (Najder 2007, 171).

2. A sailing vessel having two masts.

3. The anchor is holding the bow of the yawl in position, leaving the stern to swing freely.

4. Because there is little wind, the best time to leave downriver is after the tide starts falling, as the current will help bear the boat downstream. In this description, the tide has begun flowing in, so they will have to wait.

5. The last section of a river, stretching out to the sea (Smyth 1867, 563, 604).

6. Beyond the anchorage, toward the sea (Smyth 1867, 505).

7. In this instance, flat-bottomed vessels used for carrying cargo (Smyth 1867, 79).

8. A diagonal pole that extends a fore-and-aft sail at the uppermost corner away from the mast (Smyth 1867, 645).

9. Town on the right bank of the Thames, pop. 31,838 in 1887. This port had two piers and floating coal depots, and the town supported fisheries and the outward-bound vessels that frequently stopped there. The Thames is about 2,000 feet wide at this point (United Kingdom, Admiralty 1887, 4:12–13).

10. London; with London Bridge at 23.5 miles from Gravesend by rail (United Kingdom, Admiralty 1887, 4:13). In the latter half of the 19th century, London was the largest city in the world. Its population in 1900 was approximately 6,480,000, or almost twice as many people as the next largest city in Europe (Paris, with 3,330,000). New York (4,242,000) was the second-largest worldwide (Chandler and Fox 1974, 371).

The Director of Companies[11] was our captain and our host. We four affectionately watched his back as he stood in the bows looking to seaward. On the whole river there was nothing that looked half so nautical. He resembled a pilot,[12] which to a seaman is trustworthiness personified. It was difficult to realise his work was not out there in the luminous estuary,[13] but behind him, within the brooding gloom.

Between us there was, as I have already said somewhere, the bond of the sea. Besides holding our hearts together through long periods of separation, it had the effect of making us tolerant of each other's yarns—and even convictions. The Lawyer—the best of old fellows—had, because of his many years and many virtues, the only cushion on deck, and was lying on the only rug. The Accountant had brought out already a box of dominoes, and was toying architecturally with the bones.[14] Marlow sat cross-legged right aft, leaning against the mizzen-mast.[15] He had sunken cheeks, a yellow complexion, a straight back, an ascetic aspect, and, with his arms dropped, the palms of hands outwards, resembled an idol. The Director, satisfied the anchor had good hold, made his way aft and sat down amongst us. We exchanged a few words lazily. Afterwards there was silence on board the yacht. For some reason or other we did not begin that game of dominoes. We felt meditative, and fit for nothing but placid staring. The day was ending in a serenity of still and exquisite brilliance. The water shone pacifically; the sky, without a speck, was a benign immensity of unstained light; the very mist on the Essex[16] marshes was like a gauzy and radiant fabric, hung from the wooded rises inland, and draping the low shores in diaphanous folds. Only the gloom to the west, brooding over the upper reaches, became more sombre every minute, as if angered by the approach of the sun.

---

11. George Fountaine Weare Hope (1854–1930), owner of the historical *Nellie,* was a company director and former officer in the merchant marine (Stape and Knowles 2006, 104–16).

12. Someone licensed and qualified to sail ships in or out of a harbor or channel. Coastal navigation can be intricate and hazardous, and captains might be unfamiliar with the area. Consequently, control and responsibility for the ship is transferred to a hired pilot, who has detailed local knowledge (Smyth 1867, 528; *A Naval Encyclopaedia* 1881, 646). Because pilots had to be reliable and competent, Conrad is having the frame narrator make Marlow out to be a trustworthy teller of his tale.

13. Where the river widens into the sea.

14. Conrad's circle of friends included an accountant named William Brock Keen (1861–1941). The Lawyer does not correspond to anyone in this circle (Stape and Knowles 2006, 106–14).

15. The second mast of this boat, farther aft.

16. A county east of London, along the North Sea coast of England and along the north bank of the Thames River.

And at last, in its curved and imperceptible fall, the sun sank low, and from glowing white changed to a dull red without rays and without heat, as if about to go out suddenly, stricken to death by the touch of that gloom brooding over a crowd of men.

Forthwith a change came over the waters, and the serenity became less brilliant but more profound. The old river in its broad reach rested unruffled at the decline of day, after ages of good service done to the race that peopled its banks,[17] spread out in the tranquil dignity of a waterway leading to the uttermost ends of the earth. We looked at the venerable stream not in the vivid flush of a short day that comes and departs for ever, but in the august light of abiding memories. And indeed nothing is easier for a man who has, as the phrase goes, "followed the sea" with reverence and affection, than to evoke the great spirit of the past upon the lower reaches of the Thames. The tidal current runs to and fro in its unceasing service, crowded with memories of men and ships it has borne to the rest of home or to the battles of the sea. It had known and served all the men of whom the nation is proud, from Sir Francis Drake[18] to Sir John Franklin,[19] knights all, titled and untitled—the great knights-errant of the sea. It had borne all the ships whose names are like jewels flashing in the night of time, from the *Golden Hind* returning with her round flanks full of treasure, to be visited by the Queen's Highness and thus pass out of the gigantic tale, to the *Erebus* and *Terror,* bound on other conquests—and that never returned. It had known the ships and the men. They had sailed from Deptford, from Greenwich, from Erith[20]—the adventurers and the settlers; kings' ships

---

17. The only time the word "race" appears in *Heart of Darkness.* While today we use "race" mainly to distinguish humans by physical characteristics in common, for Conrad and his readers the word primarily meant something different: peoples descended from common ancestors, "A tribe, nation, or people," or "A group . . . forming a distinct ethnical stock" (*Oxford English Dictionary* [1884–1928]). Today we use different words for these meanings: "nation" or "ethnic group" (Firchow 2000, 5).

18. Francis Drake (c. 1540–1596) circumnavigated the globe on the *Pelican* (later renamed *Golden Hind*) in 1577–1580. Knighted by Queen Elizabeth, he was the most highly esteemed English seaman of his time.

19. Sir John Franklin (1786–1847), British naval officer and explorer. In 1845 he led an unsuccessful expedition in search of the Northwest Passage linking the Atlantic and Pacific through the Canadian Arctic. His two ships, *Erebus* and *Terror,* became trapped in the ice near King William Island in 1846, and the entire crew died without word of their fate reaching England. In 1859 a search party found the crews' remains and a written record of the expedition up to April 1848.

20. Three ports along the Thames in the London suburbs. Deptford was the site of a major royal dockyard, in use from 1513 to 1869. Charles II founded the Royal Observatory at Greenwich in 1675, primarily to advance nautical astronomy and navigation (United Kingdom, Admiralty 1887, 4:21–22).

and the ships of men on 'Change;[21] captains, admirals, the dark "interlopers" of the Eastern trade,[22] and the commissioned "generals" of East India fleets.[23] Hunters for gold or pursuers of fame, they all had gone out on that stream, bearing the sword, and often the torch, messengers of the might within the land, bearers of a spark from the sacred fire. What greatness had not floated on the ebb of that river into the mystery of an unknown earth! . . . The dreams of men, the seed of commonwealths, the germs of empires.

The sun set; the dusk fell on the stream, and lights began to appear along the shore. The Chapman lighthouse,[24] a three-legged thing erect on a mud-flat, shone strongly. Lights of ships moved in the fairway[25]—a great stir of lights going up and going down. And farther west on the upper reaches the place of the monstrous town[26] was still marked ominously on the sky, a brooding gloom in sunshine,[27] a lurid glare under the stars.

---

21. Men in finance or commerce who worked at such places as the Stock Exchange or Royal Exchange (Conrad 2010c, 440n45.1).

22. "Interlopers": smuggling traders violating royal charters and monopolies held by established trading companies (Conrad 2010c, 440n45.1).

23. The East India Company was originally founded by royal charter in 1600 to take part in the East Indian spice trade (then monopolized by Spain and Portugal) after the defeat of the Spanish Armada. Legally disbanded in 1873. Its fleet commanders were designated "Generals" (Kaye 1853, 64).

24. A 71-foot-high lighthouse painted red and erected on screw piles near Canvey Island in the Thames; in clear weather, the light was visible for 11 miles (United Kingdom, Admiralty 1887, 4:9).

25. The navigable channel in the river.

26. London.

27. Repeated references to the "gloom" overhanging London not only may point to the air pollution (due to domestic coal fires) that plagued the city at the time, but they also convey the bleak, apocalyptic outlook then in vogue: a product of anxieties about socialist and anarchist threats to society, the British Empire declining and falling like all previous empires, and the human race degenerating as suggested by Social Darwinism. Furthermore, it was a common belief in the latter half of the 19th century that because of entropy on a cosmic scale, the universe would eventually become so uniformly cold that all life would end. Conrad shared this pessimism in a letter of 14 January 1898 (the year that he began *Heart of Darkness*) (Conrad 1986, 16–17; see also Davies 2014, 147–49).

"And this also," said Marlow suddenly, "has been one of the dark places of the earth."[28]

He was the only man of us who still "followed the sea." The worst that could be said of him was that he did not represent his class. He was a seaman, but he was a wanderer too, while most seamen lead, if one may so express it, a sedentary life. Their minds are of the stay-at-home order, and their home is always with them—the ship; and so is their country—the sea. One ship is very much like another, and the sea is always the same. In the immutability of their surroundings the foreign shores, the foreign faces, the changing immensity of life, glide past, veiled not by a sense of mystery but by a slightly disdainful ignorance; for there is nothing mysterious to a seaman unless it be the sea itself, which is the mistress of his existence and as inscrutable as Destiny. For the rest, after his hours of work, a casual stroll or a casual spree on shore suffices to unfold for him the secret of a whole continent, and generally he finds the secret not worth knowing. The yarns of seamen have a direct simplicity, the whole meaning of which lies within the shell of a cracked nut. But Marlow was not typical (if his propensity to spin yarns be excepted), and to him the meaning of an episode was not inside like a kernel but outside, enveloping the tale which brought it out only as a glow brings out a haze, in the likeness of one of these misty halos that sometimes are made visible by the spectral illumination of moonshine.

His remark did not seem at all surprising. It was just like Marlow. It was accepted in silence. No one took the trouble to grunt even; and presently he said, very slow:

"I was thinking of very old times, when the Romans first came here, nineteen hundred years ago[29]—the other day. . . . Light came out of this

---

28. Psalms 74:20–21: "Have respect unto the covenant: for the dark places of the earth are full of the habitations of cruelty. That is, all places where your word does not shine, there reigns tyranny and ambition." The phrase "dark places of the earth" was well known; drawn from the Bible, it became associated with the abolitionist cause in the United States and with English and American missionary work in Asia and Africa in the latter half of the 19th century. The phrase appeared repeatedly in missionary language to describe "enlightened" Christian cultures as superior to non-Christian ones. In this opposition between darkness and light, Africa figured prominently as it was referred to as the "dark continent" in books of the period. Other writers, as well, explicitly linked England and Africa as dark places. Henry Morton Stanley published *Through the Dark Continent* in 1878 and *In Darkest Africa* in 1890. William Booth, founder of the Salvation Army, began his *In Darkest England* (1890) by writing: "As there is a darkest Africa, is there not also a darkest London?" (Booth 1890, 9, 11; see also Stape 2004, 144–46).

29. The Roman conquest of Britain began when Julius Caesar invaded in 55 or 54 BCE. Rome expanded control of this imperial province, establishing garrisons and completing Hadrian's Wall on the northern frontier ca. 122–130 CE. Roman rule ended in 410 CE.

river since—you say Knights? Yes; but it is like a running blaze on a plain, like a flash of lightning in the clouds. We live in the flicker—may it last as long as the old earth keeps rolling! But darkness was here yesterday. Imagine the feelings of a commander of a fine—what d'ye call 'em?— trireme in the Mediterranean, ordered suddenly to the north; run overland across the Gauls[30] in a hurry; put in charge of one of these craft the legion- aries—a wonderful lot of handy men they must have been too—used to build, apparently by the hundred, in a month or two, if we may believe what we read.[31] Imagine him here—the very end of the world, a sea the colour of lead, a sky the colour of smoke, a kind of ship about as rigid as a concertina—and going up this river with stores, or orders, or what you like. Sandbanks, marshes, forests, savages—precious little to eat fit for a civilised man, nothing but Thames water to drink. No Falernian[32] wine here, no going ashore. Here and there a military camp lost in a wilderness, like a needle in a bundle of hay—cold, fog, tempests, disease, exile, and death—death skulking in the air, in the water, in the bush. They must have been dying like flies here. Oh yes—he did it. Did it very well, too, no doubt, and without thinking much about it either, except afterwards to brag of what he had gone through in his time, perhaps. They were men enough to face the darkness. And perhaps he was cheered by keeping his eye on a chance of promotion to the fleet at Ravenna[33] by and by, if he had good friends in Rome and survived the awful climate. Or think of a decent young citizen in a toga—perhaps too much dice, you know—coming out here in the train of some prefect,[34] or tax-gatherer, or trader, even, to mend his fortunes. Land in a swamp, march through the woods, and in some in- land post feel the savagery, the utter savagery, had closed round him—all that mysterious life of the wilderness that stirs in the forest, in the jungles, in the hearts of wild men. There's no initiation either into such mysteries. He has to live in the midst of the incomprehensible, which is also detest- able. And it has a fascination, too, that goes to work upon him. The

---

30. Inhabitants of a region now comprising France, parts of Belgium, northern Italy, and western Germany; conquered by Julius Caesar 58–50 BCE.

31. According to Julius Caesar, legionaries in Gaul built 600 transports and 28 war- ships over one winter in preparation for the invasion of Britain (Julius Caesar, De bello gallico 5).

32. A famous wine of ancient Rome made from grapes grown in Falernus Ager, near Naples; widely praised by Roman writers (Anthon 1841, s.v. "Falernus Ager").

33. The nearby port of Classis became homeport of Rome's fleet in the Adriatic by the first century CE. Ravenna was also the capital of the Roman Empire from 402 CE until 476 CE, when the empire dissolved.

34. Roman magistrate or other official.

fascination of the abomination—you know. Imagine the growing regrets, the longing to escape, the powerless disgust, the surrender, the hate."

He paused.

"Mind," he began again, lifting one arm from the elbow, the palm of the hand outwards, so that, with his legs folded before him, he had the pose of a Buddha preaching in European clothes and without a lotus-flower— "Mind, none of us would feel exactly like this. What saves us is efficiency— the devotion to efficiency. But these chaps were not much account, really. They were no colonists; their administration was merely a squeeze, and nothing more, I suspect. They were conquerors, and for that you want only brute force—nothing to boast of, when you have it, since your strength is just an accident arising from the weakness of others. They grabbed what they could get for the sake of what was to be got. It was just robbery with violence, aggravated murder on a great scale, and men going at it blind— as is very proper for those who tackle a darkness.[35] The conquest of the earth, which mostly means the taking it away from those who have a different complexion or slightly flatter noses than ourselves, is not a pretty thing when you look into it too much.[36] What redeems it is the idea only. An idea at the back of it; not a sentimental pretence but an idea; and an unselfish belief in the idea—something you can set up, and bow down before, and offer a sacrifice to. . . ."

He broke off. Flames glided in the river, small green flames, red flames, white flames, pursuing, overtaking, joining, crossing each other— then separating slowly or hastily.[37] The traffic of the great city went on in the deepening night upon the sleepless river. We looked on, waiting patiently—there was nothing else to do till the end of the flood;[38] but it was only after a long silence, when he said, in a hesitating voice, "I suppose you fellows remember I did once turn fresh-water sailor for a bit," that we

---

35. This does not appear to be the consensus view of Roman-controlled Britain, if we judge by one popular source of Conrad's time: "The coherent civilization of the Romans was accepted by the Britons, as it was by the Gauls, with something like enthusiasm. . . . they began to speak Latin, to use the material resources of Roman civilized life, and in time to consider themselves not the unwilling subjects of a foreign empire, but the British members of the Roman state" (*Encyclopedia Britannica,* 11th ed., s.v. "Britain").

36. Marlow continues to diverge from British history as then understood. Not only were the Romans colonists (and therefore not just conquerors and administrators), but also the primarily Celtic pre-Roman Britons before did not have markedly different noses or complexions from the Romans (Firchow 2000, 91).

37. Lights shown by vessels when underway between sunset and sunrise.

38. That is, the end of the inrushing tide.

knew we were fated, before the ebb[39] began to run, to hear about one of Marlow's inconclusive experiences.

"I don't want to bother you much with what happened to me personally," he began, showing in this remark the weakness of many tellers of tales who seem so often unaware of what their audience would best like to hear; "yet to understand the effect of it on me you ought to know how I got out there, what I saw, how I went up that river to the place where I first met the poor chap. It was the farthest point of navigation and the culminating point of my experience. It seemed somehow to throw a kind of light on everything about me—and into my thoughts. It was sombre enough too—and pitiful—not extraordinary in any way—not very clear either. No, not very clear. And yet it seemed to throw a kind of light.

"I had then, as you remember, just returned to London after a lot of Indian Ocean, Pacific, China Seas—a regular dose of the East—six years or so,[40] and I was loafing about, hindering you fellows in your work and invading your homes, just as though I had got a heavenly mission to civilise you. It was very fine for a time, but after a bit I did get tired of resting. Then I began to look for a ship—I should think the hardest work on earth.[41] But the ships wouldn't even look at me. And I got tired of that game too.

"Now when I was a little chap I had a passion for maps. I would look for hours at South America, or Africa, or Australia, and lose myself in all the glories of exploration. At that time there were many blank spaces on the earth, and when I saw one that looked particularly inviting on a map (but they all look that) I would put my finger on it and say, When I grow

---

39. The beginning of the outrushing tide, after a period of slack (still) water.

40. Conrad returned to London in 1889 after having intermittently sailed to, from, and within Southeast Asia and Indian waters since 1883. Before that, he had made two voyages between England and Australia (in 1878–1879 and 1880–1881).

41. Conrad's last sea billet before going to Africa was as master of the *Otago,* an iron-hulled bark, in 1888–1889, a job from which he resigned. Upon his return to England afterward, like Marlow he too had difficulty securing a new berth at sea (Najder 2007, 134).

up I will go there.[42] The North Pole was one of these places, I remember. Well, I haven't been there yet, and shall not try now. The glamour's off.[43] Other places were scattered about the Equator, and in every sort of latitude all over the two hemispheres. I have been in some of them, and . . . well, we won't talk about that. But there was one yet—the biggest, the most blank, so to speak—that I had a hankering after.

"True, by this time it was not a blank space any more. It had got filled since my boyhood with rivers and lakes and names. It had ceased to be a blank space of delightful mystery—a white patch for a boy to dream gloriously over. It had become a place of darkness. But there was in it one river especially, a mighty big river, that you could see on the map, resembling an immense snake uncoiled, with its head in the sea, its body at rest curving afar over a vast country, and its tail lost in the depths of the land.[44] And as I looked at the map of it in a shop-window, it fascinated me as a snake

---

42. Marlow's "passion for maps" mirrors Conrad's own. In *A Personal Record* (1908–1909), Conrad wrote:

> It was in 1868, when nine years old or thereabouts, that while looking at a map of Africa of the time and putting my finger on the blank space then representing the unsolved mystery of that continent, I said to myself with absolute assurance and an amazing audacity which are no longer in my character now:
> "When I group up I will go *there*."
> And of course I thought no more about it till after a quarter of a century or so an opportunity offered to go there—as if the sin of childish audacity were to be visited on my mature head. Yes. I did go there: *There* being the region of Stanley Falls which in '68 was the blankest of blank spaces on the earth's figured surface. (Conrad 2008b, 26)

Later, in his essay "Geography and Some Explorers" (1923), Conrad revisited his childhood memories, writing:

> One day, putting my finger on a blank spot in the very middle of the, then white, heart of Africa I declared that some day I would go there. . . . Nothing was further from my wildest hopes. Yet it is a fact that about eighteen years afterwards a wretched little stern wheel steamboat I commanded lay moored to the bank of an African river. . . . I said to myself with awe "this is the very spot of my boyish boast." A great melancholy descended on me. Yes, this was the very spot. But there was no shadowy friend to stand by my side in the night of the enormous wilderness, no great haunting memory but only the unholy recollection of a prosaic newspaper stunt and the distasteful knowledge of the vilest scramble for loot that ever disfigured the history of human conscience and geographical exploration. What an end to the idealised realities of a boy's day-dreams! (Conrad 2010a, 14).

(The "prosaic newspaper stunt" would refer to Henry Morton Stanley's famous 1871 expedition, financed by the *New York Herald,* to find the lost Scottish missionary Dr. Livingstone near Lake Tanganyika.)

43. Attempts to reach the North Pole had become an international competition by the end of the 19th century, although it was not until 1909 that Robert E. Peary became the first explorer to have credibly claimed to have reached it.

44. The Congo River, explored by Henry Morton Stanley in 1876–1877; its complete course was known to Europeans by 1890.

ÉTAT INDÉPENDANT DU CONGO

This 1892 map of the Congo Free State shows, beginning at the center left, the series of points on Conrad's and Marlow's journeys. Boma, the administrative capital of the Congo Free State (in the story, "the seat of the government") is fifty miles from the Atlantic, on the Congo River. Thirty miles upriver is Matadi, the main port on the lower Congo and the site of the Société Anonyme Belge company station ("your Company's station"). From Matadi to Léopoldville, cataracts on the Lower Congo make the river impassible by water; the 230-mile overland caravan route to Kinshasa (taken by Conrad and Marlow) is marked by a solid line south of the river. The railroad between Matadi and Léopoldville, marked by the dashed line farther south, was not complete until 1898. Léopoldville was the central supply station for the Congo Free State. Five miles upriver from Léopoldville and on Stanley Pool is Kinshasa ("the Central Station"), regional operational center for the SAB ivory trade. About one thousand miles farther upriver, near the upper right corner of this map, is Stanley Falls ("the Inner Station"). (Société de Géographie de Toulouse, "État Indépendant du Congo," The University Library, University of Illinois at Urbana-Champaign.)

would a bird—a silly little bird. Then I remembered there was a big concern, a Company for trade on that river.[45] Dash it all! I thought to myself, they can't trade without using some kind of craft on that lot of fresh water— steamboats! Why shouldn't I try to get charge of one? I went on along Fleet Street,[46] but could not shake off the idea. The snake had charmed me.

"You understand it was a Continental concern, that Trading society; but I have a lot of relations living on the Continent, because it's cheap and not so nasty as it looks, they say.

"I am sorry to own I began to worry them. This was already a fresh departure for me. I was not used to get things that way, you know. I always went my own road and on my own legs where I had a mind to go. I wouldn't have believed it of myself; but, then—you see—I felt somehow I must get there by hook or by crook. So I worried them. The men said, 'My dear fellow,' and did nothing. Then—would you believe it?—I tried the women. I, Charlie Marlow, set the women to work—to get a job. Heavens! Well, you see, the notion drove me. I had an aunt, a dear enthusiastic soul.[47] She wrote: 'It will be delightful. I am ready to do anything, anything for you. It is a glorious idea. I know the wife of a very high personage in the Administration,[48] and also a man who has lots of influence with,' etc. etc. She was determined to make no end of fuss to get me appointed skipper of a river steamboat, if such was my fancy.

"I got my appointment—of course; and I got it very quick. It appears the Company had received news that one of their captains had been killed in a scuffle with the natives. This was my chance, and it made me the more

---

45. The Société Anonyme Belge pour le Commerce du Haut-Congo (Belgian Limited Company for Trade in the Upper Congo), established in 1888 (Sherry 1971, 11–14).

46. A London street known as a newspaper and publishing center; also known at the time for shops selling maps and globes (Conrad 2010c, 442n48.39).

47. Modeled on Marguerite-Blanche-Marie Poradowska (1848–1937), a novelist and cousin of Conrad's whom he addressed as his "aunt." She lived in Brussels, and the two exchanged over 100 letters, mostly between 1890 and 1895 (Knowles and Moore 2000, 288–89). However, Conrad first met her after securing his Congo command, and she was not connected with the prospect (Stape 2010, 97–116). Conrad had been negotiating with shipowners and brokers in Belgium for a billet commanding a merchant ship; G. C. de Baerdemaecker, a ship broker in Ghent, recommended Conrad to Albert Thys, managing director of the Société Anonyme Belge pour le Commerce du Haut-Congo (Najder 2007, 138).

48. That is, the Belgian administration. Likely modeled on Alphonse-Jules-Marie Wauters (1845–1916), an acquaintance of Conrad's "aunt" Marguerite Poradowska. Wauters was an author, art critic, cartographer, and geographer. The founding editor of *Le Congo Illustré* and editor-in-chief of *Le Mouvement Géographique,* he wrote at length about the Congo (although he had not ever visited it). He initially supported Leopold's colonial project in the Congo. Given his wide range of interests and accomplishments, it is possible that he too served to inspire the figure of Kurtz (Stape 2010, 99–100).

anxious to go. It was only months and months afterwards, when I made the attempt to recover what was left of the body, that I heard the original quarrel arose from a misunderstanding about some hens. Yes, two black hens. Fresleven[49]—that was the fellow's name, a Dane—thought himself wronged somehow in the bargain, so he went ashore and started to hammer the chief of the village with a stick. Oh, it didn't surprise me in the least to hear this, and at the same time to be told that Fresleven was the gentlest, quietest creature that ever walked on two legs. No doubt he was; but he had been a couple of years already out there engaged in the noble cause, you know, and he probably felt the need at last of asserting his self-respect in some way. Therefore he whacked the old nigger[50] mercilessly, while a big crowd of his people watched him, thunderstruck, till some man—I was told the chief's son—in desperation at hearing the old chap yell, made a tentative jab with a spear at the white man—and of course it went quite easy between the shoulder-blades. Then the whole population cleared into the forest, expecting all kinds of calamities to happen, while, on the other hand, the steamer Fresleven commanded left also in a bad panic, in charge of the engineer, I believe. Afterwards nobody seemed to trouble much about Fresleven's remains, till I got out and stepped into his shoes. I couldn't let it rest, though; but when an opportunity offered at last to meet my predecessor, the grass growing through his ribs was tall enough to hide his bones. They were all there. The supernatural being had not been touched after he fell. And the village was deserted, the huts gaped black, rotting, all askew within the fallen enclosures. A calamity had come to it, sure enough. The people had vanished.[51] Mad terror had scattered them, men, women, and children, through the bush, and they had never returned. What became of the hens I don't know either. I should think the cause of

---

49. Johannes Freiesleben (1861?–1890), a Dane, was captain of the *Florida,* one of the trading vessels of the Société Anonyme Belge pour le Commerce du Haut-Congo, until killed by natives on 29 January 1890 at Tchumbiri. Conrad was hired to take his place. Sources vary on Freiesleben's death: he may have been killed following an argument with natives over supplies or firewood, or (in another account) after making a gift of two brass rods (currency) to a native chief's son. The latter account has him shot rather than stabbed (Sherry 1971, 15–22, 375).

50. Conrad's use of the word "nigger" reflects practice in his time in England, although it is clear that the term was considered even then to be derogatory (*Oxford English Dictionary* [1884–1928]). However, Conrad learned colloquial English from sailors on British merchant ships, and Marlow might simply be reproducing the language or views of the sailors' world to which he (and Conrad) belonged. Conrad also may have been attempting to recreate what he thought was authentic British speech (Firchow 2000, 38–39).

51. Reprisals were carried out against the native town of Tchumbiri in response to Freiesleben's murder (Sherry 1971, 16–21).

progress got them, anyhow. However, through this glorious affair I got my appointment, before I had fairly begun to hope for it.

"I flew around like mad to get ready, and before forty-eight hours I was crossing the Channel to show myself to my employers, and sign the contract.[52] In a very few hours I arrived in a city that always makes me think of a whited sepulchre.[53] Prejudice no doubt. I had no difficulty in finding the Company's offices. It was the biggest thing in the town, and everybody I met was full of it.[54] They were going to run an oversea empire, and make no end of coin by trade.

"A narrow and deserted street in deep shadow, high houses, innumerable windows with venetian blinds, a dead silence, grass sprouting between the stones, imposing carriage archways right and left, immense double doors standing ponderously ajar. I slipped through one of these cracks, went up a swept and ungarnished staircase, as arid as a desert, and opened the first door I came to. Two women, one fat and the other slim, sat on straw-bottomed chairs, knitting black wool.[55] The slim one got up and walked straight at me—still knitting with downcast eyes—and only just as I began to think of getting out of her way, as you would for a somnambulist, stood still, and looked up. Her dress was as plain as an umbrella-cover, and she turned round without a word and preceded me into a waiting-room. I gave my name, and looked about. Deal table in the middle, plain chairs all round the walls, on one end a large shining map, marked with all the colours of a rainbow. There was a vast amount of red—good to see at

52. While Conrad, like Marlow, "flew around like mad" in this period, his travels were more complex. Conrad was interviewed by Albert Thys in Brussels in November 1889, and the next several months involved repeated trips to the continent: to negotiate for a position as ship's captain but also to see relatives in Poland and Ukraine. He returned to Brussels briefly in February 1890 to see his cousin Aleksander Poradowski and his wife, Marguerite Poradowska (the model for Marlow's aunt). He then visited relatives in Warsaw, Lublin, and Kazimierówka, returned to Lublin in April, and then came back to Brussels on 29 April 1890. At that point, news that the master of the *Florida* (Freiesleben) had been murdered had reached the headquarters of the Société Anonyme Belge, and Conrad was hurriedly appointed to the position. He rushed to London and back to Brussels in preparation for the journey to Africa, traveling to Bordeaux by train and departing for Africa on the S.S. *Ville de Maceio* on 10 May 1890 (Najder 2007, 138–44).

53. Corresponds to Brussels.

54. The offices of the Société Anonyme Belge pour le Commerce du Haut-Congo were on rue Bréderode in Brussels, along with other commercial enterprises tied to the Congo as well as the Congo office of the Department of the Interior (Administration générale de l'État indépendent du Congo). This edifice essentially formed the back entrance to the Royal Palace of King Leopold II (Stape 2010, 98).

55. Like Lachesis and Clotho, the Greek mythological Fates, who spun and measured the thread of a human's life for Atropos to cut it.

any time, because one knows that some real work is done in there, a deuce of a lot of blue, a little green, smears of orange, and, on the East Coast, a purple patch, to show where the jolly pioneers of progress drink the jolly lager-beer.[56] However, I wasn't going into any of these. I was going into the yellow. Dead in the centre. And the river was there—fascinating—deadly—like a snake. Ough! A door opened, a white-haired secretarial head, but wearing a compassionate expression, appeared, and a skinny forefinger beckoned me into the sanctuary. Its light was dim, and a heavy writing-desk squatted in the middle. From behind that structure came out an impression of pale plumpness in a frock-coat. The great man himself.[57] He was five feet six, I should judge, and had his grip on the handle-end of ever so many millions. He shook hands, I fancy, murmured vaguely, was satisfied with my French. *Bon voyage.*

"In about forty-five seconds I found myself again in the waiting-room with the compassionate secretary, who, full of desolation and sympathy, made me sign some document. I believe I undertook amongst other things not to disclose any trade secrets. Well, I am not going to.[58]

"I began to feel slightly uneasy. You know I am not used to such ceremonies, and there was something ominous in the atmosphere. It was just as though I had been let into some conspiracy—I don't know—something not quite right; and I was glad to get out. In the outer room the two women knitted black wool feverishly. People were arriving, and the younger one was walking back and forth introducing them. The old one sat on her chair. Her flat cloth slippers were propped up on a foot-warmer, and a cat reposed on her lap. She wore a starched white affair on her head, had a wart on one cheek, and silver-rimmed spectacles hung on the tip of her nose. She glanced at me above the glasses. The swift and indifferent placidity of that look troubled me. Two youths with foolish and cheery countenances were being piloted over, and she threw at them the same quick glance of unconcerned wisdom. She seemed to know all about them and about me too. An eerie feeling came over me. She seemed uncanny and fateful. Often far away there I thought of these two, guarding the door of Darkness, knitting black wool as for a warm pall, one introducing, introducing continuously to the unknown, the other scrutinising the cheery and foolish faces with unconcerned old

---

56. In 19th-century maps, colonial possessions were marked according to the color scheme of red for British, blue for French, orange for Portuguese, green for Italian, purple for German, and yellow for Belgian (Conrad 2010c, 443n50.35).

57. Corresponds to Albert Thys, managing director of Société Anonyme Belge pour le Commerce du Haut-Congo.

58. In a letter that Conrad wrote to a cousin from Sierra Leone on 22 May 1890 on the *Ville de Maceio,* he explained about the prospect of commanding a steamer that "everything is supposed to be kept secret" (Conrad 1983, 52).

eyes. *Ave!* Old knitter of black wool. *Morituri te salutant.*[59] Not many of those she looked at ever saw her again—not half, by a long way.

"There was yet a visit to the doctor. 'A simple formality,' assured me the secretary, with an air of taking an immense part in all my sorrows. Accordingly a young chap wearing his hat over the left eyebrow, some clerk I suppose—there must have been clerks in the business, though the house was as still as a house in a city of the dead—came from somewhere upstairs, and led me forth. He was shabby and careless, with ink-stains on the sleeves of his jacket, and his cravat was large and billowy, under a chin shaped like the toe of an old boot. It was a little too early for the doctor, so I proposed a drink, and thereupon he developed a vein of joviality. As we sat over our vermuths he glorified the Company's business, and by and by I expressed casually my surprise at him not going out there. He became very cool and collected all at once. 'I am not such a fool as I look, quoth Plato to his disciples,' he said sententiously, emptied his glass with great resolution, and we rose.

"The old doctor felt my pulse, evidently thinking of something else the while. 'Good, good for there,' he mumbled, and then with a certain eagerness asked me whether I would let him measure my head.[60] Rather surprised, I said Yes, when he produced a thing like calipers and got the dimensions back and front and every way, taking notes carefully. He was an unshaven little man in a threadbare coat like a gaberdine, with his feet in slippers, and I thought him a harmless fool. 'I always ask leave, in the interests of science, to measure the crania of those going out there,' he said. 'And when they come back too?' I asked. 'Oh, I never see them,' he remarked; 'and, moreover, the changes take place inside, you know.' He smiled, as if at some quiet joke. 'So you are going out there. Famous. Interesting too.' He gave me a searching glance, and made another note. 'Ever any madness in your family?' he asked, in a matter-of-fact tone. I felt very annoyed. 'Is that question in the interests of science too?' 'It would be,' he said, without taking notice of my irritation, 'interesting for science to watch the mental changes of individuals, on the spot, but . . .' 'Are you an alienist?'[61] I interrupted. 'Every doctor should be—a little,'

---

59. From "Ave, Imperator, Morituri te salutant," Latin for "Hail, Emperor, those who are about to die salute you." A well-known phrase thought to have been customarily used by gladiators on entering the arena (Suetonius, *De Vita Caesarum* 21.6).

60. Phrenology, a pseudoscientific study popular in the 19th century, involved measuring the size and shape of the skull in order to discern character traits and mental faculties. According to a letter that Conrad's uncle Tadeusz Bobrowski wrote to him in August 1881, Izydor Kopernicki (1825–1891), a physician and anthropologist famous for his work in "Craniology" (the comparative study of human races, based on examination of skulls), had asked for Conrad to bring a dozen native skulls back from his voyages (Najder 1964, 74).

61. Psychiatrist.

answered that original imperturbably. 'I have a little theory which you Messieurs who go out there must help me to prove. This is my share in the advantages my country shall reap from the possession of such a magnificent dependency. The mere wealth I leave to others. Pardon my questions, but you are the first Englishman coming under my observation. . .' I hastened to assure him I was not in the least typical. 'If I were,' said I, 'I wouldn't be talking like this with you.' 'What you say is rather profound, and probably erroneous,' he said, with a laugh. 'Avoid irritation more than exposure to the sun. Adieu. How do you English say, eh? Good-bye. Ah! Good-bye. Adieu. In the tropics one must before everything keep calm.' . . . He lifted a warning forefinger. . . . '*Du calme, du calme. Adieu.*'[62]

"One thing more remained to do—say good-bye to my excellent aunt. I found her triumphant. I had a cup of tea—the last decent cup of tea for many days—and in a room that most soothingly looked just as you would expect a lady's drawing-room to look, we had a long quiet chat by the fireside. In the course of these confidences it became quite plain to me I had been represented to the wife of the high dignitary, and goodness knows to how many more people besides, as an exceptional and gifted creature—a piece of good fortune for the Company—a man you don't get hold of every day. Good Heavens! and I was going to take charge of a twopenny-halfpenny river-steamboat with a penny whistle attached! It appeared, however, I was also one of the Workers, with a capital—you know. Something like an emissary of light, something like a lower sort of apostle.[63] There had been a lot of such rot let loose in print and talk just about that time,[64] and the excellent woman, living right in the rush of all that humbug, got carried off her feet. She talked about 'weaning those ignorant

---

62. On his way to the Congo, Conrad reported to a cousin in a letter that "60 per cent. of our Company's employees return to Europe before they have completed even six months' service. Fever and dysentery! . . . there are only 7 per cent. who can do their three years' service" (Conrad 1983, 52).

63. The influential Scottish philosopher and historian Thomas Carlyle wrote regularly of Workers (with a capital "W"), as illustrated in a passage in *Past and Present* (1843) that Marlow's comment recalls: the role of "Workers" is "To make some nook of God's Creation a little fruitfuller, better, more worthy of God; to make some human hearts a little wiser, manfuler, happier,—more blessed, less accursed!" (Carlyle 1894, 255; see Conrad 2010c, 206n113). Henry Morton Stanley drew on this passage to defend Leopold's policies in 1898 (Conrad 1988b, 79).

64. In "An Outpost of Progress" (1897), Conrad's earlier story set in Africa, the narrator describes characters reading a newspaper from home and noting, "That print discussed what it was pleased to call 'Our Colonial Expansion' in high-flown language. It spoke much of the rights and duties of civilisation, of the sacredness of the civilising work, and extolled the merits of those who went about bringing light, and faith and commerce to the dark places of the earth" (Conrad 2007, 240). Henry Morton Stanley described his purpose in exploring Africa in similarly philanthropic language (Stanley 1885, 1:30).

millions from their horrid ways,'[65] till, upon my word, she made me quite uncomfortable. I ventured to hint that the Company was run for profit.

"'You forget, dear Charlie, that the labourer is worthy of his hire,' she said, brightly.[66] It's queer how out of touch with truth women are. They live in a world of their own, and there had never been anything like it, and never can be. It is too beautiful altogether, and if they were to set it up it would go to pieces before the first sunset. Some confounded fact we men have been living contentedly with ever since the day of creation would start up and knock the whole thing over.

"After this I got embraced, told to wear flannel, be sure to write often, and so on—and I left. In the street—I don't know why—a queer feeling came to me that I was an impostor. Odd thing that I, who used to clear out for any part of the world at twenty-four hours' notice, with less thought than most men give to the crossing of a street, had a moment—I won't say of hesitation, but of startled pause, before this commonplace affair. The best way I can explain it to you is by saying that, for a second or two, I felt as though, instead of going to the centre of a continent, I were about to set off for the centre of the earth.

"I left in a French steamer, and she called in every blamed port they have out there, for, as far as I could see, the sole purpose of landing

---

65. By the late 19th century missionaries in the Congo were primarily British, American, French, and Belgian. They were dedicated not only to evangelism but also to spreading Western education, including teaching technical skills. They did considerable translation work: writing dictionaries, translating books into native languages, and promoting selected indigenous languages to be used for communication in the administration, in the army, and in education. In terms of sheer numbers, however, the missionaries' influence was not great. Furthermore, the education imparted was fairly basic, as just a small fraction of students learned even reading, writing, and arithmetic. Also, much of Christianity was so alien to natives that African fathers were reluctant to have their children brought up in its ways (Gann and Duignan 1979, 207–8).

66. Henry Morton Stanley quoted this biblical phrase (Luke 10:7) in justifying his praise of Europeans in *The Congo and the Founding of Its Free State*: "The Divine law declares that only by the sweat of his brow shall a man eat bread. There is a law pretty generally recognised among the advanced nations, that every honest labourer is worthy of his hire, but only the conspicuously meritorious deserve special commendation" (Stanley 1885, 1:xiv).

soldiers and custom-house officers.[67] I watched the coast. Watching a coast as it slips by the ship is like thinking about an enigma. There it is before you—smiling, frowning, inviting, grand, mean, insipid, or savage, and always mute with an air of whispering, Come and find out. This one was almost featureless, as if still in the making, with an aspect of monotonous grimness. The edge of a colossal jungle, so dark green as to be almost black, fringed with white surf, ran straight, like a ruled line, far, far away along a blue sea whose glitter was blurred by a creeping mist. The sun was fierce, the land seemed to glisten and drip with steam. Here and there greyish-whitish specks showed up clustered inside the white surf, with a flag flying above them perhaps—settlements some centuries old, and still no bigger than pin-heads on the untouched expanse of their background. We pounded along, stopped, landed soldiers; went on, landed custom-house clerks to levy toll in what looked like a God-forsaken wilderness, with a tin shed and a flag-pole lost in it; landed more soldiers—to take care of the custom-house clerks, presumably. Some, I heard, got drowned in the surf; but whether they did or not, nobody seemed particularly to care. They were just flung out there, and on we went. Every day the coast looked the same, as though we had not moved; but we passed various places—trading places—with names like Gran' Bassam, Little Popo;[68] names that seemed to belong to some sordid farce acted in front of a sinister back-cloth. The idleness of a passenger, my isolation amongst all these men with whom I had no point of contact, the oily and languid sea, the uniform sombreness of the coast, seemed to keep me away from the truth of things, within the toil of a mournful and senseless delusion. The voice of the surf heard now and then was a positive pleasure, like the speech of a brother. It was something natural, that had its reason, that had a meaning. Now and then a boat from the shore gave one a momentary contact with reality. It was paddled

67. Conrad sailed from Bordeaux on 10 May 1890 aboard the *Ville de Maceio,* a French steamer, which had left Antwerp on 30 April. The steamer called at Tenerife (Canary Islands, Spain), Dakar (Senegal, then a French colony), Conakry (now in Guinea, then in the part of Senegal that was separated in 1891 to become the French protectorate of Rivières du Sud), Freetown (Sierra Leone, a British colony), Grand Bassam (in Ivory Coast, which became a French colony in 1893 with Grand Bassam as its capital), Grand Popo (now in Benin, then the Kingdom of Dahomey, which was invaded by France in 1892–1894 and turned into a protectorate), Libreville (now in Gabon, from 1888 to 1904 the capital of French Equatorial Africa), Banana (a port at the mouth of the Congo River), then Boma (about 50 miles up the Congo River from the Atlantic) (Sherry 1971, 13, 23; Najder 2007, 147).

68. The *Ville de Maceio* stopped at Grand Popo, not Little Popo. Little Popo is a former name of what is now Aného in Togo (in 1890 a German protectorate, with Little Popo then its only port) (*Encyclopedia Britannica Online,* s.vv. "Lomé," "Aného," accessed 3 January 2017, https://www.britannica.com/place/Lome; https://www.britannica.com/place/Aneho).

by black fellows. You could see from afar the white of their eyeballs glistening. They shouted, sang; their bodies streamed with perspiration; they had faces like grotesque masks—these chaps; but they had bone, muscle, a wild vitality, an intense energy of movement, that was as natural and true as the surf along their coast.[69] They wanted no excuse for being there. They were a great comfort to look at. For a time I would feel I belonged still to a world of straightforward facts; but the feeling would not last long. Something would turn up to scare it away. Once, I remember, we came upon a man-of-war anchored off the coast.[70] There wasn't even a shed there, and she was shelling the bush. It appears the French had one of their wars going on thereabouts. Her ensign[71] drooped[72] limp like a rag; the muzzles of the long six-inch[73] guns stuck out all over the low hull; the greasy, slimy swell swung her up lazily and let her down, swaying her thin masts. In the empty immensity of earth, sky, and water, there she was, incomprehensible, firing into a continent. Pop, would go one of the six-inch guns; a small flame would dart and vanish, a little white smoke would

---

69. The links that Marlow makes between the natives, the surf, and the word "brother" indicates a sense of kinship that he feels with the natives, and he directly uses the word "kinship" later as well. In this respect, Conrad arguably gives Marlow attitudes about racial differences that are more generous than were common at the time. Charles Darwin had given credence to the idea that there were superior and inferior races, with whites superior to other racial groups—and therefore in a position to govern them (Brantlinger 1985b, 187). Prominent biologists T. H. Huxley and Alfred Wallace concurred with this view (Bannister 1979, 184–86).

The standard outlook of Conrad's day, encouraged by Darwinian views of evolution, was that blacks were mentally inferior. The celebrated 11th edition of the *Encyclopedia Britannica* asserted, "The negro would appear to stand on a lower evolutionary plane than the white man." Furthermore, "the mental inferiority of the negro to the white or yellow races is a fact," even if "it has often been exaggerated," and "the mental constitution of the negro is very similar to that of a child" (*Encyclopedia Britannica*, 11th ed., s.v. "Negro"). However, no conclusive evidence has surfaced that Conrad shared these prevailing opinions, and nowhere in *Heart of Darkness* does Conrad or his speaker make or imply the racist claim that Europeans are inherently superior to blacks because of biological or genetic differences. On the contrary, Conrad's fiction set in both Africa and Asia consistently ridicules ideas of white superiority (Firchow 2000, 10, 47).

70. Conrad later reported in a letter to Kazimierz Waliszewski on 16 December 1903 having seen a French warship named the *Seignelay* bombarding the African coast in 1890 (Conrad 1988a, 94). However, the *Seignelay*—while in service at the time—is not mentioned in lists of ships participating in the French blockade of the Kingdom of Dahomey (the country that included the town of Grand Popo) prior to the French invasion of 1892–1894 (Conrad 2010c, 445n55.4–6).

71. National flag.

72. Corrected from "dropped" in the 1921 published text.

73. The diameter of the gun barrel bore.

disappear, a tiny projectile would give a feeble screech—and nothing happened. Nothing could happen. There was a touch of insanity in the proceeding, a sense of lugubrious drollery in the sight; and it was not dissipated by somebody on board assuring me earnestly there was a camp of natives—he called them enemies!—hidden out of sight somewhere.

"We gave her her letters (I heard the men in that lonely ship were dying of fever at the rate of three a day) and went on. We called at some more places with farcical names, where the merry dance of death and trade goes on in a still and earthy atmosphere as of an overheated catacomb; all along the formless coast bordered by dangerous surf, as if Nature herself had tried to ward off intruders; in and out of rivers, streams of death in life, whose banks were rotting into mud, whose waters, thickened into slime, invaded the contorted mangroves, that seemed to writhe at us in the extremity of an impotent despair. Nowhere did we stop long enough to get a particularised impression, but the general sense of vague and oppressive wonder grew upon me. It was like a weary pilgrimage amongst hints for nightmares.

"It was upward of thirty days before I saw the mouth of the big river. We anchored off the seat of the government.[74] But my work would not

---

74. Boma, administrative capital of the Congo Free State, about 50 miles up the Congo River from the Atlantic. Conrad disembarked there on 12 June 1890 (Najder 2007, 148). In the early 1890s, Boma contained a Victorian mansion (with covered porches, cupola, and French windows) for the governor general of the Congo Free State, guarded by uniformed African sentries; a military post; a two-story hotel; a hospital for the Europeans; a Catholic church built out of iron; and a narrow-gauge trolley (steam engine plus cars) connecting the busy warehouses and docks on the water to the plateau above the town, where the government offices and houses for the white officials stood to take advantage of the coolness. The approximately 75 Europeans who worked there took the trolley down the hill three times a day for meals in the hotel dining room (Hochschild 1999, 115).

A description published in 1890 put the population of officials of Boma at "upwards of one hundred Belgians and foreigners (no English)." This figure does not include "a large number of Europeans in the English, French, Dutch, and Portuguese commercial houses engaged in trading with the natives, exchanging rum, powder, guns, cloth, etc., for native products, such as palm oil, palm kernels, and peanuts, which are shipped home to Liverpool, Hamburg, or Havre, and there used in the manufacture of soap, candles, etc." Boma was a bustling town: "A postal service is established, law courts exist, and a public force of Houssa soldiers are attached to the place" (Glave 1890, 619–20).

One of the significant alterations of historical fact that Conrad makes is to diminish the extent of the "seat of the government." In the published version of *Heart of Darkness,* the only detail that Marlow gives is of "the miserable little wharf." A long, much more descriptive passage appears in the manuscript of the story; it was later cut (Conrad, n.d., 40[41]–42[43]).

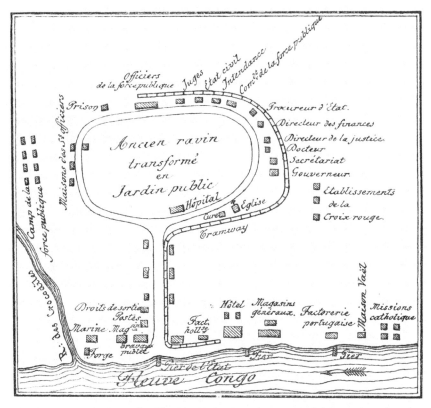

BOMA, D'APRÈS UN CROQUIS DE M. VERBRUGGHE.

Boma, the adminitstrative capital of the Congo Free State and "the seat of the government" in the story, as depicted in 1894. Conrad arrived at Boma on 12 June 1890 and was in Matadi the following day. Although reduced to "the miserable little wharf" in Marlow's tale, Boma had a Victorian mansion for the governor general, a hospital, two-story hotel, church, and numerous other buildings. In 1890 Boma had a population of a hundred Belgian officials, as well as many more Europeans engaged in the trading houses of several European countries (Glave 1890, 619–20). (From Albert Chapaux, *Le Congo.* Brussels: Charles Rozez, 1894, 433.)

begin till some two hundred miles farther on.[75] So as soon as I could I made a start for a place thirty miles higher up.[76]

---

75. Kinshasa, where Conrad was to take command of the *Florida.*

76. Matadi, about 30 miles upriver from Boma and the uppermost navigable point of the Lower Congo River. Conrad left for Matadi on a small steamer on 13 June 1890, the day after he had arrived at Boma.

Part of Boma, which Henry Morton Stanley called "the principal emporium of trade on the Congo," several years before Conrad's arrival (Stanley 1885, 91). (From Henry M. Stanley, *The Congo and the Founding of Its Free State*. New York, Harper & Brothers, 1885, opposite 1:93.)

"I had my passage on a little sea-going steamer. Her captain was a Swede,[77] and knowing me for a seaman, invited me on the bridge. He was a young man, lean, fair, and morose, with lanky hair and a shuffling gait. As we left the miserable little wharf, he tossed his head contemptuously at the shore. 'Been living there?' he asked. I said, 'Yes.' 'Fine lot these government chaps—are they not?' he went on, speaking English with great precision and considerable bitterness. 'It is funny what some people will do for a few francs a month. I wonder what becomes of that kind when it goes up country?' I said to him I expected to see that soon. 'So-o-o!' he

---

77. The seamen in the vessels plying the Congo were almost exclusively Scandinavian; most were Danish, and some were Swedish. There were three captains on the Lower Congo taking ships between Boma and Matadi from June to December 1890: the Swedish Captain Axel Tjulin (fair-haired, he may well have served as the model for the captain in Conrad's story), and two Danes (Sherry 1971, 397–98n8).

exclaimed. He shuffled athwart,[78] keeping one eye ahead vigilantly. 'Don't be too sure,' he continued. 'The other day I took up a man who hanged himself on the road.[79] He was a Swede, too.' 'Hanged himself! Why, in God's name?' I cried. He kept on looking out watchfully. 'Who knows? The sun too much for him, or the country perhaps.'

"At last we opened a reach.[80] A rocky cliff appeared, mounds of turned-up earth by the shore, houses on a hill, others with iron roofs, amongst a waste of excavations, or hanging to the declivity. A continuous noise of the rapids above hovered over this scene of inhabited devastation. A lot of people, mostly black and naked, moved about like ants. A jetty projected into the river. A blinding sunlight drowned all this at times in a sudden recrudescence of glare. 'There's your Company's station,' said the Swede, pointing to three wooden barrack-like structures on the rocky slope.[81] 'I will send your things up. Four boxes did you say? So. Farewell.'

"I came upon a boiler wallowing in the grass, then found a path leading up the hill. It turned aside for the boulders, and also for an undersized railway truck lying there on its back with its wheels in the air. One was off. The thing looked as dead as the carcass of some animal. I came upon more pieces of decaying machinery, a stack of rusty rails. To the left a clump of trees made a shady spot, where dark things seemed to stir feebly. I blinked, the path was steep. A horn tooted to the right, and I saw the black people run. A heavy and dull detonation shook the ground, a puff of smoke came out of the cliff, and that was all. No change appeared on the face of the

---

78. Nautical term: from side to side, or in a crosswise direction.

79. The only Scandinavian who committed suicide before 1891 on the caravan trail was a Dane, Captain Wass, who killed himself on 30 June 1889 at Boma; the account of this event asserts that the climate drove him to madness (Jenssen-Tusch 1902–1905, 193; Sherry 1971, 28).

80. A reach is a straight part of a navigable river; to open it is to arrive at it. The approximately 30-mile river passage from Boma to Matadi would have taken no more than a day (Sherry 1971, 397n1).

81. Matadi, where Conrad arrived on 13 June 1890, according to his diary (which starts at this point). In addition to being the site of the Société Anonyme Belge company station, Matadi held four factories and 170 European inhabitants (Sherry 1971, 30). By 1890, in one published description, Matadi was home to "large establishments belonging to the principal English, French, Dutch, Belgian, and Portuguese trading companies, and a valuable trade in ivory, rubber, palm kernels, etc., is carried on, the ivory being brought down by the middlemen dwelling around the district of Manyanga, who obtain it from the Batéké traders of Stanley Pool" (Glave 1890, 619). Matadi was an important central point on the trade network, situated at the intersection of the water route, from the sea up the Congo to its highest continuously navigable point, and the overland routes connecting by caravan to the interior (Najder 2007, 151).

rock. They were building a railway. The cliff was not in the way or anything; but this objectless blasting was all the work going on.[82]

"A slight clinking behind me made me turn my head. Six black men
advanced in a file, toiling up the path. They walked erect and slow, balanc-
ing small baskets full of earth on their heads, and the clink kept time with
their footsteps. Black rags were wound round their loins, and the short
ends behind waggled to and fro like tails. I could see every rib, the joints
of their limbs like knots in a rope; each had an iron collar on his neck,
and all were connected together with a chain whose bights[83] swung between them, rhythmically clinking. Another report from the cliff made me
think suddenly of that ship of war I had seen firing into a continent. It was
the same kind of ominous voice; but these men could by no stretch of imagination be called enemies. They were called criminals, and the outraged
law, like the bursting shells, had come to them, an insoluble mystery from
the sea. All their meagre breasts panted together, the violently dilated nostrils quivered, the eyes stared stonily uphill. They passed me within six
inches, without a glance, with that complete, deathlike indifference of unhappy savages. Behind this raw matter one of the reclaimed, the product of
the new forces at work, strolled despondently, carrying a rifle by its

---

82. Completing this railway would, in fact, significantly improve the movement of
trade on the Congo. Oceangoing steamers could ascend the river only as far as Matadi,
while river steamers were in service on the Congo, and the network of tributaries, above
Léopoldville and nearby Kinshasa. Because of the cataracts on the Lower Congo in between, the trade route in this section went overland for 230 miles, with merchandise carried
on natives' backs (Sherry 1971, 36). Construction of the railway between Matadi and Léopoldville had begun on 15 March 1890, three months before Conrad's arrival (Firchow 2000,
161), and the Ville de Maceio, with Conrad embarked, also carried sleepers and rails for the
railway (Sherry 1971, 31). Progress was slow, however, especially in the early years. Because of engineering and labor difficulties, and the high death rate among workers, the
railway would not be completed until 1898.

The impotence of the railway construction as depicted in Heart of Darkness must have
been striking to Conrad's readers. Not only did it contrast with the railway's evident bene-
fits, but also the route was completed, to general approval in Europe, eight months before
Conrad began writing his story (Firchow 2000, 161). In Conrad's hands, the railway becomes
a complex and powerful symbol that critiques promises of technological development and
the spread of civilization.

83. In 1890, Leopold issued a decree allowing the authorities in the Congo to impress
natives in the area into forced labor on the railway (Conrad 2010c, 446n56.32). Laborers were
compelled to work and chained when they were reluctant (Hochschild 1999, 171). In 1891 300
workers from Sierra Leone attacked their Zanzibari police auxiliary guards, who bludgeoned
the rioters into submission (Cornet 1948, 203–4). Bight is a nautical term for a loop.

middle.[84] He had a uniform jacket with one button off, and seeing a white man on the path, hoisted his weapon to his shoulder with alacrity. This was simple prudence, white men being so much alike at a distance that he could not tell who I might be.[85] He was speedily reassured, and with a large, white, rascally grin, and a glance at his charge, seemed to take me into partnership in his exalted trust. After all, I also was a part of the great cause of these high and just proceedings.[86]

"Instead of going up, I turned and descended to the left. My idea was to let that chain-gang get out of sight before I climbed the hill. You know I am not particularly tender; I've had to strike and to fend off. I've had to resist and to attack sometimes—that's only one way of resisting—without counting the exact cost, according to the demands of such sort of life as I had blundered into. I've seen the devil of violence, and the devil of greed, and the devil of hot desire; but, by all the stars! these were strong, lusty, red-eyed devils, that swayed and drove men—men, I tell you. But as I stood on this hillside, I foresaw that in the blinding sunshine of that land I would become acquainted with a flabby, pretending, weak-eyed devil of a rapacious and pitiless folly. How insidious he could be, too, I was only to find out several months later and a thousand miles farther. For a moment I stood appalled, as though by a warning. Finally I descended the hill, obliquely, towards the trees I had seen.

"I avoided a vast artificial hole somebody had been digging on the slope, the purpose of which I found it impossible to divine. It wasn't a quarry or a sandpit, anyhow. It was just a hole. It might have been connected with the philanthropic desire of giving the criminals something to

---

84. Corresponds to the native railway police, or possibly a member of the Force Publique, the army of natives (under white officers) that Congo Free State authorities built by recruiting from the West and East Coasts of Africa; local Congolese were also recruited and impressed into service (Gann and Duignan 1979, 73). It was primarily a fighting force and undertook countless raids and "punitive expeditions," but until 1904 it was also used for nonmilitary duties, such as building roads and government stations (Gann and Duignan 1979, 55, 65).

85. Soldiers in the Force Publique were subject to harsh discipline, including floggings of up to 100 lashes for serious offenses (Gann and Duignan 1979, 76).

86. A 26 January 1890 article in *Le Mouvement Géographique,* a periodical based in Brussels, insisted that the workers were free and hired legally and willingly. However, articles in the British press described the workers as virtual slaves (quoted in Sherry 1971, 31–32). Conditions must have been grim, even if the surviving data is from the year after Conrad's time in the Congo. The progress of the railway was hindered not only by the terrain and the climate but also by the lack of workers, many of whom were killed by disease. Fevers, beri-beri, dysentery, and smallpox decimated both natives and Europeans; 900 native laborers died of disease from November 1891 to June 1892 (Goffin 1907, 44). Officially, the total death toll was 1,800 nonwhites and 132 whites, but some estimates number the native death rate at 1,800 per year for the first two years alone (Gann and Duignan 1979, 71).

do. I don't know. Then I nearly fell into a very narrow ravine, almost no more than a scar in the hillside. I discovered that a lot of imported drainage-pipes for the settlement had been tumbled in there. There wasn't one that was not broken. It was a wanton smash-up. At last I got under the trees. My purpose was to stroll into the shade for a moment; but no sooner within than it seemed to me I had stepped into a gloomy circle of some Inferno. The rapids were near, and an uninterrupted, uniform, headlong, rushing noise filled the mournful stillness of the grove, where not a breath stirred, not a leaf moved, with a mysterious sound—as though the tearing pace of the launched earth had suddenly become audible.

"Black shapes crouched, lay, sat between the trees, leaning against the trunks, clinging to the earth, half coming out, half effaced within the dim light, in all the attitudes of pain, abandonment, and despair. Another mine on the cliff went off, followed by a slight shudder of the soil under my feet. The work was going on. The work! And this was the place where some of the helpers had withdrawn to die.[87]

"They were dying slowly—it was very clear. They were not enemies, they were not criminals, they were nothing earthly now—nothing but black shadows of disease and starvation, lying confusedly in the greenish gloom. Brought from all the recesses of the coast in all the legality of time contracts,[88] lost in uncongenial surroundings, fed on unfamiliar food, they sickened, became inefficient, and were then allowed to crawl away and rest. These moribund shapes were free as air—and nearly as thin. I began to distinguish the gleam of eyes under the trees. Then, glancing down, I saw a face near my hand. The black bones reclined at full length with one shoulder against the tree, and slowly the eyelids rose and the sunken eyes looked up at me, enormous and vacant, a kind of blind, white flicker in the depths of the orbs, which died out slowly. The man seemed young—almost a boy—but you know with them it's hard to tell. I found nothing else to do but to offer him one of my good Swede's ship's biscuits I had in my pocket. The fingers closed slowly on it and held—there was no other movement and no other glance. He had tied a bit of white worsted round his neck— Why? Where did he get it? Was it a badge—an ornament—a charm—a propitiatory act? Was there any idea at all connected with it? It looked startling round his black neck, this bit of white thread from beyond the seas.

"Near the same tree two more bundles of acute angles sat with their legs drawn up. One, with his chin propped on his knees, stared at nothing,

---

87. Louis Goffin, Engineer-in-Chief of the Congo Railway, claimed that all humane measures were taken to combat illness, but the natives would panic and flee to die in the jungle (Goffin 1907, 43).

88. Workers served for one year (Williams 1890b, 19).

in an intolerable and appalling manner: his brother phantom rested its fore-head, as if overcome with a great weariness; and all about others were scat-tered in every pose of contorted collapse, as in some picture of a massacre or a pestilence. While I stood horror-struck, one of these creatures rose to his hands and knees, and went off on all-fours towards the river to drink. He lapped out of his hand, then sat up in the sunlight, crossing his shins in front of him, and after a time let his woolly head fall on his breastbone.

"I didn't want any more loitering in the shade, and I made haste to-wards the station. When near the buildings I met a white man, in such an unexpected elegance of get-up that in the first moment I took him for a sort of vision. I saw a high starched collar, white cuffs, a light alpaca jacket, snowy trousers, a clear necktie, and varnished boots. No hat. Hair parted, brushed, oiled, under a green-lined parasol held in a big white hand. He was amazing, and had a pen-holder behind his ear.

"I shook hands with this miracle, and I learned he was the Company's chief accountant, and that all the book-keeping was done at this station. He had come out for a moment, he said, 'to get a breath of fresh air.' The expres-sion sounded wonderfully odd, with its suggestion of sedentary desk-life. I wouldn't have mentioned the fellow to you at all, only it was from his lips that I first heard the name of the man who is so indissolubly connected with the memories of that time. Moreover, I respected the fellow. Yes; I respected his collars, his vast cuffs, his brushed hair. His appearance was certainly that of a hairdresser's dummy; but in the great demoralisation of the land he kept up his appearance. That's backbone. His starched collars and got-up shirt-fronts were achievements of character. He had been out nearly three years; and, later, I could not help asking him how he managed to sport such linen. He had just the faintest blush, and said modestly, 'I've been teaching one of the native women about the station. It was difficult. She had a distaste for the work.' Thus this man had verily accomplished something. And he was de-voted to his books, which were in apple-pie order.[89]

"Everything else in the station was in a muddle,—heads, things, build-ings. Strings of dusty niggers with splay feet arrived and departed; a stream of manufactured goods, rubbishy cottons, beads, and brass-wire[90] set into the depths of darkness, and in return came a precious trickle of ivory.[91]

---

89. A nautical expression for orderly and neat.
90. Workers were paid one shilling per day (Williams 1890a, 6). The form of currency used at Léopoldville and in the Upper Congo was the *mitako,* or brass rod. Imported in 60-pound coils, at Léopoldville it was cut into pieces of regulation length (approximately two feet), resembling a stair-rod in size and appearance, each valued at 1½ pence (Twelve pence made a shilling) (Troup 1890, 103–4).
91. At the time of Conrad's visit, ivory was still the colony's most precious commodity, accounting for just over half of the country's total exports by value (Büchler 1912, 1:232).

"I had to wait in the station for ten days—an eternity.[92] I lived in a hut in the yard, but to be out of the chaos I would sometimes get into the accountant's office. It was built of horizontal planks, and so badly put together that, as he bent over his high desk, he was barred from neck to heels with narrow strips of sunlight. There was no need to open the big shutter to see. It was hot there too; big flies buzzed fiendishly, and did not sting, but stabbed. I sat generally on the floor, while, of faultless appearance (and even slightly scented), perching on a high stool, he wrote, he wrote. Sometimes he stood up for exercise. When a truckle-bed[93] with a sick man (some invalided agent from up-country) was put in there, he exhibited a gentle annoyance. 'The groans of this sick person,' he said, 'distract my attention. And without that it is extremely difficult to guard against clerical errors in this climate.'

"One day he remarked, without lifting his head, 'In the interior you will no doubt meet Mr. Kurtz.'[94] On my asking who Mr. Kurtz was, he said he was a first-class agent; and seeing my disappointment at this information,

---

92. According to his diary, Conrad was in Matadi for 15 days: from 13 to 28 June 1890. He had expected to leave on 19 June, as he wrote to his "aunt" Marguerite Poradowska from Matadi in a letter dated the day before (Conrad 1983, 56–57). However, as Conrad wrote in the first entry of his diary, he was delayed by the manager of the SAB's local trading post, Joseph-Louis-Hubert Gosse, who held him up "for some reason of his own."

93. Also called a trundle bed, a low bed usually on wheels, which could be slid or rolled under a higher bed for storage.

94. A number of real-life persons have been proposed as inspiration for Kurtz. In Conrad's manuscript of the story, the first four named instances record him as "Mr. Klein," later changed to "Mr. Kurtz." Georges Antoine Klein (1863–1890), the most obvious potential model, was a commercial agent for the SAB at the Stanley Falls "Inner Station." He went with Conrad downriver on the steamer *Roi des Belges* (*King of the Belgians*), was ill from dysentery, died along the way aboard the vessel on 21 September 1890, and was buried at Tchumbiri (Jean-Aubry 1926, 66). However, Klein was a minor subordinate agent who would have been of little particular interest to Conrad. Klein had been an agent at Stanley Falls for probably four months at the most, with a year and a half in the Congo in total (Sherry 1971, 74; Watt 1980, 142).

The Belgian Arthur Hodister (1847–1892) was an important and productive ivory agent. Energetic, courageous, and enterprising, he carried out dangerous expeditions into little-known territory and delivered detailed reports on the Upper Congo (Sherry 1971, 95–99). Hodister was also unorthodox and extraordinarily talented, using charm and theatrics instead of force. Fluent in Swahili, dressed in a turban and white robe, and surrounding himself with slaves, he ventured deep into elephant country without any black soldiers and was honored by Arab chiefs (Pakenham 2003, 434). He was nevertheless eloquent in speaking out against slave trading, and he was an authentic reformer. He was killed in 1892 in a large Arab revolt while on an expedition (Watt 1980, 142).

Emin Pasha (1840–1892) was a German physician (born Eduard Schnitzer) who had converted to Islam and was governing a province in the Sudan at the appointment of General Charles George Gordon. Isolated by the defeat of Gordon at Khartoum by the Mahdists in 1885, Emin was himself being attacked by Mahdist rebels when Henry Morton Stanley led a highly publicized relief effort in 1887. Emin, like Kurtz, declined to be rescued, and Stanley was then accused of forcibly bringing him back when they reached present-day Tanzania in December 1889. Emin was killed near Stanley Falls on an expedition in 1892 (Guerard 1958, 34; Watt 1980, 143).

Major Edmund Barttelot (1859–1888) was in charge of Stanley's rear column in the expedition to relieve Emin Pasha. Barttelot had a native lashed to death, jabbed at others with his cane tipped in steel, and bit another before he was shot and killed by a Manyema tribesman (Hochschild 1999, 97–98, 144–45). His death in 1888 resulted in great public controversy. Stanley alleged that Barttelot had lost his mind and brought about his own death (Allen 1965, 275–81; Watt 1980, 143).

Léon Rom (1860–1924) was a captain in the Force Publique, the army of the Congo Free State. He was station chief at Léopoldville when Conrad passed through on his way to Kinshasa at the beginning of August 1890, and the two may have met (Hochschild 1999, 145–46). Rom was station chief at Stanley Falls in 1895 (after Conrad's visit), where he reportedly had a gallows permanently in place. He set 21 native heads around the flowerbed of his house, as described by a British account in *Century Magazine* in 1895—reprinted in *The Saturday Review* (a magazine Conrad regularly read) on 17 December 1898, within a couple of days of when Conrad began writing *Heart of Darkness* (Hochschild 1999, 145). (For a dissenting view of this possibility, see Firchow 2000, 128–32). Furthermore, Rom was an entomologist, a painter of portraits and landscapes, and a writer. Kurtz's relations with the adoring natives and beautiful African mistress are paralleled by the later evidence of another Force Publique officer, described in 1895 as "want[ing] to play the role of a second Rom" (Leclerq 1970, 264; Hochschild 1999, 148–49).

Guillaume Van Kerckhoven (1853–1892) was a hot-tempered Force Publique officer who led violent punitive expeditions into the interior, according to a 1912 article by Camille Janssen in *Bulletin de la Société Belge d'Études Coloniales* (quoted in Hochschild 1999, 196). Roger Casement's 1904 report to the Foreign Office reports that in 1887, Van Kerckhoven described paying five brass rods for every human head that his black soldiers brought him in any of his operations (quoted in Hochschild 1999, 196). Casement met Conrad in June 1890 when the two were together in Matadi and could possibly have told him about Van Kerckhoven.

The German explorer Carl Peters (1856–1918) helped establish the German East Africa Company and was notorious for his cruelty; he was dismissed in 1897 for mistreating natives. Peters has been quoted for claiming that he "was fed up with being counted among the pariahs and wanted to belong to a master race" (Ritter 1936, preface, quoted in Arendt 1968, 189; Watt 1980, 145; Firchow 2000, 67).

Other possibilities include Casement himself (Ford 1995, 123–34). The explorer and journalist Edward James Glave (1863–1895) resembled both Marlow and Kurtz in some respects (Firchow 2000, 128–47). Additionally, the Irishman Charles Henry Stokes (1852–1895), a highly successful ivory merchant who had started as a missionary, had "gone native" and married an African woman. His hanging by the Force Publique for allegedly selling arms to the Afro-Arabs provoked an outrage in England. Paul Voulet was a French captain whose activities in Senegal were like Peters's. In terms of general morality, Kurtz resembles Henry Morton Stanley (Watt 1980, 143, 145; Pakenham 2003, 586; Firchow 2000, 67–68; Hochschild 1999, 174).

However, none of these possible historical models fits very well. Kurtz shares various characteristics with each of them, but he differs from them all in important ways. These historical models in Africa may have given Conrad details that he could later draw on in composing a composite portrait of Kurtz that represents much more than a single person. As Marlow tells us later, "All Europe contributed to the making of Kurtz," and as Conrad wrote in a letter to Kazimierz Waliszewski on 16 December 1903, he "took great care to give Kurtz a cosmopolitan origin" (Conrad 1988a, 94).

Yet another model—and one more powerfully symbolic—is Leopold himself, as we will see when Kurtz makes his appearance later in the story.

he added slowly, laying down his pen, 'He is a very remarkable person.' Further questions elicited from him that Mr. Kurtz was at present in charge of a trading-post, a very important one, in the true ivory-country, at 'the very bottom of there. Sends in as much ivory as all the others put together . . .' He began to write again. The sick man was too ill to groan. The flies buzzed in a great peace.

"Suddenly there was a growing murmur of voices and a great tramping of feet. A caravan had come in. A violent babble of uncouth sounds burst out on the other side of the planks. All the carriers were speaking together, and in the midst of the uproar the lamentable voice of the chief agent was heard 'giving it up' tearfully for the twentieth time that day. . . . He rose slowly. 'What a frightful row,' he said. He crossed the room gently to look at the sick man, and returning, said to me, 'He does not hear.' 'What! Dead?' I asked, startled. 'No, not yet,' he answered, with great composure. Then, alluding with a toss of the head to the tumult in the station-yard, 'When one has got to make correct entries, one comes to hate those savages—hate them to the death.' He remained thoughtful for a moment. 'When you see Mr. Kurtz,' he went on, 'tell him from me that everything here'—he glanced at the desk—'is very satisfactory. I don't like to write to him—with those messengers of ours you never know who may get hold of your letter—at that Central Station.'[95] He stared at me for a moment with his mild, bulging eyes. 'Oh, he will go far, very far,' he began again. 'He will be a somebody in the Administration before long. They, above—the Council in Europe, you know—mean him to be.'

"He turned to his work. The noise outside had ceased, and presently in going out I stopped at the door. In the steady buzz of flies the homeward-bound agent was lying flushed and insensible; the other, bent over his books, was making correct entries of perfectly correct transactions; and fifty feet below the doorstep I could see the still tree-tops of the grove of death.

"Next day I left that station at last, with a caravan of sixty men, for a two-hundred-mile tramp.[96]

"No use telling you much about that. Paths, paths, everywhere; a stamped-in network of paths spreading over the empty land, through long grass, through burnt grass, through thickets, down and up chilly ravines,

---

95. Kinshasa.

96. According to his diary, Conrad left Matadi on 28 June 1890. He departed on the 230-mile overland trip with Prosper Harou (1855–1893), a Belgian trader who had left Bordeaux with Conrad on the *Ville de Maceio,* and 31 men (Sherry 1971, 13, 36–37).

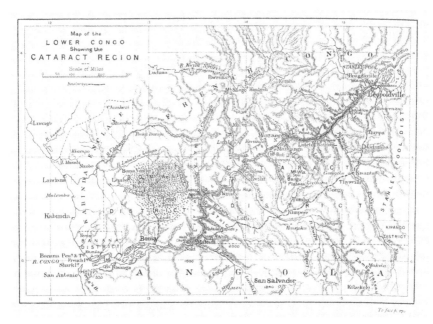

This 1908 map of the Lower Congo includes, at the lower left, Boma ("the seat of the government") and Matadi ("your Company's station"); at the upper right is Léopoldville and Kinshasa ("the Central Station"). The railway between Matadi and Léopoldville (the dashed line) is shown as complete; it was finished in 1898. Conrad took the overland caravan route between Matadi and Kinshasa, which ran closer to the river, from 28 June 1890 to 2 August on his way into the interior. (From Sir Harry Johnston, *George Grenfell and the Congo*. London: Hutchinson, 1908, opposite 1:270.)

up and down stony hills ablaze with heat; and a solitude, a solitude, nobody, not a hut. The population had cleared out a long time ago.[97] Well, if a lot of mysterious niggers armed with all kinds of fearful weapons

---

97. Two years before Conrad's visit, the trail was described as "a narrow footpath [that] runs across the hills, along rocky ridges, down into deep gorges, through rushing streams, up steep slopes, over sandy plateaux away to Stanley Pool—about 17 days continuous marching for a white man." Natives from the lower end of the trail could be persuaded to go only half way, requiring a midway station for recruiting a new set of carriers. This report also describes a difficulty in finding porters due to the sparse population in the region (Brourke 1888, quoted in Sherry 1971, 36–37). An 1890 description calls "the so-called caravan road [. . .] merely a bridle path a few inches in width," so narrow that the porters had to walk single-file. This description notes that there were "every ten or fifteen miles along the route little market places" where natives would exchange produce for "cloth and beads" (Glave 1890, 619).

suddenly took to travelling on the road between Deal[98] and Gravesend,[99] catching the yokels right and left to carry heavy loads for them, I fancy every farm and cottage thereabouts would get empty very soon. Only here the dwellings were gone too. Still, I passed through several abandoned villages. There's something pathetically childish in the ruins of grass walls. Day after day, with the stamp and shuffle of sixty pair of bare feet behind me, each pair under a 60-lb. load. Camp, cook, sleep; strike camp, march. Now and then a carrier dead in harness, at rest in the long grass near the path, with an empty water-gourd and his long staff lying by his side. A great silence around and above. Perhaps on some quiet night the tremor of far-off drums, sinking, swelling, a tremor vast, faint; a sound weird, appealing, suggestive, and wild—and perhaps with as profound a meaning as the sound of bells in a Christian country. Once a white man in an unbuttoned uniform, camping on the path with an armed escort of lank Zanzibaris,[100] very hospitable and festive—not to say drunk. Was looking after the upkeep of the road, he declared. Can't say I saw any road or any upkeep, unless the body of a middle-aged negro, with a bullet-hole in the forehead, upon which I absolutely stumbled three miles farther on, may be considered as a permanent improvement.[101] I had a white companion too,[102] not a bad chap, but rather too fleshy and with the exasperating habit of fainting on the hot hillsides, miles away from the least bit of shade and water. Annoying, you know, to hold your own coat like a parasol over a man's head while he is coming to. I couldn't help asking him once what he meant by coming there at all. 'To make money, of course. What do you think?' he said scornfully. Then he got fever, and had to be carried in a hammock slung under a pole. As he weighed sixteen stone[103] I had no end of rows with the carriers. They jibbed, ran away, sneaked off with their loads in the night—quite a mutiny. So, one evening, I made a speech in English with

---

98. A port on the Straits of Dover. Julius Caesar purportedly landed there in 55 BCE.

99. A town on the right bank of the River Thames, about 23 miles from London. The distance from Deal to Gravesend by road is approximately 60 miles.

100. Members of the Force Publique. Soldiers recruited from the East and West Coasts of Africa served for three years (Williams 1890b, 19).

101. Marlow's encounter with a white man in uniform, followed by seeing the corpse of a native, closely parallels what Conrad recorded in his diary for 3 July 1890, five days after departing from Matadi. Also, Conrad's 1 August diary entry mentions his treating the wound of a native youth who had been shot in the head.

102. Corresponds to Prosper Harou (1855–1893), the Belgian trader whom Conrad had met on the *Ville de Maceio* on the voyage from Bordeaux. Harou was seriously ill by the time they arrived at Kinshasa (Sherry 1971, 25, 38, 397n6).

103. 224 pounds. (In the British measure, one stone equals 14 pounds.)

gestures, not one of which was lost to the sixty pairs of eyes before me,[104] and the next morning I started the hammock off in front all right. An hour afterwards I came upon the whole concern wrecked in a bush—man, hammock, groans, blankets, horrors. The heavy pole had skinned his poor nose. He was very anxious for me to kill somebody, but there wasn't the shadow of a carrier near. I remembered the old doctor—'It would be interesting for science to watch the mental changes of individuals, on the spot.' I felt I was becoming scientifically interesting. However, all that is to no purpose. On the fifteenth day I came in sight of the big river again, and hobbled into the Central Station.[105] It was on a back water surrounded by scrub and forest, with a pretty border of smelly mud on one side, and on the three others enclosed by a crazy fence of rushes. A neglected gap was all the gate it had, and the first glance at the place was enough to let you see the flabby devil was running that show. White men with long staves in their hands appeared languidly from amongst the buildings, strolling up to take a look at me, and then retired out of sight somewhere. One of them, a stout, excitable chap with black moustaches, informed me with great volubility and many digressions, as soon as I told him who I was, that my

104. Conrad's diary entry for 30 July 1890 notes arguments with his carriers, followed by a speech he made that evening in anticipation of more arguments the following day. In his 1 August entry, he describes stopping an argument between carriers and a man evidently working for the government.

105. Corresponds to Kinshasa. Conrad recorded in his diary that he left Matadi on 28 June 1890 and arrived in Kinshasa on 2 August, having made a rest stop midway at Manyanga from 8 to 25 July. At Manyanga, Conrad was received by Reginald Heyn, an Englishman who was manager of the SAB transport base there, and his assistant, named Jaeger. Until that point Conrad had been in satisfactory health, but he fell ill at Manyanga, probably of fever; Harou was already sick and did not get any better. Contributing to the delay at this unscheduled stop, there may have been problems with finding replacement porters, who had to be changed there (Jean-Aubry 1927, 1:131; Najder 2007, 153).

Kinshasa was a regional operational center for the ivory trade of the Société Anonyme Belge, as well as for its Dutch competitor. On the riverbank opposite Kinshasa is Brazzaville, now the capital of the Republic of the Congo; then it was the headquarters of the French colony of the Congo, with a French company stationed nearby also engaged in the ivory trade. About five miles below Kinshasa was Léopoldville, the central supply station for the Congo Free State. Together they are now Kinshasa, capital of the Democratic Republic of the Congo. At Léopoldville by February 1890 there were about 25 Europeans, including administration officials, ship captains, engineers, and carpenters; as well as seven steamers (Glave 1890, 619–20).

Kinshasa (the "Central Station" in Marlow's tale) in 1884 or 1885: regional operational center for the Société Anonyme Belge ivory trade. On Conrad's way upriver, he arrived at Kinshasa on 2 August 1890 and left the following day. On his return from Stanley Falls, he arrived on 24 September and was back in Matadi by 16 November. (From Henry M. Stanley, *The Congo and the Founding of Its Free State*, opposite 2:185.)

steamer was at the bottom of the river.[106] I was thunderstruck. What, how, why? Oh, it was 'all right.' The 'manager himself' was there. All quite correct. 'Everybody had behaved splendidly! splendidly!'—'You must,' he said in agitation, 'go and see the general manager[107] at once. He is waiting!'

"I did not see the real significance of that wreck at once. I fancy I see it now, but I am not sure—not at all. Certainly the affair was too stupid—when I think of it—to be altogether natural. Still . . . But at the moment it presented itself simply as a confounded nuisance. The steamer was sunk.

---

106. Conrad's intended command, the *Florida,* had struck a rock and grounded at the exit of Stanley Pool on 18 July 1890. She was refloated and towed back to Kinshasa on 23 July, before Conrad's arrival on 2 August (Najder 2007, 154). Unlike Marlow, who learned of the loss of his ship only upon arriving at the Central Station (Kinshasa), Conrad recorded in his diary on 29 July, while still en route to Kinshasa, learning that one steamer was wrecked and all of them disabled (although this was not true; Sherry 1971, 398n9).

107. The Kinshasa station manager was Camille Delcommune (1859–1892) (Sherry 1971, 41).

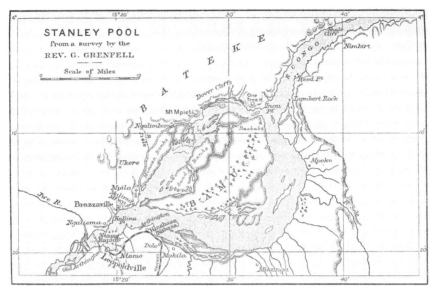

Stanley Pool and Kinshasa, where Conrad's voyage on the *Roi des Belges* began. One source records that by mid-1889, seventeen steamers were in service in the waterways above Kinshasa ("Charities, &c."); another source puts seven steamers at Léopoldville in February 1890 (Glave 1890, 619–20). This 1908 map shows the railway as completed; it was finished in 1898. (From Sir Harry Johnston, *George Grenfell and the Congo*. London: Hutchinson, 1908, 1:101.)

They had started two days before in a sudden hurry up the river with the manager on board, in charge of some volunteer skipper, and before they had been out three hours they tore the bottom out of her on stones, and she sank near the south bank.[108] I asked myself what I was to do there, now my boat was lost. As a matter of fact, I had plenty to do in fishing my command out of the river. I had to set about it the very next day. That, and the repairs when I brought the pieces to the station, took some months.[109]

"My first interview with the manager was curious. He did not ask me to sit down after my twenty-mile walk that morning. He was

---

108. The *Florida* had started upriver from Kinshasa before Conrad's arrival, with Camille Delcommune aboard. The new captain was not "some volunteer skipper," however. After the death of Freiesleben, the previous master, the Congo Free State government loaned Captain Shagerström, one of their best captains, to the Société Anonyme Belge (Sherry 1971, 41–42).

109. Conrad was not involved in salvaging the *Florida,* and his stay in Kinshasa lasted only one or two days (Sherry 1971, 42).

commonplace in complexion, in feature, in manners, and in voice. He was of middle size and of ordinary build. His eyes, of the usual blue, were perhaps remarkably cold, and he certainly could make his glance fall on one as trenchant and heavy as an axe. But even at these times the rest of his person seemed to disclaim the intention. Otherwise there was only an indefinable, faint expression of his lips, something stealthy—a smile—not a smile—I remember it, but I can't explain. It was unconscious, this smile was, though just after he had said something it got intensified for an instant. It came at the end of his speeches like a seal applied on the words to make the meaning of the commonest phrase appear absolutely inscrutable. He was a common trader, from his youth up employed in these parts— nothing more.[110] He was obeyed, yet he inspired neither love nor fear, nor even respect. He inspired uneasiness. That was it! Uneasiness. Not a definite mistrust—just uneasiness—nothing more. You have no idea how effective such a . . . a . . . faculty can be. He had no genius for organising, for initiative, or for order even. That was evident in such things as the deplorable state of the station. He had no learning, and no intelligence. His position had come to him—why? Perhaps because he was never ill . . . He had served three terms of three years out there . . . Because triumphant health in the general rout of constitutions is a kind of power in itself. When he went home on leave he rioted on a large scale—pompously. Jack ashore[111]— with a difference—in externals only. This one could gather from his casual talk. He originated nothing, he could keep the routine going—that's all. But he was great. He was great by this little thing that it was impossible to tell what could control such a man. He never gave that secret away. Perhaps there was nothing within him. Such a suspicion made one pause—for out there there were no external checks. Once when various tropical diseases had laid low almost every 'agent' in the station, he was heard to say, 'Men who come out here should have no entrails.' He sealed the utterance with that smile of his, as though it had been a door opening into a darkness he had in his keeping. You fancied you had seen things—but the seal was

---

110. Conrad wrote in a letter to Marguerite Poradowska from Kinshasa on 26 September 1890, "The manager is a common ivory dealer with base instincts who considers himself a merchant although he is only a kind of African shop-keeper. His name is Delcommune. He detests the English, and out here I am naturally regarded as such. I cannot hope for either promotion or salary increases while he is here" (Conrad 1983, 62). G. Jean-Aubry later wrote, "Conrad, who was the most generous-minded person I have ever known, despised this man heartily." Furthermore, Conrad "never showed any feeling of tenderness for the 'pilgrims' (as he called them ironically in 'Heart of Darkness'), whom he came across in the Congo, least of all for this one" (Jean-Aubry 1927, 133).

111. Jack (also "jack-tar"): familiar term for a British sailor. Jack ashore: slang for merry, reckless, spendthrift, drunk (*OED Online,* s.v. "Jack.").

on. When annoyed at meal-times by the constant quarrels of the white men about precedence, he ordered an immense round table to be made, for which a special house had to be built. This was the station's mess-room. Where he sat was the first place—the rest were nowhere. One felt this to be his unalterable conviction. He was neither civil nor uncivil. He was quiet. He allowed his 'boy'—an overfed young negro from the coast—to treat the white men, under his very eyes, with provoking insolence.

"He began to speak as soon as he saw me. I had been very long on the road. He could not wait. Had to start without me. The up-river stations had to be relieved. There had been so many delays already that he did not know who was dead and who was alive, and how they got on—and so on, and so on. He paid no attention to my explanations,[112] and, playing with a stick of sealing-wax, repeated several times that the situation was 'very grave, very grave.' There were rumours that a very important station was in jeopardy, and its chief, Mr. Kurtz, was ill. Hoped it was not true. Mr. Kurtz was . . . I felt weary and irritable. Hang Kurtz, I thought. I interrupted him by saying I had heard of Mr. Kurtz on the coast. 'Ah! So they talk of him down there,' he murmured to himself. Then he began again, assuring me Mr. Kurtz was the best agent he had, an exceptional man, of the greatest importance to the Company; therefore I could understand his anxiety. He was, he said, 'very, very uneasy.' Certainly he fidgeted on his chair a good deal, exclaimed, 'Ah, Mr. Kurtz!' broke the stick of sealing-wax and seemed dumbfounded by the accident. Next thing he wanted to know 'how long it would take to' . . . I interrupted him again. Being hungry, you know, and kept on my feet too, I was getting savage. 'How can I tell?' I said. 'I haven't even seen the wreck yet—some months, no doubt.' All this talk seemed to me so futile. 'Some months,' he said. 'Well, let us say three months before we can make a start. Yes. That ought to do the

---

112. The manager disapproves of how long it took for Marlow to arrive. Earlier in the story, Marlow notes that the overland journey took 15 days. Conrad wrote in a letter to Marguerite Poradowska dated 10 June 1890, sent from Libreville, that he expected the journey on foot to Léopoldville (about five miles downstream of Kinshasa) to take only 20 days (Conrad 1983, 56).

Conrad's overland trip from Matadi to Kinshasa lasted 35 days: from 28 June to 2 August 1890, including the rest stop of 17 days at Manyanga from 8 to 25 July. According to his diary, Conrad had also spent 15 days detained in Matadi before starting his journey. Since it therefore took him 50 days total from his arrival in Matadi to his arrival in Kinshasa, Norman Sherry has argued that the duration of the trip constituted a delay that would have given Camille Delcommune "something to complain about" (Sherry 1971, 46). However, Conrad's stop at Manyanga was made with the knowledge of Reginald Heyn, the SAB manager there, and in any event an itinerary published within a few years of Conrad's trip indicates that the length of time that Conrad took was less than typical (Najder 2007, 153).

affair.' I flung out of his hut (he lived all alone in a clay hut with a sort of verandah) muttering to myself my opinion of him. He was a chattering idiot. Afterwards I took it back when it was borne in upon me startlingly with what extreme nicety he had estimated the time requisite for the 'affair.'

"I went to work the next day, turning, so to speak, my back on that station. In that way only it seemed to me I could keep my hold on the re-deeming facts of life. Still, one must look about sometimes; and then I saw this station, these men strolling aimlessly about in the sunshine of the yard. I asked myself sometimes what it all meant. They wandered here and there with their absurd long staves in their hands, like a lot of faithless pilgrims bewitched inside a rotten fence. The word 'ivory' rang in the air, was whis-pered, was sighed. You would think they were praying to it. A taint of im-becile rapacity blew through it all, like a whiff from some corpse. By Jove! I've never seen anything so unreal in my life. And outside, the silent wil-derness surrounding this cleared speck on the earth struck me as some-thing great and invincible, like evil or truth, waiting patiently for the passing away of this fantastic invasion.

"Oh, those months! Well, never mind. Various things happened. One evening a grass shed full of calico, cotton prints, beads, and I don't know what else, burst into a blaze so suddenly that you would have thought the earth had opened to let an avenging fire consume all that trash.[113] I was smoking my pipe quietly by my dismantled steamer, and saw them all cut-ting capers in the light, with their arms lifted high, when the stout man with moustaches came tearing down to the river, a tin pail in his hand, as-sured me that everybody was 'behaving splendidly, splendidly,' dipped about a quart of water and tore back again. I noticed there was a hole in the bottom of his pail.

"I strolled up. There was no hurry. You see the thing had gone off like a box of matches. It had been hopeless from the very first. The flame had leaped high, driven everybody back, lighted up everything—and col-lapsed. The shed was already a heap of embers glowing fiercely. A nigger was being beaten near by. They said he had caused the fire in some way; be that as it may, he was screeching most horribly. I saw him, later, for several days, sitting in a bit of shade looking very sick and trying to re-cover himself: afterwards he arose and went out—and the wilderness without a sound took him into its bosom again. As I approached the glow from the dark I found myself at the back of two men, talking. I heard the name of Kurtz pronounced, then the words, 'take advantage of this

---

113. *Le Mouvement Géographique* reported on 1 November 1891 that an 1890 fire at the Kinshasa station destroyed 74,615 Francs worth of merchandise (quoted in Sherry 1971, 42).

unfortunate accident.' One of the men was the manager. I wished him a good evening. 'Did you ever see anything like it—eh? it is incredible,' he said, and walked off. The other man remained. He was a first-class agent, young, gentlemanly, a bit reserved, with a forked little beard and a hooked nose. He was stand-offish with the other agents, and they on their side said he was the manager's spy upon them. As to me, I had hardly ever spoken to him before. We got into talk, and by and by we strolled away from the hissing ruins. Then he asked me to his room, which was in the main building of the station. He struck a match, and I perceived that this young aristocrat had not only a silver-mounted dressing-case but also a whole candle all to himself. Just at that time the manager was the only man supposed to have any right to candles. Native mats covered the clay walls; a collection of spears, assegais,[114] shields, knives, was hung up in trophies. The business entrusted to this fellow was the making of bricks—so I had been informed; but there wasn't a fragment of a brick anywhere in the station, and he had been there more than a year—waiting.[115] It seems he could not make bricks without something, I don't know what—straw maybe. Anyways, it could not be found there, and as it was not likely to be sent from Europe, it did not appear clear to me what he was waiting for. An act of special creation[116] perhaps. However, they were all waiting—all the sixteen or twenty pilgrims of them—for something; and upon my word it did not seem an uncongenial occupation, from the way they took it, though the only thing that ever came to them was disease—as far as I could see. They beguiled the time by backbiting and intriguing against each other in a foolish kind of way.[117] There was an air of plotting about that station, but nothing came of it, of course. It was as unreal as everything else—as the philanthropic pretence of the whole concern, as their talk, as their government, as their show of work. The only real feeling was a desire to get appointed to a trading-post where ivory was to be had, so that they could earn percentages. They intrigued and slandered and hated each other only on that account—but as to effectually lifting a little finger—oh, no. By

---

114. A slender, iron-tipped spear or javelin made of hardwood from the assegai tree, native to South Africa.

115. There was a brickmaker in Kinshasa, who had arrived in the Congo around the time that Conrad did. According to the 22 November 1890 issue of *Le Mouvement Géographique,* by 20 August 1890 he had set up an extensive workshop and brickyard, including two ovens capable of drying 30,000 bricks each in 42 hours (quoted in Sherry 1971, 43–44).

116. That is, by God; Marlow is being sarcastic. The theory of special creation held that God created separate species individually (*Oxford Dictionary of Biology,* 7th ed., s.v. "special creation").

117. Matches what Conrad wrote in his diary entry for 24 June 1890.

Heavens! there is something after all in the world allowing one man to steal a horse while another must not look at a halter.[118] Steal a horse straight out. Very well. He has done it. Perhaps he can ride. But there is a way of looking at a halter that would provoke the most charitable of saints into a kick.

"I had no idea why he wanted to be sociable, but as we chatted in there it suddenly occurred to me the fellow was trying to get at something—in fact, pumping me. He alluded constantly to Europe, to the people I was supposed to know there—putting leading questions as to my acquaintances in the sepulchral city, and so on. His little eyes glittered like mica discs—with curiosity—though he tried to keep up a bit of superciliousness. At first I was astonished, but very soon I became awfully curious to see what he would find out from me. I couldn't possibly imagine what I had in me to make it worth his while. It was very pretty to see how he baffled himself, for in truth my body was full of chills, and my head had nothing in it but that wretched steamboat business. It was evident he took me for a perfectly shameless prevaricator. At last he got angry, and, to conceal a movement of furious annoyance, he yawned. I rose. Then I noticed a small sketch in oils, on a panel, representing a woman, draped and blindfolded, carrying a lighted torch. The background was sombre—almost black. The movement of the woman was stately, and the effect of the torchlight on the face was sinister.

"It arrested me, and he stood by civilly, holding an empty half-pint champagne bottle (medical comforts) with the candle stuck in it. To my question he said Mr. Kurtz had painted this[119]—in this very station more than a year ago—while waiting for means to go to his trading-post. 'Tell me, pray,' said I, 'who is this Mr. Kurtz?'

"'The chief of the Inner Station,' he answered in a short tone, looking away. 'Much obliged,' I said, laughing. 'And you are the brickmaker of the Central Station. Every one knows that.' He was silent for a while. 'He is a prodigy,' he said at last. 'He is an emissary of pity, and science, and progress, and devil knows what else. We want,' he began to declaim suddenly, 'for the guidance of the cause entrusted to us by Europe, so to speak, higher intelligence, wide sympathies, a singleness of purpose.' 'Who says that?' I asked. 'Lots of them,' he replied. 'Some even write that; and so *he* comes here, a special being, as you ought to know.' 'Why ought I to know?'

---

118. An old adage: "One man may steal a horse, while another may not look over a hedge": "People may take different degrees of liberty depending on our opinion of them" (Simpson and Speake 2008).

119. Captain Léon Rom of the Force Publique, one of the possible models for Kurtz, had also been a painter (Hochschild 1999, 148).

I interrupted, really surprised. He paid no attention. 'Yes. To-day he is chief of the best station, next year he will be assistant-manager, two years more and . . . but I daresay you know what he will be in two years' time. You are of the new gang—the gang of virtue. The same people who sent him specially also recommended you. Oh, don't say no. I've my own eyes to trust.' Light dawned upon me. My dear aunt's influential acquaintances were producing an unexpected effect upon that young man. I nearly burst into a laugh. 'Do you read the Company's confidential correspondence?' I asked. He hadn't a word to say. It was great fun. 'When Mr. Kurtz,' I continued severely, 'is General Manager, you won't have the opportunity.'

"He blew the candle out suddenly, and we went outside. The moon had risen. Black figures strolled about listlessly, pouring water on the glow, whence proceeded a sound of hissing; steam ascended in the moonlight, the beaten nigger groaned somewhere. 'What a row the brute makes!' said the indefatigable man with the moustaches, appearing near us. 'Serve him right. Transgression—punishment—bang! Pitiless, pitiless. That's the only way. This will prevent all conflagrations for the future. I was just telling the manager . . .' He noticed my companion, and became crestfallen all at once. 'Not in bed yet,' he said, with a kind of servile heartiness; 'it's so natural. Ha! Danger—agitation.' He vanished. I went on to the river-side, and the other followed me. I heard a scathing murmur at my ear, 'Heap of muffs[120]—go to.' The pilgrims could be seen in knots gesticulating, discussing. Several had still their staves in their hands. I verily believe they took these sticks to bed with them. Beyond the fence the forest stood up spectrally in the moonlight, and through the dim stir, through the faint sounds of that lamentable courtyard, the silence of the land went home to one's very heart—its mystery, its greatness, the amazing reality of its concealed life. The hurt nigger moaned feebly somewhere near by, and then fetched a deep sigh that made me mend my pace away from there. I felt a hand introducing itself under my arm. 'My dear sir,' said the fellow, 'I don't want to be misunderstood, and especially by you, who will see Mr. Kurtz long before I can have that pleasure. I wouldn't like him to get a false idea of my disposition. . . .'

"I let him run on, this papier-mâché Mephistopheles,[121] and it seemed to me that if I tried I could poke my forefinger through him, and would find nothing inside but a little loose dirt, maybe. He, don't you see, had been planning to be assistant-manager by and by under the present man, and I could see that the coming of that Kurtz had upset them both not a little. He talked precipitately, and I did not try to stop him. I had my shoulders against

---

120. Failures.
121. Someone who tempts a person into destruction.

the wreck of my steamer, hauled up on the slope like a carcass of some big river animal. The smell of mud, of primeval mud, by Jove! was in my nostrils, the high stillness of primeval forest was before my eyes; there were shiny patches on the black creek. The moon had spread over everything a thin layer of silver—over the rank grass, over the mud, upon the wall of matted vegetation standing higher than the wall of a temple, over the great river I could see through a sombre gap glittering, glittering, as it flowed broadly by without a murmur. All this was great, expectant, mute, while the man jabbered about himself. I wondered whether the stillness on the face of the immensity looking at us two were meant as an appeal or as a menace. What were we who had strayed in here? Could we handle that dumb thing, or would it handle us? I felt how big, how confoundedly big, was that thing that couldn't talk, and perhaps was deaf as well. What was in there? I could see a little ivory coming out from there, and I had heard Mr. Kurtz was in there. I had heard enough about it too—God knows! Yet somehow it didn't bring any image with it—no more than if I had been told an angel or a fiend was in there. I believed it in the same way one of you might believe there are inhabitants in the planet Mars. I knew once a Scotch sailmaker who was certain, dead sure, there were people in Mars. If you asked him for some idea how they looked and behaved, he would get shy and mutter something about 'walking on all-fours.' If you as much as smiled, he would—though a man of sixty—offer to fight you. I would not have gone so far as to fight for Kurtz, but I went for him near enough to a lie. You know I hate, detest, and can't bear a lie, not because I am straighter than the rest of us, but simply because it appalls me. There is a taint of death, a flavour of mortality in lies—which is exactly what I hate and detest in the world—what I want to forget. It makes me miserable and sick, like biting something rotten would do. Temperament, I suppose. Well, I went near enough to it by letting the young fool there believe anything he liked to imagine as to my influence in Europe. I became in an instant as much of a pretence as the rest of the bewitched pilgrims. This simply because I had a notion it somehow would be of help to that Kurtz whom at the time I did not see—you understand. He was just a word for me. I did not see the man in the name any more than you do. Do you see him? Do you see the story? Do you see anything? It seems to me I am trying to tell you a dream—making a vain attempt, because no relation of a dream can convey the dream-sensation, that commingling of absurdity, surprise, and bewilderment in a tremor of struggling revolt, that notion of being captured by the incredible which is of the very essence of dreams. . . ."

He was silent for a while.

". . . No, it is impossible; it is impossible to convey the life-sensation of any given epoch of one's existence—that which makes its truth, its meaning—its subtle and penetrating essence. It is impossible. We live, as we dream—alone. . . ."

He paused again as if reflecting, then added:

"Of course in this you fellows see more than I could then. You see me, whom you know. . . ."

It had become so pitch dark that we listeners could hardly see one another. For a long time already he, sitting apart, had been no more to us than a voice. There was not a word from anybody. The others might have been asleep, but I was awake. I listened, I listened on the watch for the sentence, for the word, that would give me the clue to the faint uneasiness inspired by this narrative that seemed to shape itself without human lips in the heavy night-air of the river.

The *Roi des Belges*, the steamer on which Conrad's Congo voyage took place, as seen in 1889. (From Alexandre Delcommune, *Vingt années de Vie africaine.* Brussels: Vve Ferdinand Larcier, 1922, opposite 1:286.)

". . . Yes—I let him run on," Marlow began again, "and think what he pleased about the powers that were behind me. I did! And there was nothing behind me! There was nothing but that wretched, old, mangled steamboat I was leaning against, while he talked fluently about 'the necessity for every man to get on.' 'And when one comes out here, you conceive, it is not to gaze at the moon.' Mr. Kurtz was a 'universal genius,' but even a genius would find it easier to work with 'adequate tools—intelligent men.' He did not make bricks—why, there was a physical impossibility in the way—as I was well aware; and if he did secretarial work for the manager, it was because 'no sensible man rejects wantonly the confidence of his superiors.' Did I see it? I saw it. What more did I want? What I really wanted was rivets, by Heaven! Rivets. To get on with the work—to stop the hole. Rivets I wanted. There were cases of them down at the coast—cases—piled up—burst—split! You kicked a loose rivet at every second step in that station yard on the hillside. Rivets had rolled into the grove of death. You could fill your pockets with rivets for the trouble of stooping down—and there wasn't one rivet to be found where it was wanted. We had plates that would do, but nothing to fasten them with. And every week the messenger, a lone negro, letter-bag on shoulder and staff in hand, left our station for the coast. And several times a week a coast caravan came in with trade goods—ghastly glazed calico that made you shudder only to look at it, glass beads value about a penny a quart, confounded spotted cotton hand-kerchiefs. And no rivets. Three carriers could have brought all that was wanted to set that steamboat afloat.

"He was becoming confidential now, but I fancy my unresponsive atti-tude must have exasperated him at last, for he judged it necessary to inform me he feared neither God nor devil, let alone any mere man. I said I could see that very well, but what I wanted was a certain quantity of rivets—and rivets were what really Mr. Kurtz wanted, if he had only known it. Now let-ters went to the coast every week. . . . 'My dear sir,' he cried, 'I write from dictation.' I demanded rivets. There was a way—for an intelligent man. He changed his manner; became very cold, and suddenly began to talk about a hippopotamus; wondered whether sleeping on board the steamer (I stuck to my salvage night and day) I wasn't disturbed. There was an old hippo that had the bad habit of getting out on the bank and roaming at night over the station grounds. The pilgrims used to turn out in a body and empty every rifle they could lay hands on at him. Some even had sat up o' nights for him. All this energy was wasted, though. 'That animal has a charmed life,' he said; 'but you can say this only of brutes in this country. No man—you ap-prehend me?—no man here bears a charmed life.' He stood there for a mo-ment in the moonlight with his delicate hooked nose set a little askew, and his mica eyes glittering without a wink, then, with a curt Good-night, he strode off. I could see he was disturbed and considerably puzzled, which made me feel more hopeful than I had been for days. It was a great comfort to turn from that chap to my influential friend, the battered, twisted, ruined, tin-pot steamboat. I clambered on board. She rang under my feet like an empty Huntley & Palmer biscuit-tin[122] kicked along a gutter; she was noth-ing so solid in make, and rather less pretty in shape, but I had expended enough hard work on her to make me love her. No influential friend would have served me better. She had given me a chance to come out a bit—to find

---

122. Huntley & Palmers is the name of a famous biscuit manufacturer. The tins made global distribution easy, so as the British Empire expanded, the company's biscuits made their way to the far reaches of the earth—even to the South Pole on Robert Falcon Scott's expedition in 1910–1912. Henry Morton Stanley used their biscuit tins to pacify a tribe in what is now Tanzania. Huntley & Palmers biscuits were advertised as being sold "By Ap-pointment to the King of the Belgians," and a photograph of a Belgian trading steamer on the Congo shows a large Huntley & Palmers tin (Cunningham 1994, 252–53).

out what I could do. No, I don't like work. I had rather laze about and think of all the fine things that can be done. I don't like work—no man does—but I like what is in the work—the chance to find yourself. Your own reality—for yourself, not for others—what no other man can ever know. They can only see the mere show, and never can tell what it really means.

"I was not surprised to see somebody sitting aft, on the deck, with his legs dangling over the mud. You see I rather chummed with the few mechanics there were in that station, whom the other pilgrims naturally despised—on account of their imperfect manners, I suppose. This was the foreman—a boiler-maker by trade—a good worker. He was a lank, bony, yellow-faced man, with big intense eyes. His aspect was worried, and his head was as bald as the palm of my hand; but his hair in falling seemed to have stuck to his chin, and had prospered in the new locality, for his beard hung down to his waist. He was a widower with six young children (he had left them in charge of a sister of his to come out there), and the passion of his life was pigeon-flying. He was an enthusiast and a connoisseur. He would rave about pigeons. After work hours he used sometimes to come over from his hut for a talk about his children and his pigeons; at work, when he had to crawl in the mud under the bottom of the steamboat, he would tie up that beard of his in a kind of white serviette he brought for the purpose. It had loops to go over his ears. In the evening he could be seen squatted on the bank rinsing that wrapper in the creek with great care, then spreading it solemnly on a bush to dry.

"I slapped him on the back and shouted 'We shall have rivets!' He scrambled to his feet exclaiming 'No! Rivets!' as though he couldn't believe his ears. Then in a low voice, 'You . . . eh?' I don't know why we behaved like lunatics. I put my finger to the side of my nose and nodded mysteriously. 'Good for you!' he cried, snapped his fingers above his head, lifting one foot. I tried a jig. We capered on the iron deck. A frightful clatter came out of that hulk, and the virgin forest on the other bank of the creek sent it back in a thundering roll upon the sleeping station. It must have made some of the pilgrims sit up in their hovels. A dark figure obscured the lighted doorway of the manager's hut, vanished, then, a second or so after, the doorway itself vanished too. We stopped, and the silence driven away by the stamping of our feet flowed back again from the recesses of the land. The great wall of vegetation, an exuberant and entangled mass of trunks, branches, leaves, boughs, festoons, motionless in the moonlight, was like a rioting invasion of soundless life, a rolling wave of plants, piled up, crested, ready to topple over the creek, to sweep every little man of us out of his little existence. And it moved not. A deadened burst of mighty splashes and snorts reached us from afar, as though an ichthyosaurus had been taking a bath of glitter in the great river. 'After all,' said the boiler-maker in a reasonable tone, 'why shouldn't we get the rivets?' Why not, indeed! I did not know of any reason why we shouldn't. 'They'll come in three weeks,' I said confidently.

"But they didn't. Instead of rivets there came an invasion, an infliction, a visitation. It came in sections during the next three weeks, each section headed by a donkey carrying a white man in new clothes and tan shoes, bowing from that elevation right and left to the impressed pilgrims. A quarrelsome band of footsore sulky niggers trod on the heels of the donkey; a lot of tents, camp-stools, tin boxes, white cases, brown bales would be shot down in the courtyard, and the air of mystery would deepen a little over the muddle of the station. Five such instalments came, with their absurd air of disorderly flight with the loot of innumerable outfit shops and provision stores, that, one would think, they were lugging, after a raid, into the wilderness for equitable division. It was an inextricable mess of things decent in themselves but that human folly made look like the spoils of thieving.

"This devoted band called itself the Eldorado Exploring Expedition, and I believe they were sworn to secrecy. Their talk, however, was the talk of sordid buccaneers: it was reckless without hardihood, greedy without audacity, and cruel without courage; there was not an atom of foresight or of serious intention in the whole batch of them, and they did not seem aware these things are wanted for the work of the world. To tear treasure out of the bowels of the land was their desire, with no more moral purpose at the back of it than there is in burglars breaking into a safe. Who paid the expenses of the noble enterprise I don't know; but the uncle of our manager was leader of that lot.[123]

"In exterior he resembled a butcher in a poor neighbourhood, and his eyes had a look of sleepy cunning. He carried his fat paunch with ostentation on his short legs, and during the time his gang infested the station

---

123. One possible inspiration for this expedition is the Sanford Exploring Expedition organized by Henry Shelton Sanford, an American. Established in 1886 with Leopold's permission to explore possibilities for trade in the Congo, it was dissolved in 1888 in a merger with the Compagnie du Congo pour le Commerce et l'Industrie to form the Société Anonyme Belge pour le Commerce du Haut-Congo (Gondola 2002, 66). The *Florida,* which was supposed to be Conrad's command, had passed from Sanford's group to the SAB following the merger (White 1967, 291–302).

Another possibility is the Katanga Expedition, led by Camille Delcommune's older brother Alexandre Delcommune (1855?–1922) (that is, the manager's brother rather than his uncle, as Conrad has it in his story). This expedition arrived in Kinshasa in three installments (rather than five) in September and October 1890: the first on 20 September and the second on 23 September, before Conrad and the *Roi des Belges* arrived at Kinshasa on 24 September on the downriver passage from Stanley Falls. The third detachment, with Alexandre Delcommune commanding the expedition, arrived on 5 October, before Conrad left Kinshasa (Sherry 1971, 84–85). The expedition's purpose was to occupy the Katanga area, on the Upper Congo, to make Leopold's territorial claim there effective in the face of British competition from Rhodesia to the south (Pakenham 2003, 400).

spoke to no one but his nephew.[124] You could see these two roaming about all day long with their heads close together in an everlasting confab.

"I had given up worrying myself about the rivets. One's capacity for that kind of folly is more limited than you would suppose. I said Hang!—and let things slide. I had plenty of time for meditation, and now and then I would give some thought to Kurtz. I wasn't very interested in him. No. Still, I was curious to see whether this man, who had come out equipped with moral ideas of some sort, would climb to the top after all, and how he would set about his work when there."

II

"One evening as I was lying flat on the deck of my steamboat, I heard voices approaching—and there were the nephew and the uncle strolling along the bank. I laid my head on my arm again, and had nearly lost myself in a doze, when somebody said in my ear, as it were: 'I am as harmless as a little child, but I don't like to be dictated to. Am I the manager—or am I not? I was ordered to send him there. It's incredible.' . . . I became aware that the two were standing on the shore alongside the forepart of the steamboat, just below my head. I did not move; it did not occur to me to move: I was sleepy. 'It *is* unpleasant,' grunted the uncle. 'He has asked the Administration to be sent there,' said the other, 'with the idea of showing what he could do; and I was instructed accordingly. Look at the influence that man must have. Is it not frightful?' They both agreed it was frightful, then made several bizarre remarks: 'Make rain and fine weather[125]—one man—the Council—by the nose'—bits of absurd sentences that got the better of my drowsiness, so that I had pretty near the whole of my wits about me when the uncle said, 'The climate may do away with this difficulty for you. Is he alone there?' 'Yes,' answered the manager; 'he sent his assistant down the river with a note to me in these terms: "Clear this poor devil out of the country, and don't bother sending more of that sort. I had rather be alone than have the kind of men you can dispose of with me." It was more than a year ago. Can you imagine such impudence?' 'Anything since then?' asked the other hoarsely. 'Ivory,' jerked the nephew; 'lots of it—prime sort—lots—most annoying, from him.' 'And with that?'

124. A description potentially based on Alexandre Delcommune's appearance. It is not clear whether or not Conrad had close contact with this man; if Alexandre had spoken only to his brother, as in the story, then Conrad may have felt confirmed in judging the Delcommune brothers' hostility toward him (Sherry 1971, 85–86).

125. African tribes attributed to their kings the power to control weather (Conrad 2010c, 449n74.26).

questioned the heavy rumble. 'Invoice,' was the reply fired out, so to speak. Then silence. They had been talking about Kurtz.

"I was broad awake by this time, but, lying perfectly at ease, remained still, having no inducement to change my position. 'How did that ivory come all this way?' growled the elder man, who seemed very vexed. The other explained that it had come with a fleet of canoes in charge of an English half-caste clerk Kurtz had with him; that Kurtz had apparently intended to return himself, the station being by that time bare of goods and stores, but after coming three hundred miles, had suddenly decided to go back, which he started to do alone in a small dugout with four paddlers, leaving the half-caste to continue down the river with the ivory. The two fellows there seemed astounded at anybody attempting such a thing. They were at a loss for an adequate motive. As to me, I seemed to see Kurtz for the first time. It was a distinct glimpse: the dugout, four paddling savages, and the lone white man turning his back suddenly on the headquarters, on relief, on thoughts of home—perhaps; setting his face towards the depths of the wilderness, towards his empty and desolate station. I did not know the motive. Perhaps he was just simply a fine fellow who stuck to his work for its own sake. His name, you understand, had not been pronounced once. He was 'that man.' The half-caste, who, as far as I could see, had conducted a difficult trip with great prudence and pluck, was invariably alluded to as 'that scoundrel.' The 'scoundrel' had reported that the 'man' had been very ill—had recovered imperfectly. . . . The two below me moved away then a few paces, and strolled back and forth at some little distance. I heard: 'Military post—doctor—two hundred miles—quite alone now—unavoidable delays—nine months—no news—strange rumours.' They approached again, just as the manager was saying, 'No one, as far as I know, unless a species of wandering trader—a pestilential fellow, snapping ivory from the natives.' Who was it they were talking about now? I gathered in snatches that this was some man supposed to be in Kurtz's district, and of whom the manager did not approve. 'We will not be free from unfair competition till one of these fellows is hanged for an example,' he said. 'Certainly,' grunted the other; 'get him hanged!'[126] Why not? Anything—anything can be done in this country. That's what I say; nobody here, you understand, *here*, can endanger your position. And why? You stand the climate—you outlast them all. The danger is in Europe; but there before I left I took care to——' They moved off and whispered, then their voices rose again. 'The extraordinary series of delays is not my fault. I did my possible.' The fat man sighed, 'Very sad.' 'And the pestiferous

---

126. In 1895, Charles Henry Stokes, an Irish missionary who had become a trader, was hanged by a Belgian officer for having allegedly provided ammunition to Arabs. The issue of punitive hanging in the Congo became publicized in the British press in the late 1890s (Pakenham 2003, 586).

absurdity of his talk,' continued the other; 'he bothered me enough when he was here. "Each station should be like a beacon on the road towards better things, a centre for trade of course, but also for humanising, improving, instructing." Conceive you—that ass! And he wants to be manager! No, it's——' Here he got choked by excessive indignation, and I lifted my head the least bit. I was surprised to see how near they were—right under me. I could have spat upon their hats. They were looking on the ground, absorbed in thought. The manager was switching his leg with a slender twig: his sagacious relative lifted his head. 'You have been well since you came out this time?' he asked. The other gave a start. 'Who? I? Oh! Like a charm—like a charm. But the rest—oh, my goodness! All sick. They die so quick, too, that I haven't the time to send them out of the country—it's incredible!' 'H'm. Just so,' grunted the uncle. 'Ah! my boy, trust to this—I say, trust to this.' I saw him extend his short flipper of an arm for a gesture that took in the forest, the creek, the mud, the river—seemed to beckon with a dishonouring flourish before the sunlit face of the land a treacherous appeal to the lurking death, to the hidden evil, to the profound darkness of its heart. It was so startling that I leaped to my feet and looked back at the edge of the forest, as though I had expected an answer of some sort to that black display of confidence. You know the foolish notions that come to one sometimes. The high stillness confronted these two figures with its ominous patience, waiting for the passing away of a fantastic invasion.

"They swore aloud together—out of sheer fright, I believe—then, pretending not to know anything of my existence, turned back to the station. The sun was low; and leaning forward side by side, they seemed to be tugging painfully uphill their two ridiculous shadows of unequal length, that trailed behind them slowly over the tall grass without bending a single blade.

"In a few days the Eldorado Expedition went into the patient wilderness, that closed upon it as the sea closes over a diver. Long afterwards the news came that all the donkeys were dead. I know nothing as to the fate of the less valuable animals. They, no doubt, like the rest of us, found what they deserved. I did not inquire. I was then rather excited at the prospect of meeting Kurtz very soon. When I say very soon I mean it comparatively. It was just two months from the day we left the creek when we came to the bank below Kurtz's station.[127]

---

127. Conrad's approximately 1,000-mile passage from Kinshasa to Stanley Falls on the *Roi des Belges* took 28 days (3 August to 1 September 1890), rather than the two months in the story, a speed remarked on by the 21 December 1890 issue of *Le Mouvement Géographique*. Also, while the fictional purpose is to relieve the upriver stations, according to the 2 November 1890 issue of *Le Mouvement Géographique,* the *Roi des Belges* was evidently dispatched to come to the aid of the *Ville de Bruxelles.* This larger troop-carrying steamer had run on a snag on 16 July 1890 near Upoto, about two-thirds of the way between Kinshasa and Stanley Falls. As it turned out, the *Ville de Bruxelles* managed to get under way about an hour before the *Roi des Belges* arrived on the scene (quoted in Sherry 1971, 49–50).

"Going up that river was like travelling back to the earliest beginnings of the world, when vegetation rioted on the earth and the big trees were kings. An empty stream, a great silence, an impenetrable forest.[128] The air was warm, thick, heavy, sluggish. There was no joy in the brilliance of sunshine. The long stretches of the waterway ran on, deserted, into the gloom of overshadowed distances. On silvery sandbanks hippos and alligators sunned themselves side by side. The broadening waters flowed through a mob of wooded islands; you lost your way on that river as you would in a desert, and butted all day long against shoals, trying to find the channel, till you thought yourself bewitched and cut off for ever from everything you had known once—somewhere—far away—in another existence perhaps. There were moments when one's past came back to one, as it will sometimes when you have not a moment to spare to yourself; but it came in the shape of an unrestful and noisy dream, remembered with wonder amongst the overwhelming realities of this strange world of plants, and water, and silence. And this stillness of life did not in the least resemble a

---

128. Although this depiction makes the Congo seem oppressively empty, at that time there were a total of eleven vessels, including three belonging to the SAB, sailing the upper reaches of the Congo, and Conrad passed a number of them. By the time *Roi des Belges* arrived at Bangala, midway between Kinshasa and Stanley Falls, on 19 August 1890, the ship passed four other steamers all on their way downstream. Later, Conrad would have seen one of them again, on her way back up to Stanley Falls when the *Roi des Belges* left there on her return downstream (*Le Mouvement Géographique* 28 December 1890, cited in Sherry 1971, 51). Also, all this river traffic undercuts the possibility that the real mission of the *Roi des Belges* was to bring an SAB agent down from Stanley Falls or to relieve other upriver stations, as so many other steamers were available (Sherry 1971, 51).

Numerous settlements, factories, and missionary and trading stations populated the riverbanks, such as those at Bangala, Tchumbiri, Bolobo, Coquilhatville, Upoto, Mwangi, and Basoko. According to a 21 September 1890 article in *Le Mouvement Géographique*, Basoko was "a veritable fortress" looming over the river, armed with four cannons and having walls 12 feet high [my translation]. Alexandre Delcommune's journal, cited in another *Mouvement Géographique* article on 25 August 1889, frequently reports seeing two or three settlements of some kind each day during a Congo River expedition in 1888 (quoted in Sherry 1971, 51–52).

However, Alexandre Delcommune's journal covers a relatively short section of the river (a little more than 100 miles). Other evidence indicates how isolated Conrad might have felt. A letter written by a trader on the same route six months after Conrad describes the country as "today entirely ruined," without a single inhabited village along a 200-mile stretch (four days' passage by steamer). Conrad's 28-day journey covered over 1,000 miles, during which he saw other ships at a rate of less that once every four days—that is, if he actually saw the other vessels; the Congo has a width of a few miles to 10 miles in places between its forested banks, with islands, bays, and tributaries, complicating the visual field. As for the missions they passed, they were separated by hundreds of miles, and the no more than six villages that Conrad saw were spread out over 500 miles (Najder 2007, 157).

As Conrad did, Marlow contends with snags—a significant hazard. When overhanging trees fall into the river, the trunks can become waterlogged and sink just below the surface. Striking a snag could damage a steamer's hull. (From Sir Harry Johnston, *George Grenfell and the Congo*. London: Hutchinson, 1908, 1:195.)

peace. It was the stillness of an implacable force brooding over an inscrutable intention. It looked at you with a vengeful aspect. I got used to it afterwards; I did not see it any more; I had no time. I had to keep guessing at the channel; I had to discern, mostly by inspiration, the signs of hidden banks; I watched for sunken stones; I was learning to clap my teeth smartly before my heart flew out, when I shaved by a fluke some infernal sly old snag that would have ripped the life out of the tin-pot steamboat and drowned all the pilgrims; I had to keep a look-out for the signs of dead wood we could cut up in the night for next day's steaming.[129] When you

---

129. Getting firewood for the ship's boiler was a significant task. John Rose Troup's description of sailing in the *Stanley* on the Congo in 1887 includes the daily routine, which began with getting under way at 5:30 a.m. and steaming until between 4:00 p.m. and 5:00 p.m., when the ship would stop at a suitable point for gathering firewood. Felling trees and chopping the wood took all night (Troup 1890, 124). In Conrad's "Up-river book," he made frequent notes about good locations for gathering wood along the riverbanks.

have to attend to things of that sort, to the mere incidents of the surface, the reality—the reality, I tell you—fades. The inner truth is hidden—luckily, luckily. But I felt it all the same; I felt often its mysterious stillness watching me at my monkey tricks, just as it watches you fellows performing on your respective tight-ropes for—what is it? half a crown a tumble——"

"Try to be civil, Marlow," growled a voice, and I knew there was at least one listener awake besides myself.

"I beg your pardon. I forgot the heartache which makes up the rest of the price. And indeed what does the price matter, if the trick be well done? You do your tricks very well. And I didn't do badly either, since I managed not to sink that steamboat on my first trip. It's a wonder to me yet. Imagine a blindfolded man set to drive a van over a bad road. I sweated and shivered over that business considerably, I can tell you. After all, for a seaman, to scrape the bottom of the thing that's supposed to float all the time under his care is the unpardonable sin. No one may know of it, but you never forget the thump—eh? A blow on the very heart. You remember it, you dream of it, you wake up at night and think of it—years after—and go hot and cold all over. I don't pretend to say that steamboat floated all the time. More than once she had to wade for a bit, with twenty cannibals splashing around and pushing. We had enlisted some of these chaps on the way for a crew. Fine fellows—cannibals—in their place. They were men one could work with, and I am grateful to them.[130] And, after all, they did not eat each other before my face: they had brought along a provision of hippo-meat which went rotten, and made the mystery of the wilderness stink in my nostrils. Phoo! I can sniff it now. I had the manager on board and three or four pilgrims with their staves—all complete.[131] Sometimes we came upon a station close by the bank, clinging to the skirts of the unknown, and the white men rushing out of a tumble-down hovel, with great gestures of joy and surprise and welcome, seemed very strange—had the appearance of being held there captive by a spell. The word 'ivory' would ring in the air for a while—and on we went again into the silence, along empty reaches,

---

130. Steamers were crewed by natives from the Upper Congo, primarily Bangalas, who were cannibals (Sherry 1971, 59–60). One source published in 1908 reports, "The *Bangala* were until recently such terrible cannibals that it was really difficult to induce them to bury any corpse except in their own stomachs." Still, they "were popular from the first with all Europeans in spite of occasional outbreaks of hostility," and they could be hired for lower wages than any other tribe on the Congo (Johnston 1908, 1:115n1, 2:649). The Bangala were also said to be superior pilots (Verner 1903, 79).

131. In addition to Conrad, other SAB employees aboard the *Roi des Belges* were the captain, Ludwig Rasmus Koch; Camille Delcommune (the manager); Gossens (a mechanic); and the agents Alphonse Keyaerts, Van der Heyden, and Édouard-François-Léon Rollin (Sherry 1971, 56).

The Equator Station (at Bolenge, where the equator crosses the lower Congo River) in 1883. This location is 412 miles upriver from Léopoldville, and about 600 miles downriver from Stanley Falls. Conrad left here on 16 August 1890 on his way upriver. (From Henry M. Stanley, *The Congo and the Founding of Its Free State*. New York, Harper & Brothers, 1885, opposite 2:71.)

round the still bends, between the high walls of our winding way, reverberating in hollow claps the ponderous beat of the stern-wheel. Trees, trees, millions of trees, massive, immense, running up high; and at their foot, hugging the bank against the stream, crept the little begrimed steamboat, like a sluggish beetle crawling on the floor of a lofty portico. It made you feel very small, very lost, and yet it was not altogether depressing, that feeling. After all, if you were small, the grimy beetle crawled on—which was just what you wanted it to do. Where the pilgrims imagined it crawled to I don't know. To some place where they expected to get something, I bet! For me it crawled towards Kurtz—exclusively; but when the steam-pipes started leaking we crawled very slow. The reaches opened before us and closed behind, as if the forest had stepped leisurely across the water to bar the way for our return. We penetrated deeper and deeper into the heart of darkness. It was very quiet there. At night sometimes the roll of drums behind the curtain of trees would run up the river and remain sustained faintly, as if hovering in the air high over our heads, till the first break of day. Whether it meant war, peace, or prayer we could not tell. The dawns were heralded by the descent of a chill stillness; the woodcutters slept, their fires burned low; the snapping of a twig would make you start. We were

"The Banks of the Upper Congo." Scene from Henry Morton Stanley's
expedition in 1884, showing thick walls of vegetation on the banks rising some
150 feet high. (From Henry M. Stanley, *The Congo and the Founding of Its Free
State*. New York, Harper & Brothers, 1885, opposite 2:94.)

wanderers on a prehistoric earth, on an earth that wore the aspect of an
unknown planet. We could have fancied ourselves the first of men taking
possession of an accursed inheritance, to be subdued at the cost of profound anguish and of excessive toil. But suddenly, as we struggled round a
bend, there would be a glimpse of rush walls, of peaked grass-roofs, a burst
of yells, a whirl of black limbs, a mass of hands clapping, of feet stamping,
of bodies swaying, of eyes rolling, under the droop of heavy and motionless foliage. The steamer toiled along slowly on the edge of a black and
incomprehensible frenzy. The prehistoric man was cursing us, praying to
us, welcoming us—who could tell? We were cut off from the comprehen-
sion of our surroundings; we glided past like phantoms, wondering and
secretly appalled, as sane men would be before an enthusiastic outbreak in
a madhouse. We could not understand because we were too far and could
not remember, because we were travelling in the night of first ages, of those
ages that are gone, leaving hardly a sign—and no memories.

　　"The earth seemed unearthly. We are accustomed to look upon the
shackled form of a conquered monster, but there—there you could look at
a thing monstrous and free. It was unearthly, and the men were—No, they
were not inhuman. Well, you know, that was the worst of it—this suspicion of their not being inhuman. It would come slowly to one. They howled

and leaped, and spun, and made horrid faces; but what thrilled you was just the thought of their humanity—like yours—the thought of your remote kinship with this wild and passionate uproar. Ugly. Yes, it was ugly enough; but if you were man enough you would admit to yourself that there was in you just the faintest trace of a response to the terrible frankness of that noise, a dim suspicion of there being a meaning in it which you—you so remote from the night of first ages—could comprehend. And why not? The mind of man is capable of anything—because everything is in it, all the past as well as all the future. What was there after all? Joy, fear, sorrow, devotion, valour, rage—who can tell?—but truth—truth stripped of its cloak of time. Let the fool gape and shudder—the man knows, and can look on without a wink. But he must at least be as much of a man as these on the shore.[132] He must meet that truth with his own true stuff—with his own inborn strength. Principles? Principles won't do. Acquisitions, clothes, pretty rags—rags that would fly off at the first good shake. No; you want a deliberate belief. An appeal to me in this fiendish row—is there? Very well; I hear; I admit, but I have a voice too, and for good or evil mine is the speech that cannot be silenced. Of course, a fool, what

---

132. Here Marlow appears to take back what he has just disparagingly said about the natives. Previously, he could not see any link of his similarity to them through cultural "memories," and there is not enough archaeological evidence (any "sign") to make the connection. In these ideas, Marlow expresses the prevailing view in Conrad's time that Africa effectively had no history. Yet now Marlow rejects his previous conclusion and evidently sees the truth—that he and those ashore are all men together—from behind the veil of time. Marlow evidently also refers to an anthropological theory then current, which generally held that different societies were evolving separately. Some were further along, but all were on parallel paths, with the more advanced ones having already gone through stages observed in the others. However, an opposing point of view then was that there was an essential difference between "civilized" minds and "primitive" minds, the latter ruled by mysticism rather than logic (Firchow 2000, 50–52). Marlow's assertion of a "remote kinship" navigates among these tensions in the thinking of Conrad's day, arriving at a judgment that emphasizes kindred humanity.

The details of this passage and the earlier one on the coast resemble those of a section of Henry Morton Stanley's *Through the Dark Continent* (1878), where he describes an encounter with the natives of Uhombo village (between the Upper Congo and the lakes of modern-day Uganda). Stanley writes of calling one of the elders "My brother" (the customary greeting); he then describes the elder's face as being "like an ugly and extravagant mask" (similar to Marlow's description of the coast natives as having "faces like grotesque masks"). Stanley records "the array of faces" surrounding him, those of his "humbler brothers and sisters," as "ugly—uglier—ugliest." When one of Stanley's men is injured and the native women respond with cries and expressions of pity, he sees their humanity in common: "my heart, keener than my eyes, saw through the disguise of filth, nakedness, and ochre, the human heart beating for another's suffering, and I then recognized and hailed them as indeed my own poor and degraded sisters" (Stanley 1878, 2:72–76; see also Firchow 2000, 53–54).

with sheer fright and fine sentiments, is always safe. Who's that grunt-ing?[133] You wonder I didn't go ashore for a howl and a dance? Well, no—I didn't. Fine sentiments, you say? Fine sentiments be hanged! I had no time. I had to mess about with white-lead[134] and strips of woollen blanket helping to put bandages on those leaky steam-pipes—I tell you. I had to watch the steering, and circumvent those snags, and get the tin-pot along by hook or by crook. There was surface-truth enough in these things to save a wiser man. And between whiles I had to look after the savage who was fireman. He was an improved specimen; he could fire up a vertical boiler.[135] He was there below me, and, upon my word, to look at him was as edifying as seeing a dog in a parody of breeches and a feather hat, walk-ing on his hind legs. A few months of training had done for that really fine chap. He squinted at the steam-gauge and at the water-gauge with an evi-dent effort of intrepidity—and he had filed teeth too, the poor devil, and the wool of his pate shaved into queer patterns, and three ornamental scars on each of his cheeks. He ought to have been clapping his hands and stamping his feet on the bank, instead of which he was hard at work, a thrall to strange witchcraft, full of improving knowledge. He was useful because he had been instructed; and what he knew was this—that should the water in that transparent thing disappear, the evil spirit inside the boiler would get angry through the greatness of his thirst, and take a terrible vengeance. So he sweated and fired up and watched the glass fearfully (with an impromptu charm, made of rags, tied to his arm, and a piece of polished bone, as big as a watch, stuck flatways through his lower lip), while the wooded banks slipped past us slowly, the short noise was left behind, the interminable miles of silence—and we crept on, towards Kurtz. But the snags were thick, the water was treacherous and shallow, the boiler seemed indeed to have a sulky devil in it, and thus neither that fireman nor I had any time to peer into our creepy thoughts.

"Some fifty miles below the Inner Station we came upon a hut of reeds, an inclined and melancholy pole, with the unrecognisable tatters of what had been a flag of some sort flying from it, and a neatly stacked wood-pile. This was unexpected. We came to the bank, and on the stack of firewood found a flat piece of board with some faded pencil-writing on it. When deciphered it said: 'Wood for you. Hurry up. Approach cautiously.' There was a signature, but it was illegible—not Kurtz—a much longer

---

133. Marlow is addressing his audience on the *Nellie*, not asking about the natives (Firchow 2000, 58).

134. A powder made of carbonate of lead, mixed with linseed oil to form a paste.

135. The steamer's boiler, called vertical because of the upright shape and vertical orientation of its barrel.

word. Hurry up. Where? Up the river? 'Approach cautiously.' We had not done so. But the warning could not have been meant for the place where it could be only found after approach. Something was wrong above. But what—and how much? That was the question. We commented adversely upon the imbecility of that telegraphic style. The bush around said nothing, and would not let us look very far, either. A torn curtain of red twill hung in the doorway of the hut, and flapped sadly in our faces. The dwelling was dismantled; but we could see a white man had lived there not very long ago. There remained a rude table—a plank on two posts; a heap of rubbish reposed in a dark corner, and by the door I picked up a book. It had lost its covers, and the pages had been thumbed into a state of extremely dirty softness; but the back had been lovingly stitched afresh with white cotton thread, which looked clean yet. It was an extraordinary find. Its title was, *An Inquiry into some Points of Seamanship,* by a man Towser, Towson—some such name—Master in His Majesty's Navy. The matter looked dreary reading enough, with illustrative diagrams and repulsive tables of figures, and the copy was sixty years old.[136] I handled this amazing antiquity with the greatest possible tenderness, lest it should dissolve in my hands. Within, Towson or Towser was inquiring earnestly into the breaking strain of ships' chains and tackle, and other such matters. Not a very enthralling book; but at the first glance you could see there a singleness of intention, an honest concern for the right way of going to work, which made these humble pages, thought out so many years ago, luminous with another than a professional light. The simple old sailor, with his talk of chains and purchases,[137] made me forget the jungle and the pilgrims in a delicious sensation of having come upon something unmistakably real. Such a book being there was wonderful enough; but still more astounding were the notes pencilled in the margin, and plainly referring to the text. I couldn't believe my eyes! They were in cipher! Yes, it looked like cipher. Fancy a man lugging with him a book of that description into this nowhere

---

136. Various historical sources have been proposed as the model for this book, such as a work by Alfred Henry Alston (Hay 1963, 144n78) or Nicholas Tinmouth's *An Inquiry Relative to Various Important Points of Seamanship, considered as a Branch of Practical Science* (1845) (Arnold 1976, 121–26). John Thomas Towson lived at the Sailor's Home in Liverpool and wrote and spoke on various nautical topics in the mid-1850s (Sherry 1971, 403n25). Another possibility is Anselm Griffith's *Observations on Some Points of Seamanship* (1824), whose second and final printing was exactly 60 years old in 1888, when Conrad reached the pinnacle of his career when he began his only permanent command (Larabee 2010, 70). The manuscript of *Heart of Darkness* indicates that some book was discovered in such a hut (Sherry 1971, 403n25).

137. Purchase: arrangement of pulleys, tackle, windlass, etc., that increases applied force through mechanical advantage.

and studying it—and making notes—in cipher at that! It was an extravagant mystery.

"I had been dimly aware for some time of a worrying noise, and when I lifted my eyes I saw the wood-pile was gone, and the manager, aided by all the pilgrims, was shouting at me from the river-side. I slipped the book into my pocket. I assure you to leave off reading was like tearing myself away from the shelter of an old and solid friendship.

"I started the lame engine ahead. 'It must be this miserable trader—this intruder,' exclaimed the manager, looking back malevolently at the place we had left. 'He must be English,' I said. 'It will not save him from getting into trouble if he is not careful,' muttered the manager darkly. I observed with assumed innocence that no man was safe from trouble in this world.

"The current was more rapid now, the steamer seemed at her last gasp, the stern-wheel flopped languidly, and I caught myself listening on tiptoe for the next beat of the float, for in sober truth I expected the wretched thing to give up every moment. It was like watching the last flickers of a life. But still we crawled. Sometimes I would pick out a tree a little way ahead to measure our progress towards Kurtz by, but I lost it invariably before we got abreast. To keep the eyes so long on one thing was too much for human patience. The manager displayed a beautiful resignation. I fretted and fumed and took to arguing with myself whether or no I would talk openly with Kurtz; but before I could come to any conclusion it occurred to me that my speech or my silence, indeed any action of mine, would be a mere futility. What did it matter what anyone knew or ignored? What did it matter who was manager? One gets sometimes such a flash of insight. The essentials of this affair lay deep under the surface, beyond my reach, and beyond my power of meddling.

"Towards the evening of the second day we judged ourselves about eight miles from Kurtz's station. I wanted to push on; but the manager looked grave, and told me the navigation up there was so dangerous that it would be advisable, the sun being very low already, to wait where we were till next morning. Moreover, he pointed out that if the warning to approach cautiously were to be followed, we must approach in daylight—not at dusk, or in the dark. This was sensible enough. Eight miles meant nearly three hours' steaming for us, and I could also see suspicious ripples at the upper end of the reach. Nevertheless, I was annoyed beyond expression at the delay, and most unreasonably too, since one night more could not matter much after so many months. As we had plenty of wood, and caution was the word, I brought up[138] in the middle of the stream. The reach was narrow, straight, with high sides like a railway cutting. The dusk came

---

138. Anchored.

gliding into it long before the sun had set. The current ran smooth and swift, but a dumb immobility sat on the banks. The living trees, lashed together by the creepers and every living bush of the undergrowth, might have been changed into stone, even to the slenderest twig, to the lightest leaf. It was not sleep—it seemed unnatural, like a state of trance. Not the faintest sound of any kind could be heard. You looked on amazed, and began to suspect yourself of being deaf—then the night came suddenly, and struck you blind as well. About three in the morning some large fish leaped, and the loud splash made me jump as though a gun had been fired. When the sun rose there was a white fog, very warm and clammy, and more blinding than the night. It did not shift or drive; it was just there, standing all round you like something solid. At eight or nine, perhaps, it lifted as a shutter lifts. We had a glimpse of the towering multitude of trees, of the immense matted jungle, with the blazing little ball of the sun hanging over it—all perfectly still—and then the white shutter came down again, smoothly, as if sliding in greased grooves. I ordered the chain, which we had begun to heave in, to be paid out again. Before it stopped running with a muffled rattle, a cry, a very loud cry, as of infinite desolation, soared slowly in the opaque air. It ceased. A complaining clamour, modulated in savage discords, filled our ears. The sheer unexpectedness of it made my hair stir under my cap. I don't know how it struck the others: to me it seemed as though the mist itself had screamed, so suddenly, and apparently from all sides at once, did this tumultuous and mournful uproar arise. It culminated in a hurried outbreak of almost intolerably excessive shrieking, which stopped short, leaving us stiffened in a variety of silly attitudes, and obstinately listening to the nearly as appalling and excessive silence. 'Good God! What is the meaning——?' stammered at my elbow one of the pilgrims—a little fat man, with sandy hair and red whiskers, who wore side-spring boots,[139] and pink pyjamas tucked into his socks.[140] Two others remained open-mouthed a whole minute, then dashed into the little cabin, to rush out incontinently and stand darting scared glances, with Winchesters[141] at 'ready' in their hands. What we could see was just

---

139. Boots with elastic panels on either side, allowing them to be pulled off or on more easily.

140. Most likely modeled on Alphonse Keyaerts, an agent who went upriver with Conrad on the *Roi des Belges* (Sherry 1971, 56).

141. Breech-loading repeating rifles first made around 1866 and named after D. F. Winchester, their American manufacturer.

the steamer we were on, her outlines blurred as though she had been on the point of dissolving, and a misty strip of water, perhaps two feet broad, around her—and that was all. The rest of the world was nowhere, as far as our eyes and ears were concerned. Just nowhere. Gone, disappeared; swept off without leaving a whisper or a shadow behind.

"I went forward, and ordered the chain to be hauled in short, so as to be ready to trip the anchor and move the steamboat at once if necessary.[142] 'Will they attack?' whispered an awed voice. 'We will all be butchered in this fog,' murmured another. The faces twitched with the strain, the hands trembled slightly, the eyes forgot to wink. It was very curious to see the contrast of expressions of the white men and of the black fellows of our crew, who were as much strangers to that part of the river as we, though their homes were only eight hundred miles away. The whites, of course greatly discomposed, had besides a curious look of being painfully shocked by such an outrageous row. The others had an alert, naturally interested expression; but their faces were essentially quiet, even those of the one or two who grinned as they hauled at the chain. Several exchanged short, grunting phrases, which seemed to settle the matter to their satisfaction. Their head-man, a young, broad-chested black, severely draped in dark-blue fringed cloths, with fierce nostrils and his hair all done up artfully in oily ringlets, stood near me. 'Aha!' I said, just for good fellowship's sake. 'Catch 'im,' he snapped, with a bloodshot widening of his eyes and a flash of sharp teeth—'catch 'im. Give 'im to us.' 'To you, eh?' I asked; 'what would you do with them?' 'Eat 'im!' he said curtly, and, leaning his elbow on the rail, looked out into the fog in a dignified and profoundly pensive attitude.[143] I would no doubt have been properly horrified, had it not occurred to me that he and his chaps must be very hungry: that they must have been growing increasingly hungry for at least this month past. They had been engaged for six months (I don't think a single one of them had any clear idea of time, as we at the end of countless ages have. They still belonged to the beginnings of time—had no inherited experience to teach them, as it were), and of course, as long as there was a piece of paper written over in accordance with some farcical law or other made down the river, it didn't enter anybody's head to trouble how they would live. Certainly they had brought with them some rotten hippo-meat, which couldn't

---

142. Marlow has given the order to heave in on the anchor chain until the steamer's bow is directly over the anchor and the cable is vertical. Further heaving will be enough to "trip the anchor"—lift the anchor clear of the bottom—for a quick escape (Smyth 1867, 377, 698).

143. Cannibalism was widespread among the Bangala, who predominantly crewed the SAB steamers (Sherry 1971, 59–60).

have lasted very long, anyway, even if the pilgrims hadn't, in the midst of a shocking hullabaloo, thrown a considerable quantity of it overboard. It looked like a high-handed proceeding; but it was really a case of legitimate self-defence. You can't breathe dead hippo waking, sleeping, and eating, and at the same time keep your precarious grip on existence. Besides that, they had given them every week three pieces of brass wire, each about nine inches long;[144] and the theory was they were to buy their provisions with that currency in river-side villages. You can see how *that* worked. There were either no villages, or the people were hostile, or the director, who like the rest of us fed out of tins, with an occasional old he-goat thrown in, didn't want to stop the steamer for some more or less recondite reason. So, unless they swallowed the wire itself, or made loops of it to snare the fishes with, I don't see what good their extravagant salary could be to them. I must say it was paid with a regularity worthy of a large and honourable trading company. For the rest, the only thing to eat—though it didn't look eatable in the least—I saw in their possession was a few lumps of some stuff like half-cooked dough, of a dirty lavender colour, they kept wrapped in leaves,[145] and now and then swallowed a piece of, but so small that it seemed done more for the look of the thing than for any serious purpose of sustenance. Why in the name of all the gnawing devils of hunger they didn't go for us—they were thirty to five—and have a good tuck-in for once, amazes me now when I think of it. They were big powerful men, with not much capacity to weigh the consequences, with courage, with strength, even yet, though their skins were no longer glossy and their muscles no longer hard. And I saw that something restraining, one of those human secrets that baffle probability, had come into play there. I looked at them with a swift quickening of interest—not because it occurred to me I might be eaten by them before very long, though I own to you that just then I perceived—in a new light, as it were—how unwholesome the pilgrims looked, and I hoped, yes, I positively hoped, that my aspect was not so—what shall I say?—so—unappetising: a touch of fantastic vanity which fitted well with the dream-sensation that pervaded all my days at that time. Perhaps I had a little fever too. One can't live with one's finger everlastingly on one's pulse. I had often 'a little fever,' or a little touch of other things—the playful paw-strokes of the wilderness, the preliminary

---

144. The *mitako,* brass-rod currency used to pay natives in the Congo.

145. Accurately describes the cassava (a starchy root) that Bangalas ate. According to one report of the time, this "staple food of all the riverain peoples of the Upper Congo . . . was ground into a white flour and then mixed with water till it formed a stiff dough. This was made up into rolls of sausage shape (or large round balls), wrapped in banana leaves, and boiled" (Johnston 1908, 2:605).

trifling before the more serious onslaught which came in due course. Yes; I looked at them as you would on any human being, with a curiosity of their impulses, motives, capacities, weaknesses, when brought to the test of an inexorable physical necessity. Restraint! What possible restraint? Was it superstition, disgust, patience, fear—or some kind of primitive honour? No fear can stand up to hunger, no patience can wear it out, disgust simply does not exist where hunger is; and as to superstition, beliefs, and what you may call principles, they are less than chaff in a breeze. Don't you know the devilry of lingering starvation, its exasperating torment, its black thoughts, its sombre and brooding ferocity? Well, I do.[146] It takes a man all his inborn strength to fight hunger properly. It's really easier to face bereavement, dishonour, and the perdition of one's soul—than this kind of prolonged hunger. Sad, but true. And these chaps too had no earthly reason for any kind of scruple. Restraint! I would just as soon have expected restraint from a hyena prowling amongst the corpses of a battlefield. But there was the fact facing me—the fact dazzling, to be seen, like the foam on the depths of the sea, like a ripple on an unfathomable enigma, a mystery greater—when I thought of it—than the curious, inexplicable note of desperate grief in this savage clamour that had swept by us on the river-bank, behind the blind whiteness of the fog.

"Two pilgrims were quarrelling in hurried whispers as to which bank. 'Left.' 'No, no; how can you? Right, right, of course.' 'It is very serious,' said the manager's voice behind me; 'I would be desolated if anything should happen to Mr. Kurtz before we came up.' I looked at him, and had not the slightest doubt he was sincere. He was just the kind of man who would wish to preserve appearances. That was his restraint. But when he muttered something about going on at once, I did not even take the trouble to answer him. I knew, and he knew, that it was impossible. Were we to let go our hold of the bottom, we would be absolutely in the air—in space. We wouldn't be able to tell where we were going to—whether up or down stream, or across—till we fetched against one bank or the other—and then we wouldn't know at first which it was. Of course I made no move. I had no mind for a smash-up. You couldn't imagine a more deadly place for a shipwreck. Whether drowned at once or not, we were sure to perish speedily in one way or another. 'I authorise you to take all the risks,' he said, after a short silence. 'I refuse to take any,' I said shortly; which was just the answer he expected, though its tone might have surprised him. 'Well, I must defer to your judgment. You are captain,' he said, with marked civility. I turned my shoulder to him in sign of my appreciation, and looked into

---

146. In 1902 Conrad wrote a story, "Falk," featuring starvation and cannibalism on a ship at sea.

the fog. How long would it last? It was the most hopeless look-out. The approach to this Kurtz grubbing for ivory in the wretched bush was beset by as many dangers as though he had been an enchanted princess sleeping in a fabulous castle. 'Will they attack, do you think?' asked the manager, in a confidential tone.

"I did not think they would attack, for several obvious reasons. The thick fog was one. If they left the bank in their canoes they would get lost in it, as we would be if we attempted to move. Still, I had also judged the jungle of both banks quite impenetrable—and yet eyes were in it, eyes that had seen us. The river-side bushes were certainly very thick; but the under-growth behind was evidently penetrable. However, during the short lift I had seen no canoes anywhere in the reach—certainly not abreast of the steamer. But what made the idea of attack inconceivable to me was the nature of the noise—of the cries we had heard. They had not the fierce character boding of immediate hostile intention. Unexpected, wild, and violent as they had been, they had given me an irresistible impression of sorrow. The glimpse of the steamboat had for some reason filled those sav-ages with unrestrained grief. The danger, if any, I expounded, was from our proximity to a great human passion let loose. Even extreme grief may ultimately vent itself in violence—but more generally takes the form of apathy. . . .

"You should have seen the pilgrims stare! They had no heart to grin, or even to revile me; but I believe they thought me gone mad—with fright, maybe. I delivered a regular lecture. My dear boys, it was no good bother-ing. Keep a look-out? Well, you may guess I watched the fog for the signs of lifting as a cat watches a mouse; but for anything else our eyes were of no more use to us than if we had been buried miles deep in a heap of cot-ton-wool. It felt like it too—choking, warm, stifling. Besides, all I said, though it sounded extravagant, was absolutely true to fact. What we after-wards alluded to as an attack was really an attempt at repulse. The action was very far from being aggressive—it was not even defensive, in the usual sense: it was undertaken under the stress of desperation, and in its essence was purely protective.

"It developed itself, I should say, two hours after the fog lifted, and its commencement was at a spot, roughly speaking, about a mile and a half below Kurtz's station.[147] We had just floundered and flopped round a bend, when I saw an islet, a mere grassy hummock of bright green, in the middle of the stream.[148] It was the only thing of the kind; but as we opened the

---

147. In Conrad's historical journey, the station at Stanley Falls, which he reached on 1 September 1890.

148. There were numerous islands in the 70 miles below Stanley Falls.

reach more, I perceived it was the head of a long sandbank, or rather of a chain of shallow patches stretching down the middle of the river. They were discoloured, just awash, and the whole lot was seen just under the water, exactly as a man's backbone is seen running down the middle of his back under the skin. Now, as far as I did see, I could go to the right or to the left of this. I didn't know either channel, of course. The banks looked pretty well alike, the depth appeared the same; but as I had been informed the station was on the west side,[149] I naturally headed for the western passage.

"No sooner had we fairly entered it than I became aware it was much narrower than I had supposed. To the left of us there was the long uninterrupted shoal, and to the right a high steep bank heavily overgrown with bushes. Above the bush the trees stood in serried ranks. The twigs overhung the current thickly, and from distance to distance a large limb of some tree projected rigidly over the stream. It was then well on in the afternoon, the face of the forest was gloomy, and a broad strip of shadow had already fallen on the water. In this shadow we steamed up—very slowly, as you may imagine. I sheered her well inshore—the water being deepest near the bank, as the sounding-pole[150] informed me.

"One of my hungry and forbearing friends was sounding in the bows just below me. This steamboat was exactly like a decked scow.[151] On the deck there were two little teak-wood houses, with doors and windows. The boiler was in the fore-end, and the machinery right astern. Over the whole there was a light roof, supported on stanchions.[152] The funnel[153] projected through that roof, and in front of the funnel a small cabin built of light planks served for a pilot-house.[154] It contained a couch, two campstools, a loaded Martini-Henry[155] leaning in one corner, a tiny table, and the steering-wheel. It had a wide door in front and a broad shutter at each side. All these were always thrown open, of course. I spent my days perched up

---

149. The Congo flows roughly northwest in the area of what was then Stanley Falls, making the west bank the one on the right side of the steamer, facing upstream. Conrad puts Kurtz's station on that right side, while the Stanley Falls settlement was mostly on the left side.

150. Used to determine the depth of water in order to avoid running aground.

151. A large flat-bottomed vessel. The following description closely resembles the *Roi des Belges*. The historical ship was small, with a displacement of 15 tons; a wood-fired boiler served a steam engine powering a sternwheel (Sherry 1971, 57).

152. Fixed upright posts of iron or wood.

153. Metal tube that carries smoke from the engine up and away.

154. Enclosed structure on the deck, housing the ship's wheel, from which the vessel is steered.

155. A breech-loading .45-caliber rifle.

there on the extreme fore-end of that roof, before the door. At night I slept, or tried to, on the couch. An athletic black belonging to some coast tribe, and educated by my poor predecessor, was the helmsman. He sported a pair of brass earrings, wore a blue cloth wrapper from the waist to the ankles, and thought all the world of himself. He was the most unstable kind of fool I had ever seen. He steered with no end of a swagger while you were by; but if he lost sight of you, he became instantly the prey of an abject funk, and would let that cripple of a steamboat get the upper hand of him in a minute.

"I was looking down at the sounding-pole, and feeling much annoyed to see at each try a little more of it stick out of that river, when I saw my poleman give up the business suddenly, and stretch himself flat on the deck, without even taking the trouble to haul his pole in. He kept hold on it though, and it trailed in the water. At the same time the fireman, whom I could also see below me, sat down abruptly before his furnace and ducked his head. I was amazed. Then I had to look at the river mighty quick, because there was a snag in the fairway.[156] Sticks, little sticks, were flying about—thick: they were whizzing before my nose, dropping below me, striking behind me against my pilot-house. All this time the river, the shore, the woods, were very quiet—perfectly quiet. I could only hear the heavy splashing thump of the stern-wheel and the patter of these things. We cleared the snag clumsily. Arrows, by Jove! We were being shot at![157] I stepped in quickly to close the shutter on the land-side. That fool-helmsman, his hands on the spokes, was lifting his knees high, stamping his feet, champing his mouth, like a reined-in horse. Confound him! And we were staggering within ten feet of the bank. I had to lean right out to swing the heavy shutter, and I saw a face amongst the leaves on the level with my own, looking at me very fierce and steady; and then suddenly, as though a veil had been removed from my eyes, I made out, deep in the tangled gloom, naked breasts, arms, legs, glaring eyes—the bush was swarming with human limbs in movement, glistening, of bronze colour. The twigs shook, swayed, and rustled, the arrows flew out of them, and then the shutter came to. 'Steer her straight,' I said to the helmsman. He held his head

---

156. Avoiding obstructions was a major navigational difficulty, particularly in the last 40 miles below Stanley Falls (Johnston 1908, 1:292–93).

157. It is highly unlikely that the *Roi des Belges* was attacked while Conrad was aboard. The 70 miles of river below Stanley Falls was under the control of the Congo Arabs. Thus, any such attack (while one might have occurred in the conditions two years after Conrad was there) would have been directed by them rather than Klein (or a different model for Kurtz). Furthermore, an attack this serious would no doubt have been mentioned in *Le Mouvement Géographique* and have resulted in a response from the Congo Free State, but evidently none was recorded (Sherry 1971, 53–54).

rigid, face forward; but his eyes rolled, he kept on lifting and setting down his feet gently, his mouth foamed a little. 'Keep quiet!' I said in a fury. I might just as well have ordered a tree not to sway in the wind. I darted out. Below me there was a great scuffle of feet on the iron deck; confused exclamations; a voice screamed, 'Can you turn back?' I caught shape of a V-shaped ripple on the water ahead. What? Another snag! A fusillade burst out under my feet. The pilgrims had opened with their Winchesters, and were simply squirting lead into that bush. A deuce of a lot of smoke came up and drove slowly forward. I swore at it. Now I couldn't see the ripple or the snag either. I stood in the doorway, peering, and the arrows came in swarms. They might have been poisoned, but they looked as though they wouldn't kill a cat. The bush began to howl. Our wood-cutters raised a warlike whoop; the report of a rifle just at my back deafened me. I glanced over my shoulder, and the pilot-house was yet full of noise and smoke when I made a dash at the wheel. The fool-nigger had dropped everything, to throw the shutter open and let off that Martini-Henry. He stood before the wide opening, glaring, and I yelled at him to come back, while I straightened the sudden twist out of that steamboat. There was no room to turn even if I had wanted to, the snag was somewhere very near ahead in that confounded smoke, there was no time to lose, so I just crowded her into the bank—right into the bank, where I knew the water was deep.

"We tore slowly along the overhanging bushes in a whirl of broken twigs and flying leaves. The fusillade below stopped short, as I had foreseen it would when the squirts[158] got empty. I threw my head back to a glinting whiz that traversed the pilot-house, in at one shutter-hole and out at the other. Looking past that mad helmsman, who was shaking the empty rifle and yelling at the shore, I saw vague forms of men running bent double, leaping, gliding, distinct, incomplete, evanescent. Something big appeared in the air before the shutter, the rifle went overboard, and the man stepped back swiftly, looked at me over his shoulder in an extraordinary, profound, familiar manner, and fell upon my feet. The side of his head hit the wheel twice, and the end of what appeared a long cane clattered round and knocked over a little camp-stool. It looked as though after wrenching that thing from somebody ashore he had lost his balance in the effort. The thin smoke had blown away, we were clear of the snag, and looking ahead I could see that in another hundred yards or so I would be free to sheer off, away from the bank; but my feet felt so very warm and wet that I had to look down. The man had rolled on his back and stared straight up at me; both his hands clutched that cane. It was the shaft of a spear that, either thrown or lunged through the opening, had caught him in the side just

---

158. Slang for repeating rifle (Conrad 2010c, 451n90.26).

below the ribs; the blade had gone in out of sight, after making a frightful gash; my shoes were full; a pool of blood lay very still, gleaming dark-red under the wheel; his eyes shone with an amazing lustre. The fusillade burst out again. He looked at me anxiously, gripping the spear like something precious, with an air of being afraid I would try to take it away from him. I had to make an effort to free my eyes from his gaze and attend to the steering. With one hand I felt above my head for the line of the steam whistle, and jerked out screech after screech hurriedly. The tumult of angry and warlike yells was checked instantly, and then from the depths of the woods went out such a tremulous and prolonged wail of mournful fear and utter despair as may be imagined to follow the flight of the last hope from the earth. There was a great commotion in the bush; the shower of arrows stopped, a few dropping shots rang out sharply—then silence, in which the languid beat of the stern-wheel came plainly to my ears. I put the helm hard a-starboard at the moment when the pilgrim in pink pyjamas, very hot and agitated, appeared in the doorway. 'The manager sends me——' he began in an official tone, and stopped short. 'Good God!' he said, glaring at the wounded man.

"We two whites stood over him, and his lustrous and inquiring glance enveloped us both. I declare it looked as though he would presently put to us some question in an understandable language; but he died without uttering a sound, without moving a limb, without twitching a muscle. Only in the very last moment, as though in response to some sign we could not see, to some whisper we could not hear, he frowned heavily, and that frown gave to his black death-mask an inconceivably sombre, brooding, and menacing expression. The lustre of inquiring glance faded swiftly into vacant glassiness. 'Can you steer?' I asked the agent eagerly. He looked very dubious; but I made a grab at his arm, and he understood at once I meant him to steer whether or no. To tell you the truth, I was morbidly anxious to change my shoes and socks. 'He is dead,' murmured the fellow, immensely impressed. 'No doubt about it,' said I, tugging like mad at the shoe-laces. 'And, by the way, I suppose Mr. Kurtz is dead as well by this time.'

"For the moment that was the dominant thought. There was a sense of extreme disappointment, as though I had found out I had been striving after something altogether without a substance. I couldn't have been more disgusted if I had travelled all this way for the sole purpose of talking with Mr. Kurtz. Talking with . . . I flung one shoe overboard, and became aware that that was exactly what I had been looking forward to—a talk with Kurtz. I made the strange discovery that I had never imagined him as doing, you know, but as discoursing. I didn't say to myself, 'Now I will never see him,' or 'Now I will never shake him by the hand,' but, 'Now I will never hear him.' The man presented himself as a voice. Not of course that I did not connect him with some sort of action. Hadn't I been told in all the tones of jealousy and admiration that he had collected, bartered, swindled, or stolen more ivory than all the other agents together? That was not the point. The point was in his being a gifted creature, and that of all his gifts the one that stood out pre-eminently, that carried with it a sense of real presence, was his ability to talk, his words—the gift of expression, the bewildering, the illuminating, the most exalted and the most contemptible, the pulsating stream of light, or the deceitful flow from the heart of an impenetrable darkness.

"The other shoe went flying unto the devil-god of that river. I thought, By Jove! it's all over. We are too late; he has vanished—the gift has vanished, by means of some spear, arrow, or club. I will never hear that chap speak after all—and my sorrow had a startling extravagance of emotion, even such as I had noticed in the howling sorrow of these savages in the bush. I couldn't have felt more of lonely desolation somehow, had I been robbed of a belief or had missed my destiny in life. . . . Why do you sigh in this beastly way, somebody? Absurd? Well, absurd. Good Lord! mustn't a man ever——Here, give me some tobacco." . . .

There was a pause of profound stillness, then a match flared, and Marlow's lean face appeared, worn, hollow, with downward folds and dropped eyelids, with an aspect of concentrated attention; and as he took vigorous draws at his pipe, it seemed to retreat and advance out of the night in the regular flicker of the tiny flame. The match went out.

"Absurd!" he cried. "This is the worst of trying to tell . . . Here you all are, each moored with two good addresses, like a hulk[159] with two anchors, a butcher round one corner, a policeman round another, excellent appetites, and temperature normal—you hear—normal from year's end to year's end. And you say, Absurd! Absurd be—exploded! Absurd! My dear boys, what can you expect from a man who out of sheer nervousness had just flung overboard a pair of new shoes? Now I think of it, it is amazing I did not shed tears. I am, upon the whole, proud of my fortitude. I was cut to the quick at the idea of having lost the inestimable privilege of listening to the gifted Kurtz. Of course I was wrong. The privilege was waiting for me. Oh yes, I heard more than enough. And I was right, too. A voice. He was very little more than a voice. And I heard—him—it—this voice—other voices—all of them were so little more than voices—and the memory of that time itself lingers around me, impalpable, like a dying vibration of one immense jabber, silly, atrocious, sordid, savage, or simply mean, without any kind of sense. Voices, voices—even the girl herself—now——"

He was silent for a long time.

---

159. Old vessel, no longer sent to sea but kept in place and used for various purposes such as storage or temporary quarters for crews (Smyth 1867, 395).

"I laid the ghost of his gifts at last with a lie," he began suddenly. "Girl! What? Did I mention a girl? Oh, she is out of it—completely. They—the women I mean—are out of it—should be out of it. We must help them to stay in that beautiful world of their own, lest ours gets worse. Oh, she had to be out of it. You should have heard the disinterred body of Mr. Kurtz saying, 'My Intended.' You would have perceived directly then how completely she was out of it. And the lofty frontal bone of Mr. Kurtz! They say the hair goes on growing sometimes, but this—ah—specimen was impressively bald. The wilderness had patted him on the head, and, behold, it was like a ball—an ivory ball; it had caressed him, and—lo!—he had withered; it had taken him, loved him, embraced him, got into his veins, consumed his flesh, and sealed his soul to its own by the inconceivable ceremonies of some devilish initiation. He was its spoiled and pampered favourite. Ivory? I should think so. Heaps of it, stacks of it. The old mud shanty was bursting with it. You would think there was not a single tusk left either above or below the ground in the whole country. 'Mostly fossil,' the manager had remarked disparagingly.[160] It was no more fossil than I am; but they call it fossil when it is dug up. It appears these niggers do bury the tusks sometimes—but evidently they couldn't bury this parcel deep enough to save the gifted Mr. Kurtz from his fate. We filled the steamboat with it, and had to pile a lot on the deck. Thus he could see and enjoy as long as he could see, because the appreciation of this favour had remained with him to the last. You should have heard him say, 'My ivory.' Oh yes, I heard him. 'My Intended, my ivory, my station, my river, my——' everything belonged to him. It made me hold my breath in expectation of hearing the wilderness burst into a prodigious peal of laughter that would shake the fixed stars in their places. Everything belonged to him—but that was a trifle. The thing was to know what he belonged to, how many powers of darkness claimed him for their own. That was the reflection that made you creepy all over. It was impossible—it was not good for one either—trying to imagine. He had taken a high seat amongst the devils of the land—I mean literally. You can't understand. How could you?—with solid pavement under your feet, surrounded by kind neighbours ready to cheer you or to fall on you, stepping delicately between the butcher and the policeman, in the holy terror of scandal and gallows and lunatic asylums—how can you imagine what particular region of the first ages a man's untrammeled feet may take him into by the way of solitude—utter solitude without a policeman—by the way of silence—utter silence, where no warning voice of a kind neighbour can be heard whispering of public

---

160. Fossil ivory, a term mistakenly used in this passage to describe temporarily buried ivory, properly refers to the tusks of dead mammoths, elephants, or mastodons that have been preserved in the ground from previous historical eras.

opinion? These little things make all the great difference. When they are gone you must fall back upon your own innate strength, upon your own capacity for faithfulness. Of course you may be too much of a fool to go wrong—too dull even to know you are being assaulted by the powers of darkness. I take it, no fool ever made a bargain for his soul with the devil: the fool is too much of a fool, or the devil too much of a devil—I don't know which. Or you may be such a thunderingly exalted creature as to be altogether deaf and blind to anything but heavenly sights and sounds. Then the earth for you is only a standing place—and whether to be like this is your loss or your gain I won't pretend to say. But most of us are neither one nor the other. The earth for us is a place to live in, where we must put up with sights, with sounds, with smells, too, by Jove!—breathe dead hippo, so to speak, and not be contaminated. And there, don't you see? your strength comes in, the faith in your ability for the digging of unostentatious holes to bury the stuff in—your power of devotion, not to yourself, but to an obscure, back-breaking business. And that's difficult enough. Mind, I am not trying to excuse or even explain—I am trying to account to myself for—for—Mr. Kurtz—for the shade of Mr. Kurtz. This initiated wraith from the back of Nowhere honoured me with its amazing confidence before it vanished altogether. This was because it could speak English to me. The original Kurtz had been educated partly in England, and—as he was good enough to say himself—his sympathies were in the right place. His mother was half-English, his father was half-French. All Europe contributed to the making of Kurtz;[161] and by and by I learned that, most appropriately, the International Society for the Suppression of Savage Customs[162] had entrusted him with the making of a report, for its future guidance. And he had written it too. I've seen it. I've read it. It was

---

161. Conrad wrote in a letter to Kazimierz Waliszewski on 16 December 1903, "I took great care to give Kurtz a cosmopolitan origin" (Conrad 1988a, 94).

162. Although there was apparently no society by that exact name, there was a Société Antiesclavagiste de Belgique (Antislavery Society of Belgium), founded in 1888 under the influence of the French Cardinal Charles Lavigerie (Gann and Duignan 1979, 27; Sherry 1971, 100). Arthur Hodister, the virtuous and enterprising inner station agent who was one possible inspiration for Kurtz, was opposed to barbaric customs and slavery and was associated with the Société Antiesclavagiste de Belgique. While he evidently did not write a report on native customs, he appears to have witnessed native practices such as those hinted at in *Heart of Darkness:* in particular, burning slaves alive for trying to escape, and human sacrifices carried out as part of funerary ceremonies (*Biographie Coloniale Belge* 1948–1958, 1:514, quoted in Sherry 1971, 100–101).

In 1896, in response to increasing European press attention to atrocities in the Congo, Leopold formed a new cover organization: the Commission for the Protection of the Natives (Hochschild 1999, 174).

eloquent, vibrating with eloquence, but too high-strung, I think. Seventeen pages of close writing he had found time for! But this must have been be- fore his—let us say—nerves went wrong, and caused him to preside at certain midnight dances ending with unspeakable rites, which—as far as I reluctantly gathered from what I heard at various times—were offered up to him—do you understand?—to Mr. Kurtz himself. But it was a beautiful piece of writing. The opening paragraph, however, in the light of later in- formation, strikes me now as ominous. He began with the argument that we whites, from the point of development we had arrived at, 'must neces- sarily appear to them [savages] in the nature of supernatural beings—we approach them with the might as of a deity,' and so on, and so on. 'By the simple exercise of our will we can exert a power for good practically un- bounded,' etc. etc. From that point he soared and took me with him. The peroration was magnificent, though difficult to remember, you know. It gave me the notion of an exotic Immensity ruled by an august Benevo- lence. It made me tingle with enthusiasm. This was the unbounded power of eloquence—of words—of burning noble words. There were no practi- cal hints to interrupt the magic current of phrases, unless a kind of note at the foot of the last page, scrawled evidently much later, in an unsteady hand, may be regarded as the exposition of a method. It was very simple, and at the end of that moving appeal to every altruistic sentiment it blazed at you, luminous and terrifying, like a flash of lightning in a serene sky: 'Exterminate all the brutes!'[163] The curious part was that he had apparently forgotten all about that valuable postscriptum, because, later on, when he in a sense came to himself, he repeatedly entreated me to take good care of 'my pamphlet' (he called it), as it was sure to have in the future a good influence upon his career. I had full information about all these things, and, besides, as it turned out, I was to have the care of his memory. I've done enough for it to give me the indisputable right to lay it, if I choose, for an everlasting rest in the dust-bin of progress, amongst all the sweepings and, figuratively speaking, all the dead cats of civilisation. But then, you see, I can't choose. He won't be forgotten. Whatever he was, he was not com- mon. He had the power to charm or frighten rudimentary souls into an aggravated witch-dance in his honour; he could also fill the small souls of the pilgrims with bitter misgivings: he had one devoted friend at least, and he had conquered one soul in the world that was neither rudimentary nor

---

163. Such an attitude conformed with mid-19th-century discussions of evolution ex- emplified by Charles Darwin's observation, in *The Descent of Man* (1871): "At some future period, not very distant as measured by centuries, the civilised races of man will almost certainly exterminate, and replace, the savage races throughout the world" (Darwin 2006, 891; Conrad 2010c, 452n95.39–40).

tainted with self-seeking. No; I can't forget him, though I am not prepared to affirm the fellow was exactly worth the life we lost in getting to him. I missed my late helmsman awfully—I missed him even while his body was still lying in the pilot-house. Perhaps you will think it passing strange this regret for a savage who was no more account than a grain of sand in a black Sahara. Well, don't you see, he had done something, he had steered; for months I had him at my back—a help—an instrument. It was a kind of partnership. He steered for me—I had to look after him, I worried about his deficiencies, and thus a subtle bond had been created, of which I only became aware when it was suddenly broken. And the intimate profundity of that look he gave me when he received his hurt remains to this day in my memory—like a claim of distant kinship affirmed in a supreme moment.

"Poor fool! If he had only left that shutter alone. He had no restraint, no restraint—just like Kurtz—a tree swayed by the wind. As soon as I had put on a dry pair of slippers, I dragged him out, after first jerking the spear out of his side, which operation I confess I performed with my eyes shut tight. His heels leaped together over the little door-step; his shoulders were pressed to my breast; I hugged him from behind desperately. Oh! he was heavy, heavy; heavier than any man on earth, I should imagine. Then without more ado I tipped him overboard. The current snatched him as though he had been a wisp of grass, and I saw the body roll over twice before I lost sight of it for ever. All the pilgrims and the manager were then congregated on the awning-deck about the pilot-house, chattering at each other like a flock of excited magpies, and there was a scandalised murmur at my heartless promptitude. What they wanted to keep that body hanging about for I can't guess. Embalm it, maybe. But I had also heard another, and a very ominous, murmur on the deck below. My friends the wood-cutters were likewise scandalised, and with a better show of reason—though I admit that the reason itself was quite inadmissible. Oh, quite! I had made up my mind that if my late helmsman was to be eaten, the fishes alone should have him. He had been a very second-rate helmsman while alive, but now he was dead he might have become a first-class temptation, and possibly cause some startling trouble. Besides, I was anxious to take the wheel, the man in pink pyjamas showing himself a hopeless duffer at the business.

"This I did directly the simple funeral was over. We were going half-speed, keeping right in the middle of the stream, and I listened to the talk about me. They had given up Kurtz, they had given up the station; Kurtz was dead, and the station had been burnt—and so on, and so on. The red-haired pilgrim was beside himself with the thought that at least this poor Kurtz had been properly revenged. 'Say! We must have made a glorious slaughter of them in the bush. Eh? What do you think? Say?' He positively danced, the bloodthirsty little gingery beggar. And he had nearly fainted

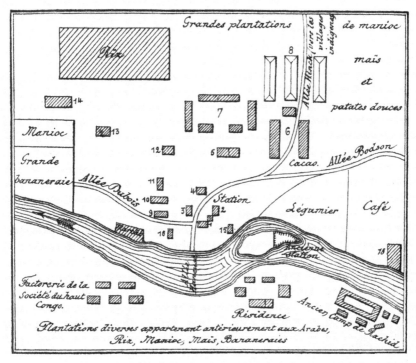

Grandes plantations

de manioc

maïs

et

patates douces

Riz

Manioc

Grande
bananeraie

Allée Dubois

Allée Henn (vers les villages indigènes)

8

7

6

5

Cacao. Allée Bodson

Station

Légumier

Café

Factorerie de la
Société du haut
Congo.

Résidence

Ancienne
Station

Ancien Camp de Rachid

Plantations diverses appartenant antérieurement aux Arabes,
Riz, Manioc, Maïs, Bananeraies

STANLEY-FALLS, D'APRÈS DES CROQUIS DE MM. HINCK ET DAENEN.

Stanley Falls (site of Kurtz's "Inner Station") by 1893 or 1894. Farthest point of Conrad's journey upriver; he arrived on 1 September 1890 and left on probably 7 or 8 September. A major hub in the ivory trade, Stanley Falls was about 1,300 miles up the Congo River and at the river's highest navigable point above Kinshasa. Above the settlement of Stanley Falls were the falls themselves (now Boyoma Falls). In contrast with the solitude of the "Inner Station" as portrayed in *Heart of Darkness*, Stanley Falls was a thriving trade settlement with dozens of buildings, cultivated fields, and a banana plantation. Now Kisangani, Democratic Republic of the Congo. (From Albert Chapaux, *Le Congo.* Brussels: Charles Rozez, 1894, 447.)

when he saw the wounded man! I could not help saying, 'You made a glorious lot of smoke, anyhow.' I had seen, from the way the tops of the bushes rustled and flew, that almost all the shots had gone too high. You can't hit anything unless you take aim and fire from the shoulder; but these chaps fired from the hip with their eyes shut. The retreat, I maintained—and I was right—was caused by the screeching of the steam-whistle. Upon this they forgot Kurtz, and began to howl at me with indignant protests.

"The manager stood by the wheel murmuring confidentially about the necessity of getting well away down the river before dark at all events, when I saw in the distance a clearing on the river-side and the outlines of some sort of building. 'What's this?' I asked. He clapped his hands in wonder. 'The station!' he cried. I edged in at once, still going half-speed.

"Through my glasses[164] I saw the slope of a hill interspersed with rare trees and perfectly free from undergrowth. A long decaying building on the summit was half buried in the high grass; the large holes in the peaked roof gaped black from afar; the jungle and the woods made a background. There was no enclosure or fence of any kind; but there had been one apparently, for near the house half a dozen slim posts remained in a row, roughly trimmed, and with their upper ends ornamented with round carved balls. The rails, or whatever there had been between, had disappeared. Of course the forest surrounded all that.[165] The river-bank was clear, and on the water side I saw a white man under a hat like a cart-wheel beckoning persistently with his whole arm. Examining the edge of the forest above and below, I was almost certain I could see movements—human forms gliding here and there. I steamed past prudently, then stopped the engines and let her drift down. The man on the shore began to shout, urging us to land. 'We have been attacked,' screamed the manager. 'I know—I know. It's all right,' yelled back the other, as cheerful as you please. 'Come along. It's all right. I am glad.'

---

164. Binoculars.

165. The settlement of Stanley Falls is now Kisangani, Democratic Republic of the Congo. The settlement was just downstream of the seven cataracts of Stanley Falls (now Boyoma Falls), extending over the next 60 miles upriver, which made the location, approximately 1,300 miles up the Congo from the sea, the river's highest navigable point.

Conrad makes major departures from historical reality in transforming Stanley Falls into the Inner Station of his narrative. First, the river falls do not appear in *Heart of Darkness,* thereby making the river seem to extend indefinitely into the interior. Also, Kurtz's station is on the right side facing upriver, while (except for the SAB factory and some other structures) most of the major buildings at Stanley Falls were on the other side. More important, in sharp contrast to the solitary and decaying hut in the story, Stanley Falls was a major hub in a thriving ivory trade. In 1893, it had dozens of buildings, many of stone, extending along both riverbanks—including warehouses; factories; a prison; residences; different habitations for workers, freed slaves, and the Force Publique; structures for transportation and ammunition; a kitchen; a hospital; and arbors of passion fruit vines. There were also fields for cassava, corn, sweet potatoes, rice, cocoa, coffee, and vegetables. Just downstream, a banana plantation covered many hundreds of acres. Upstream, cultivation of coffee and cocoa included more than 2,000 plants (Chapaux 1894, 446–47). Historical evidence indicates that this 1893 description was generally accurate for 1890 as well (Sherry 1971, 66). Despite the isolation in which Conrad portrays Kurtz, according to *Le Mouvement Géographique* on 16 July 1890 there were seven State officials present at Stanley Falls, in addition to an unknown number of commercial agents (quoted in Sherry 1971, 64).

"His aspect reminded me of something I had seen—something funny I had seen somewhere. As I manœuvred to get alongside, I was asking myself, 'What does this fellow look like?' Suddenly I got it. He looked like a harlequin.[166] His clothes had been made of some stuff that was brown holland[167] probably, but it was covered with patches all over, with bright patches, blue, red, and yellow—patches on the back, patches on the front, patches on elbows, on knees; coloured binding round his jacket, scarlet edging at the bottom of his trousers; and the sunshine made him look extremely gay and wonderfully neat withal, because you could see how beautifully all this patching had been done. A beardless, boyish face, very fair, no features to speak of, nose peeling, little blue eyes, smiles and frowns chasing each other over that open countenance like sunshine and shadow on a wind-swept plain. 'Look out, captain!' he cried; 'there's a snag lodged in here last night.' What! Another snag? I confess I swore shamefully. I had nearly holed my cripple, to finish off that charming trip. The harlequin on the bank turned his little pug-nose up to me. 'You English?' he asked, all smiles. 'Are you?' I shouted from the wheel. The smiles vanished, and he shook his head as if sorry for my disappointment. Then he brightened up. 'Never mind!' he cried encouragingly. 'Are we in time?' I asked. 'He is up there,' he replied, with a toss of the head up the hill, and becoming gloomy all of a sudden. His face was like the autumn sky, overcast one moment and bright the next.

"When the manager, escorted by the pilgrims, all of them armed to the teeth, had gone to the house, this chap came on board. 'I say, I don't like this. These natives are in the bush,' I said. He assured me earnestly it was all right. 'They are simple people,' he added; 'well, I am glad you came. It took me all my time to keep them off.' 'But you said it was all right,' I cried. 'Oh, they meant no harm,' he said; and as I stared he corrected himself, 'Not exactly.' Then vivaciously, 'My faith, your pilot-house wants a clean-up!' In the next breath he advised me to keep enough steam on the boiler to blow the whistle in case of any trouble. 'One good screech will do more for you than all your rifles. They are simple people,' he repeated. He rattled away at such a rate he quite overwhelmed me. He seemed to be trying to make up for lots of silence, and actually hinted, laughing, that such was the case. 'Don't you talk with Mr. Kurtz?' I said. 'You don't talk with that man—you listen to him,' he exclaimed with severe exaltation. 'But now——' He waved his arm, and in the twinkling of an eye was in the uttermost depths of despondency. In a moment he came up again with

---

166. A character in Italian and French light comedy; a mute, clownlike character in English pantomime; usually wearing multicolored clothing.
167. Unbleached linen.

a jump, possessed himself of both my hands, shook them continuously, while he gabbled: 'Brother sailor . . . honour . . . pleasure . . . delight . . . introduce myself . . . Russian . . . son of an arch-priest . . . Government of Tambov[168] . . . What? Tobacco! English tobacco; the excellent English tobacco! Now, that's brotherly. Smoke? Where's a sailor that does not smoke?'

"The pipe soothed him, and gradually I made out he had run away from school, had gone to sea in a Russian ship; ran away again; served some time in English ships; was now reconciled with the arch-priest. He made a point of that. 'But when one is young one must see things, gather experience, ideas; enlarge the mind.' 'Here!' I interrupted. 'You can never tell! Here I met Mr. Kurtz,' he said, youthfully solemn and reproachful. I held my tongue after that. It appears he had persuaded a Dutch trading-house on the coast[169] to fit him out with stores and goods, and had started for the interior with a light heart, and no more idea of what would happen to him than a baby. He had been wandering about that river for nearly two years alone, cut off from everybody and everything. 'I am not so young as I look. I am twenty-five,' he said. 'At first old Van Shuyten[170] would tell me to go to the devil,' he narrated with keen enjoyment; 'but I stuck to him, and talked and talked, till at last he got afraid I would talk the hind-leg off his favourite dog, so he gave me some cheap things and a few guns, and told me he hoped he would never see my face again. Good old Dutchman, Van Shuyten. I sent him one small lot of ivory a year ago, so that he can't call me a little thief when I get back. I hope he got it. And for the rest, I don't care. I had some wood stacked for you. That was my old house. Did you see?'

"I gave him Towson's book. He made as though he would kiss me, but restrained himself. 'The only book I had left, and I thought I had lost it,' he said, looking at it ecstatically. 'So many accidents happen to a man going

---

168. City and regional capital in western Russia.

169. The Dutch African Trading Company (Nieuwe Afrikaansche Handels-Vennootsc-hap), based at Banana Point at the Congo River mouth (Stanley 1885, 1:72–76). This company was perhaps the most significant competitor to the Société Anonyme Belge, and evidently the two were in a fierce competition (Sherry 1971, 69). In an account in *Le Mouvement Géographique* on 31 May 1889, the Dutch were described as increasing the number of their personnel and trading establishments, which at the time consisted of five stations and fourteen white agents (with three new Europeans on the way). There was just one steamer (the *Holland*), but it was considered probable that more would be added (quoted in Sherry 1971, 69).

170. The manager of the Nieuwe Afrikaansche Handels-Vennootschap was Antoine Greshoff; Conrad may have taken the name of Van Shuyten from a Belgian named Schouten, who accompanied Arthur Hodister on his disastrous 1892 expedition (Sherry 1971, 69, 117).

about alone, you know. Canoes get upset sometimes—and sometimes you've got to clear out so quick when the people get angry.' He thumbed the pages. 'You made notes in Russian?' I asked. He nodded. 'I thought they were written in cipher,' I said. He laughed, then became serious. 'I had lots of trouble to keep these people off,' he said. 'Did they want to kill you?' I asked. 'Oh no!' he cried, and checked himself. 'Why did they attack us?' I pursued. He hesitated, then said shamefacedly, 'They don't want him to go.' 'Don't they?' I said curiously. He nodded a nod full of mystery and wisdom. 'I tell you,' he cried, 'this man has enlarged my mind.' He opened his arms wide, staring at me with his little blue eyes that were perfectly round."

III

"I looked at him, lost in astonishment. There he was before me, in motley, as though he had absconded from a troupe of mimes, enthusiastic, fabulous. His very existence was improbable, inexplicable, and altogether bewildering. He was an insoluble problem. It was inconceivable how he had existed, how he had succeeded in getting so far, how he had managed to remain—why he did not instantly disappear. 'I went a little farther,' he said, 'then still a little farther—till I had gone so far that I don't know how I'll ever get back. Never mind. Plenty time. I can manage. You take Kurtz away quick—quick—I tell you.' The glamour of youth enveloped his parti-coloured rags, his destitution, his loneliness, the essential desolation of his futile wanderings. For months—for years—his life hadn't been worth a day's purchase; and there he was gallantly, thoughtlessly alive, to all appearance indestructible solely by the virtue of his few years and of his unreflecting audacity. I was seduced into something like admiration—like envy. Glamour urged him on, glamour kept him unscathed. He surely wanted nothing from the wilderness but space to breathe in and to push on through. His need was to exist, and to move onwards at the greatest possible risk, and with a maximum of privation. If the absolutely pure, uncalculating, unpractical spirit of adventure had ever ruled a human being, it ruled this be-patched youth. I almost envied him the possession of this modest and clear flame. It seemed to have consumed all thought of self so completely, that, even while he was talking to you, you forgot that it was he—the man before your eyes—who had gone through these things. I did not envy him his devotion to Kurtz, though. He had not meditated over it. It came to him, and he accepted it with a sort of eager fatalism. I must say that to me it appeared about the most dangerous thing in every way he had come upon so far.

"They had come together unavoidably, like two ships becalmed near each other, and lay rubbing sides at last. I suppose Kurtz wanted an audience, because on a certain occasion, when encamped in the forest, they had talked all night, or more probably Kurtz had talked. 'We talked of everything,' he said, quite transported at the recollection. 'I forgot there was such a thing as sleep. The night did not seem to last an hour. Everything! Everything! . . . Of love too.' 'Ah, he talked to you of love!' I said, much amused. 'It isn't what you think,' he cried, almost passionately. 'It was in general. He made me see things—things.'

"He threw his arms up. We were on deck at the time, and the head-man of my wood-cutters, lounging near by, turned upon him his heavy and glittering eyes. I looked around, and I don't know why, but I assure you that never, never before, did this land, this river, this jungle, the very arch of this blazing sky, appear to me so hopeless and so dark, so impenetrable to human thought, so pitiless to human weakness. 'And, ever since, you have been with him, of course?' I said.

"On the contrary. It appears their intercourse had been very much broken by various causes. He had, as he informed me proudly, managed to nurse Kurtz through two illnesses (he alluded to it as you would to some risky feat), but as a rule Kurtz wandered alone, far in the depths of the forest. 'Very often coming to this station, I had to wait days and days before he would turn up,' he said. 'Ah, it was worth waiting for!—sometimes.' 'What was he doing? exploring or what?' I asked. 'Oh yes, of course'; he had discovered lots of villages, a lake too—he did not know exactly in what direction; it was dangerous to inquire too much—but mostly his expeditions had been for ivory. 'But he had no goods to trade with by that time,' I objected. 'There's a good lot of cartridges left even yet,' he answered, looking away. 'To speak plainly, he raided the country,' I said. He nodded. 'Not alone, surely!' He muttered something about the villages round that lake. 'Kurtz got the tribe to follow him, did he?' I suggested. He fidgeted a little. 'They adored him,' he said. The tone of these words was so extraordinary that I looked at him searchingly. It was curious to see his mingled eagerness and reluctance to speak of Kurtz. The man filled his life, occupied his thoughts, swayed his emotions. 'What can you expect?' he burst out; 'he came to them with thunder and lightning, you know—and they had never seen anything like it—and very terrible. He could be very terrible. You can't judge Mr. Kurtz as you would an ordinary man. No, no, no! Now—just to give you an idea—I don't mind telling you, he wanted to shoot me too one day—but I don't judge him.' 'Shoot you!' I cried. 'What for?' 'Well, I had a small lot of ivory the chief of that village near my house gave me. You see I used to shoot game for them. Well, he wanted it, and wouldn't hear reason. He declared he would shoot me unless I gave him the ivory and then cleared out of the country, because he could do so, and had a fancy for it, and there was nothing on earth to prevent him killing whom he jolly well pleased. And it was true too. I gave him the ivory. What did I care! But I didn't clear out. No, no. I couldn't leave him. I had to be careful, of course, till we got friendly again for a time. He had his second illness then. Afterwards I had to keep out of the way; but I didn't mind. He was living for the most part in those villages on the lake. When he came down to the river, sometimes he would take to me, and sometimes it was better for me to be careful. This man suffered too much. He hated all this, and somehow he couldn't get away. When I had a chance I begged him to try and leave while there was time; I offered to go back with him. And he would say yes, and then he would remain; go off on another ivory hunt; disappear for weeks; forget himself amongst these people—forget himself—you know.' 'Why! he's mad,' I said. He protested indignantly. Mr. Kurtz couldn't be mad. If I had heard him talk, only two days ago, I wouldn't dare hint at such a thing. . . . I had taken up my binoculars while we talked, and was looking at the shore, sweeping the limit of the forest at each side and at the back of the house. The consciousness of there being people in that bush, so silent, so quiet—as silent and quiet as the ruined house on the hill—made me uneasy. There was no sign on the face of nature of this amazing tale that was not so much told as suggested to me in desolate exclamations, completed by shrugs, in interrupted phrases, in hints ending in deep sighs. The woods were unmoved, like a mask—heavy, like the closed door of a prison—they looked with their air of hidden knowledge, of patient expectation, of unapproachable silence. The Russian was explaining to me that it was only lately that Mr. Kurtz had come down to the river, bringing along with him all the fighting men of that lake tribe. He had been absent for several months—getting himself adored, I suppose—and had come down unexpectedly, with the intention to all appearance of making a raid either across the river or down stream. Evidently the appetite for more ivory had got the better of the—what shall I say?—less material aspirations. However, he had got much worse suddenly. 'I heard he was lying helpless, and so I came up—took my chance,' said the Russian. 'Oh, he is bad, very bad.' I directed my glass to the house. There were no signs of life, but there was the ruined roof, the long mud wall peeping above the grass, with three little square window-holes, no two of the same size; all this brought within reach of my hand, as it were. And then I made a brusque movement, and one of the remaining posts of that vanished fence leaped up in the field of my glass. You remember I told you I had been struck at the distance by certain attempts at ornamentation, rather remarkable in the ruinous aspect of the place. Now I had suddenly a nearer view, and its first result was to make me throw my head back as if before a blow. Then I went carefully from post to post with my glass, and I saw my mistake. These round knobs were not ornamental but symbolic; they were expressive and puzzling, striking and disturbing—food for thought and also for the vultures if there had been any looking down from the sky; but at all events for such ants as were industrious enough to ascend the pole. They would have been even more impressive, those heads on the stakes, if their faces had not been turned to the house. Only one, the first I had made out, was facing my way. I was not so shocked as you may think. The start back I had given was really nothing but a movement of surprise. I had expected to see a knob of wood there, you know. I returned deliberately to the first I had seen—and there it was, black, dried, sunken, with closed eyelids—a head that seemed to sleep at the top of that pole, and, with the shrunken dry lips showing a narrow white line of the teeth, was smiling too, smiling continuously at some end-less and jocose dream of that eternal slumber.[171]

"I am not disclosing any trade secrets. In fact the manager said after-wards that Mr. Kurtz's methods had ruined the district. I have no opinion on that point, but I want you clearly to understand that there was nothing ex-actly profitable in these heads being there. They only showed that Mr. Kurtz lacked restraint in the gratification of his various lusts, that there was some-thing wanting in him—some small matter which, when the pressing need arose, could not be found under his magnificent eloquence. Whether he knew of this deficiency himself I can't say. I think the knowledge came to him at last—only at the very last. But the wilderness had found him out early, and had taken on him a terrible vengeance for the fantastic invasion. I think it had whispered to him things about himself which he did not know, things of which he had no conception till he took counsel with this great solitude—and the whisper had proved irresistibly fascinating. It echoed loudly within him because he was hollow at the core. . . . I put down the glass, and the head that had appeared near enough to be spoken to seemed at once to have leaped away from me into inaccessible distance.

"The admirer of Mr. Kurtz was a bit crestfallen. In a hurried, indistinct voice he began to assure me he had not dared to take these—say, symbols—down. He was not afraid of the natives; they would not stir till Mr. Kurtz gave the word. His ascendency was extraordinary. The camps of these people surrounded the place, and the chiefs came every day to see

---

171. Two possible models for Kurtz are joined in this scene. Captain Léon Rom was station chief at Stanley Falls in 1895. Within a few days of Conrad's beginning to write *Heart of Darkness,* the *Century Magazine* and *The Saturday Review* (among Conrad's admired reading) carried descriptions of Rom's expeditions to punish African rebels, which culmi-nated in the capture of women and children, and 21 native heads being placed as decora-tion around the flowerbed of his house (Hochschild 1999, 145; but see Firchow 2000, 128–29 for a dissenting view of this link). Arthur Hodister's 1892 expedition ended in the capture, torture, and death of Hodister and his men on the Lomani River. Accounts of the disaster appeared in *London Times* articles from September to December 1892, including descrip-tions of the bodies being cannibalized and the heads put on poles (Sherry 1971, 109–10, 117). Nor were these instances the only ones; a September 1892 article in *Mouvement Antiescla-vagiste* describes the post at Yanga surrounded by 52 heads of bandits, mounted on poles (Sherry 1971, 117–18).

him. They would crawl . . . 'I don't want to know anything of the ceremonies used when approaching Mr. Kurtz,' I shouted. Curious, this feeling that came over me that such details would be more intolerable than those heads drying on the stakes under Mr. Kurtz's windows. After all, that was only a savage sight, while I seemed at one bound to have been transported into some lightless region of subtle horrors, where pure, uncomplicated savagery was a positive relief, being something that had a right to exist—obviously—in the sunshine. The young man looked at me with surprise. I suppose it did not occur to him that Mr. Kurtz was no idol of mine. He forgot I hadn't heard any of these splendid monologues on, what was it? on love, justice, conduct of life—or what not. If it had come to crawling before Mr. Kurtz, he crawled as much as the veriest savage of them all. I had no idea of the conditions, he said: these heads were the heads of rebels. I shocked him excessively by laughing. Rebels! What would be the next definition I was to hear? There had been enemies, criminals, workers—and these were rebels. Those rebellious heads looked very subdued to me on their sticks. 'You don't know how such a life tries a man like Kurtz,' cried Kurtz's last disciple. 'Well, and you?' I said. 'I! I! I am a simple man. I have no great thoughts. I want nothing from anybody. How can you compare me to . . .?' His feelings were too much for speech, and suddenly he broke down. 'I don't understand,' he groaned. 'I've been doing my best to keep him alive, and that's enough. I had no hand in all this. I have no abilities. There hasn't been a drop of medicine or a mouthful of invalid food for months here.[172] He was shamefully abandoned. A man like this, with such ideas. Shamefully! Shamefully! I—I—haven't slept for the last ten nights. . . .'

"His voice lost itself in the calm of the evening. The long shadows of the forests had slipped downhill while we talked, had gone far beyond the ruined hovel, beyond the symbolic row of stakes. All this was in the gloom, while we down there were yet in the sunshine, and the stretch of the river abreast of the clearing glittered in a still and dazzling splendour, with a murky and overshadowed bend above and below. Not a living soul was seen on the shore. The bushes did not rustle.

"Suddenly round the corner of the house a group of men appeared, as though they had come up from the ground. They waded waist-deep in the grass, in a compact body, bearing an improvised stretcher in their midst. Instantly, in the emptiness of the landscape, a cry arose whose shrillness pierced the still air like a sharp arrow flying straight to the very heart of the

---

172. When Conrad arrived in Stanley Falls, Klein was probably ill with dysentery, which can be life threatening if left untreated. Klein's sickness would not have been unusual, as dysentery was endemic in the Congo region in general, and there was an outbreak in Stanley Falls and Basoko at the time of Conrad's visit (Sherry 1971, 74).

land; and, as if by enchantment, streams of human beings—of naked human beings—with spears in their hands, with bows, with shields, with wild glances and savage movements, were poured into the clearing by the dark-faced and pensive forest. The bushes shook, the grass swayed for a time, and then everything stood still in attentive immobility.

"'Now, if he does not say the right thing to them we are all done for,' said the Russian at my elbow. The knot of men with the stretcher had stopped too, half-way to the steamer, as if petrified. I saw the man on the stretcher sit up, lank and with an uplifted arm, above the shoulders of the bearers. 'Let us hope that the man who can talk so well of love in general will find some particular reason to spare us this time,' I said. I resented bitterly the absurd danger of our situation, as if to be at the mercy of that atrocious phantom had been a dishonouring necessity. I could not hear a sound, but through my glasses I saw the thin arm extended commandingly, the lower jaw moving, the eyes of that apparition shining darkly far in its bony head that nodded with grotesque jerks. Kurtz—Kirtz—that means 'short' in German—don't it?[173] Well, the name was as true as everything else in his life—and death. He looked at least seven feet long. His covering had fallen off, and his body emerged from it pitiful and appalling as from a winding-sheet. I could see the cage of his ribs all astir, the bones of his arm waving. It was as though an animated image of death carved out of old ivory had been shaking its hand with menaces at a motionless crowd of men made of dark and glittering bronze. I saw him open his mouth wide—it gave him a weirdly voracious aspect, as though he had wanted to swallow all the air, all the earth, all the men before him.[174] A deep voice reached me faintly. He

---

173. "Kurtz" means "short" in German; "klein," in the name of Georges Antoine Klein, means "small." Thus, Conrad may have drawn on the linguistic parallel between the names as he originally used "Klein" in the manuscript and later changed it to "Kurtz." However, there is no surviving evidence to support any characterization of Klein's physical or other qualities (Knowles and Moore 2000, 194; Sherry 1971, 74–75).

174. Leopold himself is another possible model for Kurtz. In a 17 November 1877 letter to Baron Solvyns (the Belgian Ambassador in London), Leopold wrote that in approaching Stanley he did not want to spoil "a good chance to procure for us a portion of this magnificent African cake" (quoted in van Zuylen 1959, 43–44, cited in Newman 2004, 157, my translation). Stanley, in a 4 March 1884 letter to Henry Shelton Sanford, complained of his employer Leopold that he had "the enormous voracity to swallow a million of square miles with a gullet that will not take in a herring" (reprinted in Bontinck 1966, 300, quoted in Hochschild 1999, 74). Toward the end of the century, regarding his 1897 investment of Congo Free State profits on a railway line in China, Leopold exclaimed, "This is the spine of China; if they give it to me I'll also take some cutlets" (Stinglhamber and Dresse 1945, 88, translated and quoted in Hochschild 1999, 169). Whether or not Conrad knew of Leopold's statements, when Marlow describes Kurtz in such strikingly similar terms in this passage, Conrad makes events in the Congo seem like the product of an immense hunger on the part of Europeans.

must have been shouting. He fell back suddenly. The stretcher shook as the bearers staggered forward again, and almost at the same time I noticed that the crowd of savages was vanishing without any perceptible movement of retreat, as if the forest that had ejected these beings so suddenly had drawn them in again as the breath is drawn in a long aspiration.

"Some of the pilgrims behind the stretcher carried his arms—two shot-guns, a heavy rifle, and a light revolver-carbine—the thunderbolts of that pitiful Jupiter. The manager bent over him murmuring as he walked beside his head. They laid him down in one of the little cabins—just a room for a bed-place and a camp-stool or two, you know. We had brought his belated correspondence, and a lot of torn envelopes and open letters littered his bed. His hand roamed feebly amongst these papers. I was struck by the fire of his eyes and the composed languor of his expression. It was not so much the exhaustion of disease. He did not seem in pain. This shadow looked satiated and calm, as though for the moment it had had its fill of all the emotions.

"He rustled one of the letters, and looking straight in my face said, 'I am glad.' Somebody had been writing to him about me. These special rec-ommendations were turning up again. The volume of tone he emitted without effort, almost without the trouble of moving his lips, amazed me. A voice! a voice! It was grave, profound, vibrating, while the man did not seem capable of a whisper. However, he had enough strength in him—factitious no doubt—to very nearly make an end of us, as you shall hear directly.

"The manager appeared silently in the doorway; I stepped out at once and he drew the curtain after me. The Russian, eyed curiously by the pil-grims, was staring at the shore. I followed the direction of his glance.

"Dark human shapes could be made out in the distance, flitting indis-tinctly against the gloomy border of the forest, and near the river two bronze figures, leaning on tall spears, stood in the sunlight under fantastic head-dresses of spotted skins, warlike and still in statuesque repose. And from right to left along the lighted shore moved a wild and gorgeous ap-parition of a woman.

"She walked with measured steps, draped in striped and fringed cloths, treading the earth proudly, with a slight jingle and flash of barbarous orna-ments. She carried her head high; her hair was done in the shape of a hel-met; she had brass leggings to the knee, brass wire gauntlets to the elbow, a crimson spot on her tawny cheek, innumerable necklaces of glass beads on her neck; bizarre things, charms, gifts of witch-men, that hung about her, glittered and trembled at every step. She must have had the value of several elephant tusks upon her. She was savage and superb, wild-eyed and magnificent; there was something ominous and stately in her deliber-ate progress. And in the hush that had fallen suddenly upon the whole sor-rowful land, the immense wilderness, the colossal body of the fecund and

mysterious life seemed to look at her, pensive, as though it had been looking at the image of its own tenebrous and passionate soul.

"She came abreast of the steamer, stood still, and faced us. Her long
shadow fell to the water's edge. Her face had a tragic and fierce aspect of
wild sorrow and of dumb pain mingled with the fear of some struggling,
half-shaped resolve. She stood looking at us without a stir, and like the
wilderness itself, with an air of brooding over an inscrutable purpose. A
whole minute passed, and then she made a step forward. There was a low
jingle, a glint of yellow metal, a sway of fringed draperies, and she stopped
as if her heart had failed her. The young fellow by my side growled. The
pilgrims murmured at my back. She looked at us all as if her life had
depended upon the unswerving steadiness of her glance. Suddenly she
opened her bared arms and threw them up rigid above her head, as though
in an uncontrollable desire to touch the sky, and at the same time the swift
shadows darted out on the earth, swept around on the river, gathering the
steamer into a shadowy embrace. A formidable silence hung over the
scene.

"She turned away slowly, walked on, following the bank, and passed
into the bushes to the left. Once only her eyes gleamed back at us in the
dusk of the thickets before she disappeared.

"'If she had offered to come aboard I really think I would have tried to
shoot her,' said the man of patches nervously. 'I had been risking my life
every day for the last fortnight to keep her out of the house. She got in
one day and kicked up a row about those miserable rags I picked up in
the storeroom to mend my clothes with. I wasn't decent. At least it must
have been that, for she talked like a fury[175] to Kurtz for an hour, pointing
at me now and then. I don't understand the dialect of this tribe. Luckily for
me, I fancy Kurtz felt too ill that day to care, or there would have been
mischief. I don't understand. . . . No—it's too much for me. Ah, well, it's
all over now.'

"At this moment I heard Kurtz's deep voice behind the curtain: 'Save
me!—save the ivory, you mean. Don't tell me. Save *me!* Why, I've had to
save you. You are interrupting my plans now. Sick! Sick! Not so sick as
you would like to believe. Never mind. I'll carry my ideas out yet—I will
return. I'll show you what can be done. You with your little peddling
notions—you are interfering with me. I will return. I . . .'

---

175. An angry or malevolent woman. In Greek mythology, the Furies were avenging
deities who had their home in Hades. In some accounts, such as in Virgil's *Aeneid,* they
were the daughters of Night. Just and pitiless, they avenged crime, particularly murder, and
they especially punished bloodguilt within a family. They were considered significant in
representing the idea of a moral order of justice to a primitive society (Morford and Lenardon 1999, 45, 271–72).

"The manager came out. He did me the honour to take me under the arm and lead me aside. 'He is very low, very low,' he said. He considered it necessary to sigh, but neglected to be consistently sorrowful. 'We have done all we could for him—haven't we? But there is no disguising the fact, Mr. Kurtz has done more harm than good to the Company. He did not see the time was not ripe for vigorous action. Cautiously, cautiously—that's my principle. We must be cautious yet. The district is closed to us for a time. Deplorable! Upon the whole, the trade will suffer.[176] I don't deny there is a remarkable quantity of ivory—mostly fossil. We must save it, at all events—but look how precarious the position is—and why? Because the method is unsound.' 'Do you,' said I, looking at the shore, 'call it "unsound method"?' 'Without doubt,' he exclaimed hotly. 'Don't you?' . . . 'No method at all,' I murmured after a while. 'Exactly,' he exulted. 'I anticipated this. Shows a complete want of judgment. It is my duty to point it out in the proper quarter.' 'Oh,' said I, 'that fellow—what's his name?— the brickmaker, will make a readable report for you.' He appeared confounded for a moment. It seemed to me I had never breathed an atmosphere so vile, and I turned mentally to Kurtz for relief—positively for relief. 'Nevertheless, I think Mr. Kurtz is a remarkable man,' I said with emphasis. He started, dropped on me a cold heavy glance, said very quietly, 'He *was,*' and turned his back on me. My hour of favour was over; I found myself lumped along with Kurtz as a partisan of methods for which the time was not ripe: I was unsound! Ah! but it was something to have at least a choice of nightmares.

"I had turned to the wilderness really, not to Mr. Kurtz, who, I was ready to admit, was as good as buried. And for a moment it seemed to me as if I also were buried in a vast grave full of unspeakable secrets. I felt an intolerable weight oppressing my breast, the smell of the damp earth, the unseen presence of victorious corruption, the darkness of an impenetrable night. . . . The Russian tapped me on the shoulder. I heard him mumbling and stammering something about 'brother seaman—couldn't conceal— knowledge of matters that would affect Mr. Kurtz's reputation.' I waited. For him evidently Mr. Kurtz was not in his grave; I suspect that for him Mr. Kurtz was one of the immortals. 'Well!' said I at last, 'speak out. As it happens, I am Mr. Kurtz's friend—in a way.'

"He stated with a good deal of formality that had we not been 'of the same profession,' he would have kept the matter to himself without regard

---

176. No evidence suggests that trading was closed at Stanley Falls or in the surrounding area anytime around Conrad's visit. On the contrary, Alexandre Delcommune's account of his arrival at Stanley Falls on 16 December 1890 (three months after Conrad left) portrays a settled and thriving community (Delcommune 1922, 2:15–16; Sherry 1971, 70).

to consequences. He suspected 'there was an active ill-will towards him on the part of these white men that——' 'You are right,' I said, remembering a certain conversation I had overheard. 'The manager thinks you ought to be hanged.' He showed a concern at this intelligence which amused me at first. 'I had better get out of the way quietly,' he said earnestly. 'I can do no more for Kurtz now, and they would soon find some excuse. What's to stop them? There's a military post three hundred miles from here.' 'Well, upon my word,' said I, 'perhaps you had better go if you have any friends amongst the savages near by.' 'Plenty,' he said. 'They are simple people— and I want nothing, you know.' He stood biting his lips, then: 'I don't want any harm to happen to these whites here, but of course I was thinking of Mr. Kurtz's reputation—but you are a brother seaman and——' 'All right,' said I, after a time. 'Mr. Kurtz's reputation is safe with me.' I did not know how truly I spoke.

"He informed me, lowering his voice, that it was Kurtz who had ordered the attack to be made on the steamer. 'He hated sometimes the idea of being taken away—and then again . . . But I don't understand these matters. I am a simple man. He thought it would scare you away—that you would give it up, thinking him dead. I could not stop him. Oh, I had an awful time of it this last month.' 'Very well,' I said. 'He is all right now.' 'Ye-e-es,' he muttered, not very convinced apparently. 'Thanks,' said I; 'I shall keep my eyes open.' 'But quiet—eh?' he urged anxiously. 'It would be awful for his reputation if anybody here——' I promised a complete discretion with great gravity. 'I have a canoe and three black fellows waiting not very far. I am off. Could you give me a few Martini-Henry cartridges?' I could, and did, with proper secrecy. He helped himself, with a wink at me, to a handful of my tobacco. 'Between sailors—you know— good English tobacco.' At the door of the pilot-house he turned round—'I say, haven't you a pair of shoes you could spare?' He raised one leg. 'Look.' The soles were tied with knotted strings sandal-wise under his bare feet. I rooted out an old pair, at which he looked with admiration before tucking it under his left arm. One of his pockets (bright red) was bulging with cartridges, from the other (dark blue) peeped 'Towson's Inquiry,' etc. etc. He seemed to think himself excellently well equipped for a renewed encounter with the wilderness. 'Ah! I'll never, never meet such a man again. You ought to have heard him recite poetry—his own too it was, he told me. Poetry!' He rolled his eyes at the recollection of these delights. 'Oh, he enlarged my mind!' 'Good-bye,' said I. He shook hands and vanished in the night. Sometimes I ask myself whether I had ever really seen him—whether it was possible to meet such a phenomenon! . . .

"When I woke up shortly after midnight his warning came to my mind with its hint of danger that seemed, in the starred darkness, real enough to make me get up for the purpose of having a look round. On the hill a big fire burned, illuminating fitfully a crooked corner of the station-house.

One of the agents with a picket of a few of our blacks, armed for the purpose, was keeping guard over the ivory; but deep within the forest, red gleams that wavered, that seemed to sink and rise from the ground amongst confused columnar shapes of intense blackness, showed the exact position of the camp where Mr. Kurtz's adorers were keeping their uneasy vigil. The monotonous beating of a big drum filled the air with muffled shocks and a lingering vibration. A steady droning sound of many men chanting each to himself some weird incantation came out from the black, flat wall of the woods as the humming of bees comes out of a hive, and had a strange narcotic effect upon my half-awake senses. I believe I dozed off leaning over the rail, till an abrupt burst of yells, an overwhelming outbreak of a pent-up and mysterious frenzy, woke me up in a bewildered wonder. It was cut short all at once, and the low droning went on with an effect of audible and soothing silence. I glanced casually into the little cabin. A light was burning within, but Mr. Kurtz was not there.

"I think I would have raised an outcry if I had believed my eyes. But I didn't believe them at first—the thing seemed so impossible. The fact is, I was completely unnerved by a sheer blank fright, pure abstract terror, unconnected with any distinct shape of physical danger. What made this emotion so overpowering was—how shall I define it?—the moral shock I received, as if something altogether monstrous, intolerable to thought and odious to the soul, had been thrust upon me unexpectedly. This lasted of course the merest fraction of a second, and then the usual sense of commonplace, deadly danger, the possibility of a sudden onslaught and massacre, or something of the kind, which I saw impending, was positively welcome and composing. It pacified me, in fact, so much, that I did not raise an alarm.

"There was an agent buttoned up inside an ulster[177] and sleeping on a chair on deck within three feet of me. The yells had not awakened him; he snored very slightly; I left him to his slumbers and leaped ashore. I did not betray Mr. Kurtz—it was ordered I should never betray him—it was written I should be loyal to the nightmare of my choice. I was anxious to deal with this shadow by myself alone—and to this day I don't know why I was so jealous of sharing with anyone the peculiar blackness of that experience.

"As soon as I got on the bank I saw a trail—a broad trail through the grass. I remember the exultation with which I said to myself, 'He can't walk—he is crawling on all-fours—I've got him.' The grass was wet with dew. I strode rapidly with clenched fists. I fancy I had some vague notion of falling upon him and giving him a drubbing. I don't know. I had some imbecile thoughts. The knitting old woman with the cat obtruded herself

---

177. A loose, long, and heavy overcoat, often belted; introduced in Belfast.

upon my memory as a most improper person to be sitting at the other end of such an affair. I saw a row of pilgrims squirting lead in the air out of Winchesters held to the hip. I thought I would never get back to the steamer, and imagined myself living alone and unarmed in the woods to an advanced age. Such silly things—you know. And I remember I confounded the beat of the drum with the beating of my heart, and was pleased at its calm regularity.

"I kept to the track though—then stopped to listen. The night was very clear; a dark blue space, sparkling with dew and starlight, in which black things stood very still. I thought I could see a kind of motion ahead of me. I was strangely cocksure of everything that night. I actually left the track and ran in a wide semicircle (I verily believe chuckling to myself) so as to get in front of that stir, of that motion I had seen—if indeed I had seen anything. I was circumventing Kurtz as though it had been a boyish game.

"I came upon him, and, if he had not heard me coming, I would have fallen over him too, but he got up in time. He rose, unsteady, long, pale, indistinct, like a vapour exhaled by the earth, and swayed slightly, misty and silent before me; while at my back the fires loomed between the trees, and the murmur of many voices issued from the forest. I had cut him off cleverly; but when actually confronting him I seemed to come to my senses, I saw the danger in its right proportion. It was by no means over yet. Suppose he began to shout? Though he could hardly stand, there was still plenty of vigour in his voice. 'Go away—hide yourself,' he said, in that profound tone. It was very awful. I glanced back. We were within thirty yards from the nearest fire. A black figure stood up, strode on long black legs, waving long black arms, across the glow. It had horns—antelope horns, I think—on its head. Some sorcerer, some witch-man, no doubt: it looked fiend-like enough. 'Do you know what you are doing?' I whispered. 'Perfectly,' he answered, raising his voice for that single word: it sounded to me far off and yet loud, like a hail through a speaking-trumpet. If he makes a row we are lost, I thought to myself. This clearly was not a case for fisticuffs, even apart from the very natural aversion I had to beat that Shadow—this wandering and tormented thing. 'You will be lost,' I said—'utterly lost.' One gets sometimes such a flash of inspiration, you know. I did say the right thing, though indeed he could not have been more irretrievably lost than he was at this very moment, when the foundations of our intimacy were being laid—to endure—to endure—even to the end—even beyond.

"'I had immense plans,' he muttered irresolutely. 'Yes,' said I; 'but if you try to shout I'll smash your head with——' There was not a stick or a stone near. 'I will throttle you for good,' I corrected myself. 'I was on the threshold of great things,' he pleaded, in a voice of longing, with a wistfulness of tone that made my blood run cold. 'And now for this stupid scoundrel——' 'Your success in Europe is assured in any case,' I affirmed steadily. I did not want to have the throttling of him, you understand—and indeed it would have been very little use for any practical purpose. I tried to break the spell—the heavy, mute spell of the wilderness—that seemed to draw him to its pitiless breast by the awakening of forgotten and brutal instincts, by the memory of gratified and monstrous passions. This alone, I was convinced, had driven him out to the edge of the forest, to the bush, towards the gleam of fires, the throb of drums, the drone of weird incantations; this alone had beguiled his unlawful soul beyond the bounds of permitted aspirations. And, don't you see, the terror of the position was not in being knocked on the head—though I had a very lively sense of that danger too—but in this, that I had to deal with a being to whom I could not appeal in the name of anything high or low. I had, even like the niggers, to invoke him—himself—his own exalted and incredible degradation. There was nothing either above or below him, and I knew it. He had kicked himself loose of the earth. Confound the man! he had kicked the very earth to pieces. He was alone, and I before him did not know whether I stood on the ground or floated in the air. I've been telling you what we said—repeating the phrases we pronounced—but what's the good? They were common everyday words—the familiar, vague sounds exchanged on every waking day of life. But what of that? They had behind them, to my mind, the terrific suggestiveness of words heard in dreams, of phrases spoken in nightmares. Soul! If anybody had ever struggled with a soul, I am the man. And I wasn't arguing with a lunatic either. Believe me or not, his intelligence was perfectly clear—concentrated, it is true, upon himself with horrible intensity, yet clear; and therein was my only chance—barring, of course, the killing him there and then, which wasn't so good, on account of unavoidable noise. But his soul was mad. Being alone in the wilderness, it had looked within itself, and, by Heavens! I tell you, it had gone mad. I had—for my sins, I suppose, to go through the ordeal of looking into it myself. No eloquence could have been so withering to one's belief in mankind as his final burst of sincerity. He struggled with himself too. I saw it—I heard it. I saw the inconceivable mystery of a soul that knew no restraint, no faith, and no fear, yet struggling blindly with itself. I kept my head pretty well; but when I had him at last stretched on the couch, I wiped my forehead, while my legs shook under me as though I had carried half a ton on my back down that hill. And yet I had only supported him, his bony arm clasped round my neck—and he was not much heavier than a child.

"When next day we left at noon, the crowd, of whose presence behind the curtain of trees I had been acutely conscious all the time, flowed out of the woods again, filled the clearing, covered the slope with a mass of naked, breathing, quivering, bronze bodies. I steamed up a bit, then swung downstream, and two thousand eyes followed the evolutions of the splashing, thumping, fierce river-demon beating the water with its terrible tail and breathing black smoke into the air. In front of the first rank, along the river, three men, plastered with bright red earth from head to foot, strutted to and fro restlessly. When we came abreast again, they faced the river, stamped their feet, nodded their horned heads, swayed their scarlet bodies; they shook towards the fierce river-demon a bunch of black feathers, a mangy skin with a pendent tail—something that looked like a dried gourd; they shouted periodically together strings of amazing words that resembled no sounds of human language; and the deep murmurs of the crowd, interrupted suddenly, were like the response of some satanic litany.[178]

"We had carried Kurtz into the pilot-house: there was more air there. Lying on the couch, he stared through the open shutter. There was an eddy in the mass of human bodies, and the woman with helmeted head and tawny cheeks rushed out to the very brink of the stream. She put out her hands, shouted something, and all that wild mob took up the shout in a roaring chorus of articulated, rapid, breathless utterance.

"'Do you understand this?' I asked.

"He kept on looking out past me with fiery, longing eyes, with a mingled expression of wistfulness and hate. He made no answer, but I saw a smile, a smile of indefinable meaning, appear on his colourless lips that a moment after twitched convulsively. 'Do I not?' he said slowly, gasping, as if the words had been torn out of him by a supernatural power.

"I pulled the string of the whistle, and I did this because I saw the pilgrims on deck getting out their rifles with an air of anticipating a jolly lark. At the sudden screech there was a movement of abject terror through that wedged mass of bodies. 'Don't! Don't you frighten them away,' cried some one on deck disconsolately. I pulled the string time after time. They broke and ran, they leaped, they crouched, they swerved, they dodged the flying terror of the sound. The three red chaps had fallen flat, face down on the shore, as though they had been shot dead.[179] Only the barbarous and superb woman did not so much as flinch, and stretched tragically her bare arms after us over the sombre and glittering river.

"And then that imbecile crowd down on the deck started their little fun, and I could see nothing more for smoke.

---

178. When the Resident at Stanley Falls departed on 7 April 1889 to return to Europe, the natives staged a demonstration including fighting scenes enacted in canoes on the river, with the natives dressed and painted for war, and a mock attack on the riverbank at the station, followed by gifts given to the warriors. The departure of the Kinshasa manager and the Belgian agent at Stanley Falls would not have merited such an impressive display, but perhaps Conrad witnessed an event that was something along these lines (Jenssen-Tusch 1902–1905, 599; Sherry 1971, 75).

179. Ships' steam whistles had been used this way before in the Congo, to similar effect: by George Grenfell in 1886 on Lake Leopold (now Mai-Ndombe) (Johnston 1908, 1:167) and on the Quango River (Wissmann 1891, 20), and by Henry Morton Stanley in 1887 at Yumbaya on the Aruwimi (Stanley 1890, 1:114).

George Grenfell using the ship's steam whistle on the Quango in 1886. (From Hermann von Wissmann, *My Second Journey through Equatorial Africa.* London: Chatto & Windus, 1891, opposite 20.)

"The brown current ran swiftly out of the heart of darkness, bearing us down towards the sea with twice the speed of our upward progress;[180] and Kurtz's life was running swiftly too, ebbing, ebbing out of his heart into the sea of inexorable time. The manager was very placid, he had no vital anxieties now, he took us both in with a comprehensive and satisfied glance: the 'affair' had come off as well as could be wished. I saw the time approaching when I would be left alone of the party of 'unsound method.' The pilgrims looked upon me with disfavour. I was, so to speak, numbered with the dead. It is strange how I accepted this unforeseen partnership, this choice of nightmares forced upon me in the tenebrous land invaded by these mean and greedy phantoms.[181]

"Kurtz discoursed. A voice! a voice! It rang deep to the very last. It survived his strength to hide in the magnificent folds of eloquence the

---

180. Approximates the historical record. The *Roi des Belges* left Stanley Falls on probably 7 or 8 September 1890, stopped at Bangala (about halfway between Stanley Falls and Kinshasa) for one night on 15–16 September, and reached Kinshasa on 24 September. This made a passage of 16 or 17 days, compared with 28 days on the upriver passage (Najder 2007, 156, 159).

181. Conrad's feelings for Klein could not have been as strong, as they had only just met (Sherry 1971, 76).

barren darkness of his heart. Oh, he struggled! he struggled! The wastes of his weary brain were haunted by shadowy images now—images of wealth and fame revolving obsequiously round his unextinguishable gift of noble and lofty expression. My Intended, my station, my career, my ideas—these were the subjects for the occasional utterances of elevated sentiments. The shade of the original Kurtz frequented the bedside of the hollow sham, whose fate it was to be buried presently in the mould of primeval earth. But both the diabolic love and the unearthly hate of the mysteries it had penetrated fought for the possession of that soul satiated with primitive emotions, avid of lying fame, of sham distinction, of all the appearances of success and power.

"Sometimes he was contemptibly childish. He desired to have kings meet him at railway stations[182] on his return from some ghastly Nowhere, where he intended to accomplish great things. 'You show them you have in you something that is really profitable, and then there will be no limits to the recognition of your ability,' he would say. 'Of course you must take care of the motives—right motives—always.' The long reaches that were like one and the same reach, monotonous bends that were exactly alike, slipped past the steamer with their multitude of secular[183] trees looking patiently after this grimy fragment of another world, the forerunner of change, of conquest, of trade, of massacres, of blessings. I looked ahead—piloting. 'Close the shutter,' said Kurtz suddenly one day; 'I can't bear to look at this.' I did so. There was a silence. 'Oh, but I will wring your heart yet!' he cried at the invisible wilderness.

"We broke down—as I had expected—and had to lie up for repairs at the head of an island. This delay was the first thing that shook Kurtz's confidence. One morning he gave me a packet of papers and a photo-graph—the lot tied together with a shoe-string. 'Keep this for me,' he said. 'This noxious fool' (meaning the manager) 'is capable of prying into my boxes when I am not looking.' In the afternoon I saw him. He was lying on his back with closed eyes, and I withdrew quietly, but I heard him mutter, 'Live rightly, die, die . . .'[184] I listened. There was nothing more. Was he

---

182. May allude to Henry Morton Stanley's arrival at the Marseilles railway station in January 1878 upon returning from Africa; Leopold's envoys formally received him. Also, when Stanley attended an 1889 antislavery conference in Brussels, he stayed in Royal Palace rooms usually reserved for visiting royalty (Hochschild 1999, 94; Conrad 2010c, 453–54n116.4).

183. Belonging to a long period of time, or living or lasting for ages, or (for trees, for example), centuries old.

184. Conrad's manuscript completes Kurtz's phrase as "Live rightly, die nobly" (Conrad n.d, 204[208]).

rehearsing some speech in his sleep, or was it a fragment of a phrase from some newspaper article? He had been writing for the papers and meant to do so again, 'for the furthering of my ideas. It's a duty.'

"His was an impenetrable darkness. I looked at him as you peer down at a man who is lying at the bottom of a precipice where the sun never shines. But I had not much time to give him, because I was helping the engine-driver to take to pieces the leaky cylinders, to straighten a bent connecting-rod,[185] and in other such matters. I lived in an infernal mess of rust, filings, nuts, bolts, spanners, hammers, ratchet-drills—things I abominate, because I don't get on with them. I tended the little forge we fortunately had aboard; I toiled wearily in a wretched scrap-heap—unless I had the shakes too bad to stand.

"One evening coming in with a candle I was startled to hear him say a little tremulously, 'I am lying here in the dark waiting for death.' The light was within a foot of his eyes. I forced myself to murmur, 'Oh, nonsense!' and stood over him as if transfixed.

"Anything approaching the change that came over his features I have never seen before, and hope never to see again. Oh, I wasn't touched. I was fascinated. It was as though a veil had been rent. I saw on that ivory face the expression of sombre pride, of ruthless power, of craven terror—of an intense and hopeless despair. Did he live his life again in every detail of desire, temptation, and surrender during that supreme moment of complete knowledge? He cried in a whisper at some image, at some vision—he cried out twice, a cry that was no more than a breath:

"'The horror! The horror!'[186]

"I blew the candle out and left the cabin. The pilgrims were dining in the mess-room, and I took my place opposite the manager, who lifted his eyes to give me a questioning glance, which I successfully ignored. He leaned back, serene, with that peculiar smile of his sealing the unexpressed depths of his meanness. A continuous shower of small flies streamed upon the lamp, upon the cloth, upon our hands and faces. Suddenly the manager's

---

185. Steam engine part joining the crank to the side-lever, turning the motion of the piston into a rotary force to turn a driveshaft (Smyth 1867, 209).

186. May allude to Psalms 45:4–5: "My heart is sore pained within me: and the terrors of death are fallen upon me. Fearfulness and trembling are come upon me, and horror hath overwhelmed me" (Conrad 2008a, 215–16n178; Conrad 2010c, 454n117.14). Conrad may also possibly have been inspired by Arthur Hodister's paper on slavery and native customs published in *Le Mouvement Géographique* on 4 October 1891, describing the outcome of a slaving raid between tribes. After detailing the cries of the wounded and prisoners, the corpses, and the acrid-smelling puddles of blood, Hodister exclaims, "Ah! quel tableau, qui donc pourra en dire l'horreur?" ("Ah! What a sight; who can tell the horror of it?") (quoted in Sherry 1971, 102, and Chapaux 1894, 807, my translation).

boy put his insolent black head in the doorway, and said in a tone of scathing contempt:

"'Mistah Kurtz—he dead.'

"All the pilgrims rushed out to see. I remained, and went on with my dinner. I believe I was considered brutally callous. However, I did not eat much. There was a lamp in there—light, don't you know—and outside it was so beastly, beastly dark. I went no more near the remarkable man who had pronounced a judgment upon the adventures of his soul on this earth. The voice was gone. What else had been there? But I am of course aware that next day the pilgrims buried something in a muddy hole.[187]

"And then they very nearly buried me.[188]

"However, as you see, I did not go to join Kurtz there and then. I did not. I remained to dream the nightmare out to the end, and to show my loyalty to Kurtz once more. Destiny. My destiny! Droll thing life is—that mysterious arrangement of merciless logic for a futile purpose. The most you can hope from it is some knowledge of yourself—that comes too late—a crop of unextinguishable regrets. I have wrestled with death. It is the most unexciting contest you can imagine. It takes place in an impalpable greyness, with nothing underfoot, with nothing around, without spectators, without clamour, without glory, without the great desire of victory,

---

187. Klein was sick aboard the *Roi des Belges* when it left Stanley Falls. He died on 21 September 1890 and was buried at Tchumbiri (now Tsumbiri), an American Baptist mission about 150 miles upriver from Kinshasa (after most of the 1,000-mile journey from Stanley Falls downriver to Kinshasa). The European graveyard at Tchumbiri was approximately 150 yards from the river, and at the time Conrad may well have been able to see the burial from his vantage point on the *Roi des Belges* (Sherry 1971, 77–78).

188. Conrad reported to his "aunt" Marguerite Poradowska in a letter from Kinshasa on 26 September 1890 that he had suffered a five-day attack of dysentery while at Stanley Falls, and he had had a fever four times over a two-month period while ascending the river (Conrad 1983, 62). Captain Koch, the master of the *Roi des Belges*, was also sick. A letter from Camille Delcommune dated 6 September 1890—just before the *Roi des Belges* descended the river from Stanley Falls—requested that Conrad take command of the vessel temporarily until Koch recovered. There is as yet no other basis for Conrad's later claim to have had command of a "steamer" during his sea career. It is not yet known how long Conrad was in command, if at all; Koch was back in command when the *Roi des Belges* arrived in Bangala on 15 September (Najder 2007, 159).

Sometime after his return to England and before writing *Heart of Darkness*, Conrad told Edward Garnett at length about his experiences in the Congo. Garnett marveled at Conrad's powers of memory, and when Garnett later read the published story, he found that much of what he had previously heard had been left out, while new episodes had been added. "I regretted the omission of various scenes," Garnett later wrote, "one of which descried the hero lying sick to death in a native hut, tended by an old negress who brought him water from day to day, when he had been abandoned by all the Belgians. 'She saved my life,' Conrad said; 'the white men never came near me'" (Garnett 1928, 14).

without the great fear of defeat, in a sickly atmosphere of tepid scepticism, without much belief in your own right, and still less in that of your adversary. If such is the form of ultimate wisdom, then life is a greater riddle than some of us think it to be. I was within a hair's-breadth of the last opportunity for pronouncement, and I found with humiliation that probably I would have nothing to say. This is the reason why I affirm that Kurtz was a remarkable man. He had something to say. He said it. Since I had peeped over the edge myself, I understand better the meaning of his stare, that could not see the flame of the candle, but was wide enough to embrace the whole universe, piercing enough to penetrate all the hearts that beat in the darkness. He had summed up—he had judged. 'The horror!' He was a remarkable man. After all, this was the expression of some sort of belief; it had candour, it had conviction, it had a vibrating note of revolt in its whisper, it had the appalling face of a glimpsed truth—the strange commingling of desire and hate. And it is not my own extremity I remember best—a vision of greyness without form filled with physical pain, and a careless contempt for the evanescence of all things—even of this pain itself. No! It is his extremity that I seem to have lived through. True, he had made that last stride, he had stepped over the edge, while I had been permitted to draw back my hesitating foot. And perhaps in this is the whole difference; perhaps all the wisdom, and all truth, and all sincerity, are just compressed into that inappreciable moment of time in which we step over the threshold of the invisible. Perhaps! I like to think my summing-up would not have been a word of careless contempt. Better his cry—much better. It was an affirmation, a moral victory paid for by innumerable defeats, by abominable terrors, by abominable satisfactions. But it was a victory! That is why I have remained loyal to Kurtz to the last, and even beyond, when a long time after I heard once more, not his own voice, but the echo of his magnificent eloquence thrown to me from a soul as translucently pure as a cliff of crystal.

"No, they did not bury me, though there is a period of time which I remember mistily, with a shuddering wonder, like a passage through some inconceivable world that had no hope in it and no desire.[189] I found myself back in the sepulchral city resenting the sight of people hurrying through the streets to filch a little money from each other, to devour their infamous

---

189. After Conrad returned to Kinshasa on 24 September 1890, he expected to take part in a new expedition on the Kasai River, commanding the steamer carrying Alexandre Delcommune and his party. However, those hopes were dashed by the continuing opposition of Camille Delcommune. Alexandre had not arrived in Kinshasa when Conrad wrote a letter to Poradowska on 26 September 1890, explaining that he "could hope for neither promotion nor increase of salary while he [Camille Delcommune] remains here." He added, "Likewise I can look forward to nothing, as I have no vessel to command" even aside from the Kasai

cookery, to gulp their unwholesome beer, to dream their insignificant and silly dreams. They trespassed upon my thoughts. They were intruders whose knowledge of life was to me an irritating pretence, because I felt so sure they could not possibly know the things I knew. Their bearing, which was simply the bearing of commonplace individuals going about their business in the assurance of perfect safety, was offensive to me like the outrageous flauntings of folly in the face of a danger it is unable to comprehend. I had no particular desire to enlighten them, but I had some difficulty in restraining myself from laughing in their faces, so full of stupid importance. I daresay I was not very well at that time. I tottered about the streets—there were various affairs to settle—grinning bitterly at perfectly respectable persons. I admit my behaviour was inexcusable, but then my temperature was seldom normal in these days. My dear aunt's endeavours to 'nurse up my strength' seemed altogether beside the mark.[190] It was not my strength that wanted nursing, it was my imagination that wanted soothing. I kept the bundle of papers given me by Kurtz, not knowing exactly what to do with it. His mother had died lately,[191] watched over, as I was told, by his Intended.[192] A clean-shaved man, with an official manner and wearing gold-rimmed spectacles, called on me one day and made inquiries, at first circuitous, afterwards suavely pressing, about what he was pleased to denominate certain 'documents.' I was not surprised, because I had had two rows with the manager on the subject out there. I had refused to give up the smallest scrap out of that package, and I took the same attitude with the spectacled man. He became darkly menacing at last, and

---

River expedition. As for Camille Delcommune, Conrad explained that he "has taken the trouble of telling a good many people that I displease him intensely" (Conrad 1983, 62; Sherry 1971, 82–83). By 19 October 1890 Conrad had decided to return to Europe. Not much is known of his return journey from Kinshasa to the coast, although apparently the approximately five-mile leg from Kinshasa to Léopoldville was by native canoe (Conrad 2008b, 27; Sherry 1971, 87). Conrad was in Matadi by 4 December 1890, having taken over six weeks to get there from Kinshasa after deciding to leave—longer than the 35 days of his trip from Matadi to Kinshasa—likely due to renewed illness, which was then at its most serious. Records indicating which ship Conrad took to return to Europe have not survived. The first available vessels arrived at Boma on 8 and 14 December 1890 (Sherry 1971, 86–89).

190. Conrad was in Brussels for two days sometime in January 1891, spending the time with Marguerite Poradowska (Sherry 1971, 89; Knowles 2014, 22). In March 1891 he was treated for neuralgia, malaria, and rheumatism at the German Hospital, Dalston (in London), followed by a month of hydrotherapy at Champel-les-Bains, near Geneva, Switzerland, in May–June 1891 (Knowles 2014, 22).

191. Klein's mother was still alive (Sherry 1971, 89).

192. Marlow's visit to Kurtz's fiancée is unlikely to have paralleled any visit that Conrad made during his two days in Brussels, as Klein was born in Paris and had lived there (Sherry 1971, 89).

with much heat argued that the Company had the right to every bit of information about its 'territories.' And, said he, 'Mr. Kurtz's knowledge of unexplored regions must have been necessarily extensive and peculiar—owing to his great abilities and to the deplorable circumstances in which he had been placed: therefore——' I assured him Mr. Kurtz's knowledge, however extensive, did not bear upon the problems of commerce or administration. He invoked then the name of science. 'It would be an incalculable loss if,' etc. etc. I offered him the report on the 'Suppression of Savage Customs,' with the postscriptum torn off. He took it up eagerly, but ended by sniffing at it with an air of contempt. 'This is not what we had a right to expect,' he remarked. 'Expect nothing else,' I said. 'There are only private letters.' He withdrew upon some threat of legal proceedings, and I saw him no more; but another fellow, calling himself Kurtz's cousin, appeared two days later, and was anxious to hear all the details about his dear relative's last moments. Incidentally he gave me to understand that Kurtz had been essentially a great musician. 'There was the making of an immense success,' said the man, who was an organist, I believe, with lank grey hair flowing over a greasy coat-collar. I had no reason to doubt his statement; and to this day I am unable to say what was Kurtz's profession, whether he ever had any—which was the greatest of his talents. I had taken him for a painter who wrote for the papers, or else for a journalist who could paint—but even the cousin (who took snuff during the interview) could not tell me what he had been—exactly. He was a universal genius—on that point I agreed with the old chap, who thereupon blew his nose noisily into a large cotton handkerchief and withdrew in senile agitation, bearing off some family letters and memoranda without importance. Ultimately a journalist anxious to know something of the fate of his 'dear colleague' turned up. This visitor informed me Kurtz's proper sphere ought to have been politics 'on the popular side.' He had furry straight eyebrows, bristly hair cropped short, an eyeglass on a broad ribbon, and, becoming expansive, confessed his opinion that Kurtz really couldn't write a bit—'but Heavens! how that man could talk! He electrified large meetings. He had faith—don't you see?—he had the faith. He could get himself to believe anything—anything. He would have been a splendid leader of an extreme party.' 'What party?' I asked. 'Any party,' answered the other. 'He was an—an—extremist.' Did I not think so? I assented. Did I know, he asked, with a sudden flash of curiosity, 'what it was that had induced him to go out there?' 'Yes,' said I, and forthwith handed him the famous Report for publication, if he thought fit. He glanced through it hurriedly, mumbling all the time, judged 'it would do,' and took himself off with this plunder.

"Thus I was left at last with a slim packet of letters and the girl's portrait. She struck me as beautiful—I mean she had a beautiful expression. I know that the sunlight can be made to lie too, yet one felt that no manipulation of light and pose could have conveyed the delicate shade of truthfulness upon those features. She seemed ready to listen without mental reservation, without suspicion, without a thought for herself. I concluded I would go and give her back her portrait and those letters myself. Curiosity? Yes; and also some other feeling perhaps. All that had been Kurtz's had passed out of my hands: his soul, his body, his station, his plans, his ivory, his career. There remained only his memory and his Intended—and I wanted to give that up too to the past, in a way—to surrender personally all that remained of him with me to that oblivion which is the last word of our common fate. I don't defend myself. I had no clear perception of what it was I really wanted. Perhaps it was an impulse of unconscious loyalty, or the fulfillment of one of those ironic necessities that lurk in the facts of human existence. I don't know. I can't tell. But I went.

"I thought his memory was like the other memories of the dead that accumulate in every man's life—a vague impress on the brain of shadows that had fallen on it in their swift and final passage; but before the high and ponderous door, between the tall houses of a street as still and decorous as a well-kept alley in a cemetery, I had a vision of him on the stretcher, opening his mouth voraciously, as if to devour all the earth with all its mankind. He lived then before me; he lived as much as he had ever lived—a shadow insatiable of splendid appearances, of frightful realities; a shadow darker than the shadow of the night, and draped nobly in the folds of a gorgeous eloquence. The vision seemed to enter the house with me—the stretcher, the phantom-bearers, the wild crowd of obedient worshipers, the gloom of the forests, the glitter of the reach between the murky bends, the beat of the drum, regular and muffled like the beating of a heart—the heart of a conquering darkness. It was a moment of triumph for the wilderness, an invading and vengeful rush which, it seemed to me, I would have to keep back alone for the salvation of another soul. And the memory of what I had heard him say afar there, with the horned shapes stirring at my back, in the glow of fires, within the patient woods, those broken phrases came back to me, were heard again in their ominous and terrifying simplicity. I remembered his abject pleading, his abject threats, the colossal scale of his vile desires, the meanness, the torment, the tempestuous anguish of his soul. And later on I seemed to see his collected languid manner, when he said one day, 'This lot of ivory now is really mine. The Company did not pay for it. I collected it myself at a very great personal risk. I am afraid they will try to claim it as theirs though. H'm. It is a difficult case. What do you think I ought to do—resist? Eh? I want no more than justice.' . . . He wanted no more than justice—no more than justice. I rang the bell before a mahogany door on the first floor, and while I waited he seemed to stare at me out of the glassy panel—stare with that wide and immense stare embracing, condemning, loathing all the universe. I seemed to hear the whispered cry, 'The horror! The horror!'

"The dusk was falling. I had to wait in a lofty drawing-room with three long windows from floor to ceiling that were like three luminous and be-draped columns. The bent gilt legs and backs of the furniture shone in indistinct curves. The tall marble fireplace had a cold and monumental whiteness. A grand piano stood massively in a corner; with dark gleams on the flat surfaces like a sombre and polished sarcophagus. A high door opened—closed. I rose.

"She came forward, all in black, with a pale head, floating towards me in the dusk. She was in mourning. It was more than a year since his death, more than a year since the news came;[193] she seemed as though she would remember and mourn for ever. She took both my hands in hers and mur-mured, 'I had heard you were coming.' I noticed she was not very young— I mean not girlish. She had a mature capacity for fidelity, for belief, for suffering. The room seemed to have grown darker, as if all the sad light of the cloudy evening had taken refuge on her forehead. This fair hair, this pale visage, this pure brow, seemed surrounded by an ashy halo from which the dark eyes looked out at me. Their glance was guileless, pro-found, confident, and trustful. She carried her sorrowful head as though she were proud of that sorrow, as though she would say, I—I alone know how to mourn for him as he deserves. But while we were still shaking hands, such a look of awful desolation came upon her face that I perceived she was one of those creatures that are not the playthings of Time. For her he had died only yesterday. And, by Jove! the impression was so powerful that for me too he seemed to have died only yesterday—nay, this very minute. I saw her and him in the same instant of time—his death and her sorrow—I saw her sorrow in the very moment of his death. Do you under-stand? I saw them together—I heard them together. She had said, with a deep catch of the breath, 'I have survived'; while my strained ears seemed to hear distinctly, mingled with her tone of despairing regret, the sum-ming-up whisper of his eternal condemnation. I asked myself what I was doing there, with a sensation of panic in my heart as though I had blun-dered into a place of cruel and absurd mysteries not fit for a human being to behold. She motioned me to a chair. We sat down. I laid the packet gently on the little table, and she put her hand over it. . . . 'You knew him well,' she murmured, after a moment of mourning silence.

---

193. The timeline at the end of the story departs significantly from Conrad's own chro-nology. Aside from Conrad's two days in Brussels sometime in January 1891, little is known of his travel between being in Matadi on 4 December 1890 and being in London on 1 Febru-ary 1891 (Najder 2007, 162). However, by January 1891 it had been only four months since Klein's death on 21 September and only a little longer since Conrad's time on the *Roi des Belges* in August–September—not "more than a year."

"'Intimacy grows quickly out there,' I said. 'I knew him as well as it is possible for one man to know another.'

"'And you admired him,' she said. 'It was impossible to know him and not to admire him. Was it?'

"'He was a remarkable man,' I said unsteadily. Then before the appealing fixity of her gaze, that seemed to watch for more words on my lips, I went on, 'It was impossible not to——'

"'Love him,' she finished eagerly, silencing me into an appalled dumbness. 'How true! how true! But when you think that no one knew him so well as I! I had all his noble confidence. I knew him best.'

"'You knew him best,' I repeated. And perhaps she did. But with every word spoken the room was growing darker, and only her forehead, smooth and white, remained illumined by the unextinguishable light of belief and love.

"'You were his friend,' she went on. 'His friend,' she repeated, a little louder. 'You must have been, if he had given you this, and sent you to me. I feel I can speak to you—and oh! I must speak. I want you—you who have heard his last words—to know I have been worthy of him. . . . It is not pride. . . . Yes! I am proud to know I understood him better than any one on earth—he told me so himself. And since his mother died I have had no one—no one—to—to——'

"I listened. The darkness deepened. I was not even sure whether he had given me the right bundle. I rather suspect he wanted me to take care of another batch of his papers which, after his death, I saw the manager examining under the lamp. And the girl talked, easing her pain in the certitude of my sympathy; she talked as thirsty men drink. I had heard that her engagement with Kurtz had been disapproved by her people. He wasn't rich enough or something. And indeed I don't know whether he had not been a pauper all his life. He had given me some reason to infer that it was his impatience of comparative poverty that drove him out there.

"'. . . Who was not his friend who had heard him speak once?' she was saying. 'He drew men towards him by what was best in them.' She looked at me with intensity. 'It is the gift of the great,' she went on, and the sound of her low voice seemed to have the accompaniment of all the other sounds, full of mystery, desolation, and sorrow, I had ever heard—the ripple of the river, the soughing of the trees swayed by the wind, the murmurs of the crowds, the faint ring of incomprehensible words cried from afar, the whisper of a voice speaking from beyond the threshold of an eternal darkness. 'But you have heard him! You know!' she cried.

"'Yes, I know,' I said with something like despair in my heart, but bowing my head before the faith that was in her, before that great and saving illusion that shone with an unearthly glow in the darkness, in the triumphant darkness from which I could not have defended her—from which I could not even defend myself.

"'What a loss to me—to us!'—she corrected herself with beautiful generosity; then added in a murmur, 'To the world.' By the last gleams of twilight I could see the glitter of her eyes, full of tears—of tears that would not fall.

"'I have been very happy—very fortunate—very proud,' she went on. 'Too fortunate. Too happy for a little while. And now I am unhappy for—for life.'

"She stood up; her fair hair seemed to catch all the remaining light in a glimmer of gold. I rose too.

"'And of all this,' she went on mournfully, 'of all his promise, and of all his greatness, of his generous mind, of his noble heart, nothing remains—nothing but a memory. You and I——'

"'We shall always remember him,' I said, hastily.

"'No!' she cried. 'It is impossible that all this should be lost—that such a life should be sacrificed to leave nothing—but sorrow. You know what vast plans he had. I knew of them too—I could not perhaps understand—but others knew of them. Something must remain. His words, at least, have not died.'

"'His words will remain,' I said.

"'And his example,' she whispered to herself. 'Men looked up to him—his goodness shone in every act. His example——'

"'True,' I said; 'his example too. Yes, his example. I forgot that.'

"'But I do not. I cannot—I cannot believe—not yet. I cannot believe that I shall never see him again, that nobody will see him again, never, never, never.'

"She put out her arms as if after a retreating figure, stretching them black[194] and with clasped pale hands across the fading and narrow sheen of the window. Never see him! I saw him clearly enough then. I shall see this eloquent phantom as long as I live, and I shall see her too, a tragic and familiar Shade, resembling in this gesture another one, tragic also, and bedecked with powerless charms, stretching bare brown arms over the glitter of the infernal stream, the stream of darkness. She said suddenly very low, 'He died as he lived.'

"'His end,' said I, with dull anger stirring in me, 'was in every way worthy of his life.'

"'And I was not with him,' she murmured. My anger subsided before a feeling of infinite pity.

"'Everything that could be done——' I mumbled.

"'Ah, but I believed in him more than any one on earth—more than his own mother, more than—himself. He needed me! Me! I would have treasured every sigh, every word, every sign, every glance.'

---

194. Corrected from "back" in the 1921 published text.

"I felt like a chill grip on my chest. 'Don't,' I said, in a muffled voice.

"'Forgive me. I—I—have mourned so long in silence—in silence. . . . You were with him—to the last? I think of his loneliness. Nobody near to understand him as I would have understood. Perhaps no one to hear . . .'

"'To the very end,' I said shakily. 'I heard his very last words. . . .' I stopped in a fright.

"'Repeat them,' she murmured in a heart-broken tone. 'I want—I want—something—something—to—to live with.'

"I was on the point of crying at her, 'Don't you hear them?' The dusk was repeating them in a persistent whisper all around us, in a whisper that seemed to swell menacingly like the first whisper of a rising wind. 'The horror! The horror!'

"'His last word—to live with,' she insisted. 'Don't you understand I loved him—I loved him—I loved him!'

"I pulled myself together and spoke slowly.

"'The last word he pronounced was—your name.'

"I heard a light sigh and then my heart stood still, stopped dead short by an exulting and terrible cry, by the cry of inconceivable triumph and of unspeakable pain. 'I knew it—I was sure!' . . . She knew. She was sure. I heard her weeping; she had hidden her face in her hands. It seemed to me that the house would collapse before I could escape, that the heavens would fall upon my head. But nothing happened. The heavens do not fall for such a trifle. Would they have fallen, I wonder, if I had rendered Kurtz that justice which was his due? Hadn't he said he wanted only justice? But I couldn't. I could not tell her. It would have been too dark—too dark altogether. . . ."

Marlow ceased, and sat apart, indistinct and silent, in the pose of a meditating Buddha. Nobody moved for a time. "We have lost the first of the ebb," said the Director suddenly. I raised my head. The offing was barred by a black bank of clouds, and the tranquil waterway leading to the uttermost ends of the earth flowed sombre under an overcast sky—seemed to lead into the heart of an immense darkness.

Author's Note

The three stories in this volume[195] lay no claim to unity of artistic purpose. The only bond between them is that of the time in which they were written. They belong to the period immediately following the publication of the *Nigger of the Narcissus,* and preceding the first conception of *Nostromo,* two books which, it seems to me, stand apart and by themselves in the body of my work. It is also the period during which I contributed to "Maga";[196] a period dominated by *Lord Jim* and associated in my grateful memory with the late Mr. William Blackwood's encouraging and helpful kindness.

Youth was not my first contribution to "Maga." It was the second. But that story marks the first appearance in the world of the man Marlow, with whom my relations have grown very intimate in the course of years. The origins of that gentleman (nobody as far as I know had ever hinted that he was anything but that)—his origins have been the subject of some literary speculation of, I am glad to say, a friendly nature.

One would think that I am the proper person to throw a light on the matter; but in truth I find that it isn't so easy. It is pleasant to remember that nobody had charged him with fraudulent purposes or looked down on him as a charlatan; but apart from that he was supposed to be all sorts of things: a clever screen, a mere device, a "personator," a familiar spirit, a whispering "dæmon." I myself have been suspected of a meditated plan for his capture.

---

195. "Youth," *Heart of Darkness*, and *The End of the Tether.* Conrad's "Author's Note" was added in 1917 at the beginning of a collected edition of *Youth: A Narrative and Two Other Stories,* containing the three tales. The book had first appeared in Britain in 1902 and in America (as *Youth and Two Other Stories*) in 1903. Before then, *Heart of Darkness* had first been published in magazine form in 1899 (as "The Heart of Darkness," in *Blackwood's Edinburgh Magazine*). The textual history of *Heart of Darkness* is complicated, and there were differences among the magazine versions and successive book versions. The 1921 Heinemann edition of *Youth: A Narrative and Two Other Stories,* which includes this "Author's Note," is the copy text for this edition of *Heart of Darkness,* on the grounds that readers during and soon after Conrad's lifetime believed it to be his choice of final text (Curle 1928, 64) (although that belief now increasingly appears to have been mistaken [Stape and Sullivan 2002, 72–87]).

196. *Blackwood's Edinburgh Magazine.*

That is not so. I made no plans. The man Marlow and I came together in the casual manner of those health-resort acquaintances which sometimes ripen into friendships. This one has ripened. For all his assertiveness in matters of opinion he is not an intrusive person. He haunts my hours of solitude, when, in silence, we lay our heads together in great comfort and harmony; but as we part at the end of a tale I am never sure that it may not be for the last time. Yet I don't think that either of us would care much to survive the other. In his case, at any rate, his occupation would be gone and he would suffer from that extinction, because I suspect him of some vanity. I don't mean vanity in the Solomonian sense. Of all my people he's the one that has never been a vexation to my spirit. A most discreet, understanding man. . . .

Even before appearing in book-form *Youth* was very well received. It lies on me to confess at last, and this is as good a place for it as another, that I have been all my life—all my two lives—the spoiled adopted child of Great Britain and even of the Empire; for it was Australia that gave me my first command. I break out into this declaration not because of a lurking tendency to megalomania, but, on the contrary, as a man who has no very notable illusions about himself. I follow the instincts of vain-glory and humility natural to all mankind. For it can hardly be denied that it is not their own deserts that men are most proud of, but rather of their prodigious luck, of their marvellous fortune: of that in their lives for which thanks and sacrifices must be offered on the altars of the inscrutable gods.

Heart of Darkness also received a certain amount of notice from the first; and of its origins this much may be said: it is well known that curious men go prying into all sorts of places (where they have no business) and come out of them with all kinds of spoil. This story, and one other, not in this volume,[197] are all the spoil I brought out from the centre of Africa, where, really, I had no sort of business. More ambitious in its scope and longer in the telling, *Heart of Darkness* is quite as authentic in fundamentals as *Youth*. It is, obviously, written in another mood. I won't characterise the mood precisely, but anybody can see that it is anything but the mood of wistful regret, of reminiscent tenderness.

One more remark may be added. *Youth* is a feat of memory. It is a record of experience; but that experience, in its facts, in its inwardness and in its outward colouring, begins and ends in myself. *Heart of Darkness* is experience too; but it is experience pushed a little (and only very little) beyond the actual facts of the case for the perfectly legitimate, I believe, purpose of bringing it home to the minds and bosoms of the readers. There it was no longer a matter of sincere colouring. It was like another

---

197. "An Outpost of Progress," written in 1896 and published in 1897.

art altogether. That sombre theme had to be given a sinister resonance, a tonality of its own, a continued vibration that, I hoped, would hang in the air and dwell on the ear after the last note had been struck.

After saying so much there remains the last tale of the book, still untouched. *The End of the Tether* is a story of sea-life in a rather special way; and the most intimate thing I can say of it is this: that having lived that life fully, amongst its men, its thoughts and sensations, I have found it possible, without the slightest misgiving, in all sincerity of heart and peace of conscience, to conceive the existence of Captain Whalley's personality and to relate the manner of his end. This statement acquires some force from the circumstance that the pages of that story—a fair half of the book—are also the product of experience. That experience belongs (like *Youth's*) to the time before I ever thought of putting pen to paper. As to its "reality," that is for the readers to determine. One had to pick up one's facts here and there. More skill would have made them more real and the whole composition more interesting. But here we are approaching the veiled region of artistic values which it would be improper and indeed dangerous for me to enter. I have looked over the proofs, have corrected a misprint or two, have changed a word or two—and that's all. It is not very likely that I shall ever read *The End of the Tether* again. No more need be said. It accords best with my feelings to part from Captain Whalley in affectionate silence.

J. C.

1917.

glad

"The Congo Diary"

By Joseph Conrad

With Annotations
by Mark D. Larabee

Conrad kept a private account of his time in the Congo in two small leather-bound notebooks that were not published until after his death. The first notebook, unlabeled by Conrad but given the title "The Congo Diary" by Richard Curle (coexecutor of Conrad's estate), was initially published in 1925. "The Congo Diary" has entries from 13 June to 1 August 1890, covering the period from Conrad's arrival at Matadi on the Lower Congo through the overland journey on the caravan route to Nselemba, near Kinshasa on Stanley Pool. In this diary, Conrad recorded impressions of the people he met, the landscape he passed through, and the difficulties of the journey, along with a dozen sketches of the terrain and notes on the meanings of native words. The notebook's entries give us a window onto not only the details of the country through which he passed, but also his thinking and the mentality of the Europeans in the Congo—all furthermore meaningful when placed alongside the fictional telling in *Heart of Darkness*. Conrad gave the title "Up-river book" to the second notebook (not reproduced in this volume), which Conrad evidently created for future reference navigating the Congo River. It begins on 3 August and covers about half of the upriver journey. Unlike "The Congo Diary," which shows us natives and Europeans and their interactions, the "Up-river book" focuses primarily on a set of navigational descriptions, maps and sketches, and instructions for safely ascending the river.

THE CONGO DIARY[1]

Arrived at Matadi[2] on the 13th of June 1890. –
Mr Gosse[3] chief of the station (O.K.) retaining us for some reason of his own.

---

1. Transcription of Conrad 1890, vol. 2 (Joseph Conrad, 1890, *Up-river book: manuscript, 1890*, 2 vols, Houghton Library, Harvard University, MS Eng 46).

2. Port on the Lower Congo and site of the Société Anonyme Belge company station. The farthest navigable point upriver from the Atlantic below the cataracts, Matadi was the starting point of the railway line to Léopoldville and the caravan route to Kinshasa.

3. Joseph-Louis-Hubert Gosse (1860–1891), manager of the SAB trading post at Matadi (Najder 2007, 148; Conrad 2010b 453n123.5).

Made the acquaintance of Mr Roger Casement,[4] which I should consider as a great pleasure under any circumstances and now it becomes a positive piece of luck.

Thinks, speaks well, most intelligent and very sympathetic. –

feel considerably in doubt about the future. Think just now that my life amongst the people (white) around here can not be very comfortable. Intend avoid acquaintances as much as possible.

Through Mr R. C. Have made the acquain[tan]^{ce} of Mr Underwood the manager of the English factory (Hatton & Cookson,[5] in Kalla Kalla – av[era]^{ge} com[merci]^{al} – Hearty and kind. Lunched there on the 21st. –

24th – Gosse and R. C. gone with a large lot of ivory down to Boma.[6] On G. return intend to start up the river. Have been myself busy packing ivory in casks. Idiotic employement [sic]. Health good up to now.

Wrote to Simpson, to Gov. B. to Purd. to Hope, to Cap Froud, and to Mar.[7] Prominent characteristic of the social life here: People speaking ill of each other. –

Saturday 28th June left Matadi with Mr Harou[8] and a caravan of 31 men. Parted with Casement in a very friendly manner. Mr Gosse saw us off as far as the State station. –

First halt. M'poso. 2 Danes in Comp[a]ny.

Sund: 29th. Ascent of Palaballa[.] Sufficiently fatiguing. – Camped at 11^{h} am at Nsoke-River[.] Mosquitos –

Monday 30th. to Congo da Lemba after passing black rocks long ascent. Harou giving up. Bother. Camp bad. Water far. Dirty[.] At night Harou better.

---

4. Roger Casement (1864–1916), then a supervisor for the Compagnie du Chemin de Fer du Congo, working on building the Matadi to Léopoldville railway line. He became British Consul for the Congo Free State in 1898; in 1903 he wrote a report on the Congo, published in 1904, that criticized Leopold's administration of the colony (Najder 2007, 149, 337).

5. British trading company, based in Liverpool.

6. Seat of the Congo Free State government; about 50 miles up the Congo River from the Atlantic and about 30 miles downriver from Matadi.

7. James L. Simpson (1844–1899) was the head of an Australian shipping firm; Conrad had been master of one of the firm's ships, the *Otago,* in 1888–1889 (Najder 2007, 133; Conrad 2010b, 454n123.23). "Gov. B." may refer to Tadeusz Bobrowski (1829–1894), Conrad's maternal uncle and his guardian after his parents died; "Purd." may be master mariner Robins Purdy (1844–1932) (Conrad 2010c, 454n123.23). George Fountaine Ware Hope (1854–1930) was a friend of Conrad's since 1880, a company director and former merchant marine officer (Stape and Knowles 2006, 104–16). Captain A. G. Froud (1831–1901) was secretary of the London Ship-Master's Society (Conrad 2010c, 455n123.23). "Mar.": Marguerite Poradowska (1848–1937), Conrad's cousin in Brussels whom he called his "aunt" the two exchanged many letters during Conrad's time in the Congo (Knowles and Moore 2000, 288–89).

8. Prosper Harou (1855–1893), the Belgian trader who had arrived with Conrad from Bordeaux on the *Ville de Maceio* (Sherry 1971, 13).

1st <u>July</u>.

<u>Tuesday</u>. 1ˢᵗ. Left early in a heavy mist marching towards Lufu River. – Part route through forest on the sharp slope of a high mountain. Very long descent. Then market place, from where short walk to the bridge (good) and camp. V[ery].G[ood]. Bath. Clear river. Feel well[.] Harou all right. 1st chicken. <u>2p.</u>[m.] [Written in the left margin:] no sunshine today

<u>Wednesday</u> 2ᵈ July.

Started at 5ʰ30 after a sleepless night. Country more open – gently andulating [*sic*] hills. Road good in perfect order – (District of Lukungu). Great market at 9.30. bought eggs & chickens.

feel not well today. Heavy cold in the head. Arrived at 11ʰ at Banza Manteka. Camped on the market place. Not well enough to call on the missionary.⁹ Water scarce and bad – Camp[in]ᵍ place dirty. –

2 Danes still in company

Thursday 3ᵈ July.

Left at 6am. after a good night's rest. Crossed a low range of hills and entered a broad valley or rather plain with a break in the middle – Met an off[ic]er of the State inspecting; a few minutes afterwards saw at a camp[in]ᵍ place the dead body of a Backongo.¹⁰ Shot? Horrid smell. – Crossed a a [*sic*] range of mountains running NW–SE. by a low pass. Another broad flat valley with a deep ravine through the centre. – Clay and gravel. Another range parallel to the first-mentioned with a chain of low foothills running close to it. Between the two came to camp on the banks of Luinzono River. Camp[in]ᵍ place clean. River clear. Govt. Zanzibari with register. Canoe. 2 danes camp[in]ᵍ on the other bank. – Health good.

General tone of landscape grey yellowish. (Dry grass) with reddish patches (soil) and clumps of dark green vegetation scattered sparsely about. Mostly in steep gorges between the higher mountains or in ravines cutting the plain – Noticed Palma Christi¹¹ – Oil palm. Very straight tall and thick trees in some places. Name not known to me – Villages quite invisible. Infer their existence from cal[a]bashes¹² suspended to palm trees for the "malafu".¹³ – Good many caravans and travellers. No women unless on the market place. –

---

9. Rev. Charles E. Ingham (d. 1890s), formerly of the Livingstone Inland Mission (American Baptist Mission Union) (Conrad 2010c, 456n124.21).

10. The Bakongo tribe, natives of the cataract region, served as porters on the overland route (Glave 1890, 619).

11. Castor oil plant.

12. Gourds.

13. Kikongo word for palm wine (Conrad 2010c, 457n125.13).

Bird notes charming – One especially a flute-like note. Another kind of "boom" ressembling [*sic*] the very distant baying of a hound. – Saw only pigeons and a few green parroquets; very small and not many[.] No birds of prey seen by me. Up to 9am – Sky clouded and calm – Afterwards gentle breeze from the N[or]ᵗʰ generally and sky clearing – Nights damp and cool. – White mists on the hills up about half way. Water effects, very beautiful, this morning. Mists generally raising before sky clears.

[Sketch at foot of the page:] Section of day's road –

[From left to right, above drawing of landscape:] Luinzono River[,] 3. Hills[,] Banza Manteka

[Below sketch:] Distance 15 miles. General Direction NNE<<<SSW
Friday – 4ᵗʰ July. –

Left camp at 6ʰ am. after a very unpleasant night – Marching across a chain of hills and then in a maze of hills – At 8.15 opened out into an an-dulating [*sic*] plain[.] Took bearings[14] of a break in the chain of mountains on the other side – Bearing NNE – Road passes through that. Sharp as-cents up very steep hills not very high. The higher mountains recede sharply and show a low hilly country –

At 9.30 Market Place.

At 10ʰ passed R. Lukanga and at 10.30 Camped on the Mpwe R.

[Sketch at top of the page:] To day's march.

[Above sketch:] Direction NNE½N [<—<< underneath] Dist[an]ᶜᵉ
13 miles

[Sketch of hills, labeled at left:] Camp [At right:] Luinzono

Saw another dead body lying by the path in an attitude of meditative repose. –

In the evening 3 women of whom one albino passed our camp. Horrid chalky white with pink blotches. Red eyes. Red hair. Features very negroid and ugly. – Mosquitos. At night when the moon rose heard shouts and drumming in distant villages[.] Passed a bad night.

Saturday 5th July. [18]90.

Left at 6.15. Morning cool, even cold and very damp – Sky densely overcast. Gentle breeze from NE. Road through a narrow plain up to R. Kwilu. Swift flowing and deep 50y[ar]ds wide – Passed in canoes – After[war]ᵈˢ up and down very steep hills intersected by deep ravines – Main chain of heights running mostly NW – SE or W and E (at times[)]. Stopped at Manyamba – Camp[in]ᵍ place bad – in a hollow – Water very indifferent. Tent set at 10ʰ15ᵐ.

[Sketch at foot of the page:] Section of to day's road

[Above sketch:] NNE <–<< Distᵃ[ⁿᶜᵉ] 12ᵐ[ⁱˡᵉˢ]

---

14. Measured the direction by using a compass.

[Sketch of hills, labeled at left:] Camp[,] Manyamba [In center:] Kwilu River

To day fell into a muddy puddle – Beastly. The fault of the man that carried me. After camp[in]^g went to a small stream bathed and washed clothes. – Getting jolly well sick of this fun. –

To morrow expect a long march to get to Nsona. 2 days from Manyanga. –

No sunshine to-day

Sunday 6th July –

Started at 5.40. – the route at first hilly then after a sharp descent traversing a broad plain. At the end of it a large market place[.] at 10^h. Sun came out. –

After leaving the market passed another plain then walking on the crest of a chain of hills passed 2 villages and at 11^h arrived at Nsona. – Village invisible –

[Sketch at foot of the page:] Section of day's march.

[Sketch of hills, labeled at left:] Camp Nsona [In center:] Market.

[Below sketch:] Direction about NNE <—<<

Distance—18 miles

In this camp (Nsona –) there is a good camp[in]^g place[.] Shady. Water far and not very good. – This night no mosquitos owing to large fires lit all round our tent. –

Afternoon very close

Night clear and starry.

Monday – 7th July. –

Left at 6^h after a good night's rest on the road to Inkandu which is some distance past Lukungu gov[ernmen]^t station. –

Route very accidented.[15] Succession of round steep hills. At times walking along the crest of a chain of hills. –

Just before Lukunga our carriers took a wide sweep to the southward till the station bore N[or]th. – Walking through long grass for 1½ hours. – Crossed a broad river about 100 feet wide and 4 deep. – After another ½ hours walk through manioc[16] plantations in good order rejoined our route to the E[astwar]^d of the Lukunga Sta[ti]^{on} – Walking along an undulating plain towards the Inkandu market on a hill. – Hot, thirsty and tired. At 11^h arrived on the m[ar]ketplace – About 200 people. – Business brisk. No water. No camp[in]^g place – After remaining for one hour left in search of a resting place. –

---

15. From the French "accidenté" (uneven or hilly) (Conrad 2010b, 458n127.26). Conrad used Gallicisms in his writing.

16. Another term for the cassava plant, whose starchy root, boiled, was a staple food; the leaves were sometimes also boiled and eaten (Johnston 1908, 2:605).

Row with carriers – No water.

At last about 1 ½ p.m. camped on an exposed hill side near a muddy creek. No shade. Tent on a slope. Sun heavy. Wretched.

[Sketch of hills, labeled from left to right:] Camp[,] <u>Inkandu</u>[,] River bearing N[or]th. Lukunga[,] Nsona

[Below sketch:] Direction NE by N. <—<<

Distance 22 miles

Night miserably cold. –

No sleep. Mosquitos –

Tuesday 8th July

Left at 6^h. am

About ten minutes from camp left main gov[ernmen]^t path for the Manyanga track. Sky overcast[.] Road up and down all the time – Passing a couple of villages

The country presents a confused wilderness of hills[,] land slips on their side showing red. Fine effect of red hill covered in places by dark green vegetation

½ hour before beginning the descent got a glimpse of the Congo. – Sky clouded.

[Sketch at top of page:] To day's march – 3^h

[Sketch of hills, labeled left to right:] Manyanga[,] Congo[,] Hill[,] River[,] Camp

[Below sketch:] NbyE <—<< SbyW

General direction NbyE –

Dist[an]<u>ce</u> 9½ miles –

Arrived at Manyanga at 9^h a.m.

Received most kindly by Messr[s] Heyn & Jaeger.[17] –

Most comfortable and pleasant halt. –

Stayed here till the 25. Both have been sick. – Most kindly care taken of us. Leave with sincere regret.

(Mafiela)

Frid^y 25th	–	Nkenghe[18]	–	<u>left</u>
Sat. 26		Nsona		Nkendo.k
Sund. 27		Nkandu		<u>Luasi</u>

---

17. Reginald Heyn was an Englishman who was manager of the SAB transport base at Manyanga; Jaeger was his assistant (Jean-Aubry 1927, 1:131; Najder 2007, 153).

18. This table shows the four-day week observed in the Congo. Markets were held every four or eight days. The words in the middle column are the names of the days of the week; the right column names the town near which the market would be held on that day (Bentley 1900, 1:358, 1:399).

Mond 28	Nkonzo		Nzungi (Ngoma)
Tues. 29	Nkenghe		Inkissi
Wedn: 30	Nsona	mercredi –	Stream
Thurs: 31.	Nkandu		Luila
Frid[y] 1st Aug.	Nkonzo		Nselenba
Sat[y] 2[d]	Nkenghe		
Sund. 3[d]	Nsona		
Mond. 4th	Nkandu		
Tuesd: 5th	Nkonzo.		
Wedn[y] 6th	Nkenghe.		

Friday the 25th July 1890. –
Left Manyanga at 2½ p.m – with plenty of hammock carriers. H[arou].
lame and not in very good form. Myself ditto but not lame. Walked as far
as Mafiela and camped – 2[h]
Saturday – 26th
Left very early. – Road ascending all the time. – Passed villages.
Country seems thickly inhabited. At 11[h] arrived at large Market place. Left
at noon and camped at 1[h] pm.
[Sketch of hills at foot of page; labeled above, left to right:] Camp[,] a
white man died here – [,] Market[,] gov[ernmen]t. path.[,] mount[,] Croco-
dile pond[,] Mafiela
[Below sketch:] General direction E½N <—<< N½S
Sun visible at 8 am. very hot
distance – 18 miles
Sunday. 27th.
Left at 8[h] am. Sent luggage carriers straight on to Luasi and went our-
selves round by the Mission of Sutili.
Hospitable reception by Mrs Comber[19] – All the missio[naries].
absent. –
The looks of the whole establishment eminently civilized and very
refreshing to see after the lot of tumble down hovels in which the state &
Company agents are content to live – fine buildings. Position on a hill.
Rather breezy. –

---

19. Annie Comber (d. 1890), wife of missionary Rev. Percy E. Comber at the Sutili Baptist mission (Conrad 2010c, 458n130.5).

Left at 3[h] pm. At the first heavy ascent met Mr Davis[20] Miss[ionary]. returning from a preaching trip. Rev. Bentley[21] away in the South with his wife. –

This being off the road no section given – Distance traversed about 15 miles – Gen[eral]. direction ENE. –

At Luasi we get on again on to the gov[ernmen][t] road. –

Camped at 4½ pm. with M[r] Heche[22] in company. –

To day no sunshine –

Wind remarkably cold –

Gloomy day. –

Monday. 28th

Left camp at 6.30 after breakfasting with Heche –

Road at first hilly. Then walking along the ridges of hill chains with valleys on both sides. – The country more open and there is much more trees growing in large clumps in the ravines. –

Passed Nzungi and camped 11[h] on the right bank of Ngoma. A rapid little river with rocky bed. Village on a hill to the right. –

[Sketch at foot of page, labeled left to right:] Camp[,] Ngoma River[,] Nzungi[,] [flag] Wooded valleys[,] Ridge.[,] River.[,] Luasi.[,] Camp

[Below sketch:] General direction ENE <—<<

　　　　　　　　Distance——14 miles

　　　　　　　　No sunshine. Gloomy cold day. Squalls.

Tuesday – 29th

Left camp at 7[h] after a good night's rest. Continuous ascent; rather easy at first. – Crossed wooded ravines and the river Lunzadi by a very decent bridge –

At 9[h] met Mr Louette escorting a sick agent of the Comp[an][y] back to Matadi – Looking very well – Bad news from up the river – All the steamers disabled. One wrecked.[23] – Country wooded – at 10.30 camped at Inkissi

[Sketch at foot of page, labeled left to right:] [flag] Camp[,] Inkissi River[,] Met Mr Louette.[,] Lunzadi River[,] Ngoma

　　　　　　　　General direction ENE <—<<

　　　　　　　　Dist[an]ce 15 miles

　　　　　　　　Sun visible at 6.30. Very warm day. –

29[th]

---

20. Baptist missionary Rev. Philip Davis (Conrad 2010c, 458n130.11).

21. Baptist missionary W. Holman Bentley (1855–1905) (Conrad 2010c, 458–59n130.14–15).

22. Perhaps Conrad's misnaming of Ernest-Albert-Louis-Adolphe Stache (1856–1897), principal agent for the SAB (Conrad 2010c, 459n130.19).

23. Not all steamers were disabled; Conrad's statement is inaccurate (Sherry 1971, 398n9). However, the *Florida,* Conrad's intended command, had struck a rock and grounded at the exit of Stanley Pool on 18 July 1890. She was refloated and towed back to Kinshasa on 23 July (Najder 2007, 154).

Inkissi River very rapid, is about 100 yards broad. Passage in canoes. – Banks wooded very densely and valley of the river rather deep but very narrow. –

To day did not set the tent but put up in gov[ernmen]ᵗ shimbek.[24]

Zanzibari in charge – Very obliging. – Met ripe pineapple for the first time. –

On the road to day passed a skeleton tied-up to a post. Also white man's grave – No name. Heap of stones in the form of a cross.

Health good now –

Wednesday – 30ᵗʰ.

Left at 6 am intending to camp at Kinfumu – Two hours sharp walk brought me to Nsona na Nsefe – Market – ½ hour after Harou arrived very ill with billious [*sic*] attack and fever. – Laid him down in gov[ernmen]ᵗ shimbek – Dose of Ipeca.[25] Vomiting bile in enormous quantities. At 11ʰ gave him 1 gramme of quinine and lots of hot tea. Hot fit ending in heavy perspiration. At 2ʰ p.m. put him in hammock and started for Kinfumu – Row with carriers all the way. Harou suffering much through the jerks of the hammock[.] Camped at a small stream. –

At 4ʰ Harou better. Fever gone.

[Sketch, labeled left to right:] Camp/grass[,] [flag] Nsona [n]a Nsefe[,] Stream[,] Wood[,] open[,] A remarkable conical mountain bearing NE visible from here[,] Lulufu river[,] wood[,] Inkissi[?]

[Below sketch:] General direction NEbyE½E –

　　　　　　Distance 13 miles –

Up till noon, sky clouded and strong NW wind very chilling. from 1ʰ pm to 4ʰ pm sky clear and a very hot day. Expect lots of bother with carriers to-morrow – Had them all called and made a speech which they did not understand. They promise good behaviour

Thursday – 31st

Left at 6ʰ. – Sent Harou ahead and followed in ½ an hour. – Road presents several sharp ascents and a few others easier but rather long. Notice in places sandy surface soil instead of hard clay as heretofore; think however that the layer of sand is not very thick and that the clay would be found under it[.] Great difficulty in carrying Harou. – Too heavy. Bother! Made two long halts to rest the carriers. Country wooded in valleys and on many of the ridges.

31ˢᵗ

[Sketch at top of page:] Section of to-day's road

---

24. African word for a temporary shelter, housing people all engaged in the same work (Conrad 2010c, 459n131.19).

25. Ipecac or ipecacuanha, an herbal drug used to induce vomiting.

[Labeled left to right:] Luila River[,] Kinzilu River[,] Congo [River,] Kimfumu River[,] [flag] Nkenghe[,] Camp

[Below sketch:] NE½E <—<<

At 2.30 pm reached Luila at last and camped on right bank. – Breeze from SW

General direction of march about NE½E

Distance est[imate]^d 16 miles

Congo very narrow and rapid[.] Kinzilu rushing in. A short distance up from the mouth fine waterfall. –

– Sun rose red – from 9^h a.m. infernally hot day. –

Harou very little better.

Self rather seedy. Bathed.

Luila about 60 feet wide. Shallow

<u>Friday – 1st of August 1890</u>

Left at 6.30 am after a very indifferently passed night – Cold, Heavy mists – Road in long ascents and sharp dips all the way to Mfumu Mbé –

After leaving there a long and painful climb up a very steep hill; then a long descent to Mfumu Koko where a long halt was made.

Left at 12.30 pm – towards Nselemba. – Many ascents – The aspect of the country entirely changed – Wooded hills with openings. – Path almost all the afternoon thro' a forest of light trees with dense undergrowth. –

After a halt on a wooded hillside reached Nselemba at 4^{h}10^m p.m.

[Sketch, labeled left to right:] Camp[,] Nselemba[,] [flag] Stream[,] mostly wooded[,] Stream[,] Koko[,] Stream[,] grass[,] woods[?] Mfumu Mbé[,] Camp

Put up at gov[ernmen]^t shanty. –

Row between the carriers and a man stating himself in gov[ernmen]^t employ, about a mat. – Blows with sticks raining hard – Stopped it. Chief came with a youth about 13 suffering from gunshot wound in the head. Bullet entered about an inch above the right eyebrow and came out a little inside the roots of the hair, fairly in the middle of the brow in a line with the bridge of the nose – Bone not damaged apparently. Gave him a little glycerine to put on the wound made by the bullet on coming out.

Harou not very well. Mosquitos – Frogs – Beastly. Glad to see the end of this stupid tramp. feel rather seedy.

Sun rose red – Very hot day – Wind Sth

<u>General direction of march – NEbyN</u>

<u>Distance about   17 miles^{26}</u>

---

26. Conrad arrived at Kinshasa on the following day, 2 August 1890. He departed upriver on the *Roi des Belges* on 3 August, and he began entries in his second diary notebook, which he titled his "Up-river book," on the same day. The rest of the first notebook, "The Congo Diary," is undated and consists mostly of a few unlabeled sketches, lists of oil and paint containers, translations of native words, and nautical calculations from at least a year later.

Bibliography

Achebe, Chinua. 1977. "An Image of Africa." *The Massachusetts Review* 18 (4): 782–94.

Achebe, Chinua. 1988. "An Image of Africa." In *Heart of Darkness*, 3rd ed., edited by Robert Kimbrough, 251–62. Norton Critical Editions. New York: W. W. Norton.

Allen, James Smith. 1983. "History and the Novel: Mentalité in Modern Popular Fiction." *History and Theory* 22 (3): 233–52.

Allen, Jerry. 1965. *The Sea Years of Joseph Conrad*. New York: Doubleday.

Anthon, Charles. 1841. *A Classical Dictionary: Containing an Account of The Principal Proper Names Mentioned in Ancient Authors, and Intended to Elucidate all the Important Points Connected with the Geography, History, Biography, Mythology, and Fine Arts of the Greeks and Romans. Together with An Account of Coins, Weights, and Measures, With Tabular Values of the Same.* New York: Harper & Brothers.

Arendt, Hannah. 1968. *The Origins of Totalitarianism*. Orlando: Harcourt.

Arnold, J. A. 1976. "The Young Russian's Book in Conrad's *Heart of Darkness*." *Conradiana* 8: 121–26.

Bannister, Robert C. 1979. *Social Darwinism: Science and Myth in Anglo-American Social Thought*. Philadelphia: Temple University Press.

Bentley, Rev. W. Holman. 1900. *Pioneering on the Congo*. 2 vols. [London]: The Religious Tract Society.

Biographie Coloniale Belge. 1948–1958. 5 vols. Brussels: Falk van Campenhout.

Bontinck, François. 1966. *Aux Origines de l'État Indépendant du Congo. Document tirés d'Archives Américaines.* Publications de l'Université Lovanium de Léopoldville. Louvain: Éditions Nauwelaerts.

Booth, General [William]. 1890. *In Darkest England: And the Way Out*. New York: Funk & Wagnalls.

Brantlinger, Patrick. 1985a. "*Heart of Darkness:* Anti-Imperialism, Racism, or Impressionism?" *Criticism* 27 (4): 363–85.

Brantlinger, Patrick. 1985b. "Victorians and Africans: The Genealogy of the Myth of the Dark Continent." *Critical Inquiry* 12 (Autumn): 166–203.

Brassey, Thomas. 1877. *British Seamen: As Described in Recent Parliamentary and Official Documents*. London: Longmans, Green.

Brourke, G. W. 1888. Memorandum, 22 June 1888. Suggestions for Surmounting the Congo Transport Difficulty. Baptist Missionary Society Headquarters, London.

Büchler, Max. 1912. *Der Kongostaat Leopolds II.* 2 vols. Zurich: Rascher. https://babel.hathitrust.org/cgi/pt?id=uc1.a0009008145;view=1up;seq=5.

Carlyle, Thomas. 1894. *Past and Present.* London: Chapman and Hall.

Chandler, Tertius, and Gerald Fox. 1974. *3000 Years of Urban Growth.* New York and London: Academic Press.

Chapaux, Albert. 1894. *Le Congo: Historique, diplomatique, physique; politique, économique, humanitaire & colonial; ouvrage contenant une grande carte en quatre feuilles, tirée en couleurs; 6 cartes, croquis et plans, intercalés dans le texte; 163 portraits, types d'indigènes, vues, etc.* Brussels: Charles Rozez, Éditeur.

Conrad, Joseph. 1890. *Up-river book: manuscript, 1890.* 2 vols. MS Eng 46. Houghton Library, Harvard University.

Conrad, Joseph. 1921a. "Author's Note." In *Youth: A Narrative and Two Other Stories,* ix–xiii. London: William Heinemann.

Conrad, Joseph. 1921b. *Heart of Darkness.* In *Youth: A Narrative and Two Other Stories,* 53–199. London: William Heinemann.

Conrad, Joseph. 1983. *The Collected Letters of Joseph Conrad. Vol. 1: 1861–1897.* Edited by Frederick R. Karl and Laurence Davies. Cambridge: Cambridge University Press.

Conrad, Joseph. 1986. *The Collected Letters of Joseph Conrad. Vol. 2: 1898–1902.* Edited by Frederick R. Karl and Laurence Davies. Cambridge: Cambridge University Press.

Conrad, Joseph. 1988a. *The Collected Letters of Joseph Conrad. Vol. 3: 1903–1907.* Edited by Frederick R. Karl and Laurence Davies. Cambridge: Cambridge University Press.

Conrad, Joseph. 1988b. *Heart of Darkness.* 3rd ed. Edited by Robert Kimbrough. New York: Norton.

Conrad, Joseph. 2007. "An Outpost of Progress." In *The Nigger of the "Narcissus" and Other Stories,* edited by J. H. Stape and Allan H. Simmons, 231–57. London: Penguin.

Conrad, Joseph. 2008a. *Heart of Darkness and Other Tales.* Edited by Cedric Watts. Oxford: Oxford University Press.

Conrad, Joseph. 2008b. *A Personal Record.* Edited by Zdzisław Najder and J. H. Stape. Cambridge: Cambridge University Press.

Conrad, Joseph. 2010a. "Geography and Some Explorers." In *Last Essays,* edited by Harold Ray Stevens and J. H. Stape, 3–22. Cambridge: Cambridge University Press.

Conrad, Joseph. 2010b. *Last Essays.* Edited by Harold Ray Stevens and J. H. Stape. Cambridge: Cambridge University Press.

Conrad, Joseph. 2010c. *Youth, Heart of Darkness, The End of the Tether.* Edited by Owen Knowles. Cambridge: Cambridge University Press.

Conrad, Joseph. 2016. "Author's Note." In *Victory: An Island Tale,* edited by J. H. Stape and Alexandre Fachard, with Aaron Zacks, 7–13. Cambridge: Cambridge University Press.

Conrad, Joseph. n.d. "Heart of Darkness," Beinecke Rare Book and Manuscript Library, Yale University.

Cornet, René J. 1948. *La bataille du rail: La construction du chemin de fer de Matadi au Stanley Pool.* 2nd ed. Brussels: Éditions L. Cuypers.

Cornewall-Jones, R. J. 1898. *The British Merchant Service: Being a History of the British Mercantile Marine from the Earliest Times to the Present Day.* London: Sampson Low, Marston.

Cunningham, Valentine. 1994. *In the Reading Gaol: Postmodernity, Texts, and History.* Oxford: Blackwell.

Darwin, Charles. 2006. *From So Simple a Beginning: Four Great Books of Charles Darwin.* New York: W. W. Norton.

Davies, Laurence. 2014. "Fin de siècle." In *Joseph Conrad in Context,* edited by Allan H. Simmons, 147–54. Cambridge: Cambridge University Press.

Delcommune, Alexandre. 1922. *Vingt années de Vie africaine: Récits de Voyages, d'Aventures et d'Exploration au Congo Belge 1874–1893.* 2 vols. Brussels: Vve Ferdinand Larcier.

Eaglestone, Robert. 2003. "Critical Knowledge, Scientific Knowledge and the Truth of Literature." In *The New Aestheticism,* edited John J. Joughin and Simon Malpas, 151–66. Manchester and New York: Manchester University Press.

Firchow, Peter Edgerly. 2000. *Envisioning Africa: Racism and Imperialism in Conrad's* Heart of Darkness. Lexington: The University Press of Kentucky.

Fleishman, Avrom. 1967. *Conrad's Politics: Community and Anarchy in the Fiction of Joseph Conrad.* Baltimore: Johns Hopkins University Press.

Ford, Jane. 1995. "An African Encounter, a British Traitor, and *Heart of Darkness.*" *Conradiana* 27: 123–34.

Gann, Lewis H., and Peter Duignan. 1979. *The Rulers of Belgian Africa, 1884–1914.* Princeton: Princeton University Press.

Garnett, Edward. 1928. Introduction to *Letters from Joseph Conrad: 1895 to 1924,* by Joseph Conrad, 1–28. Indianapolis: Bobbs-Merrill.

Glave, E. J. 1890. "The Congo River To-Day." *The Century Illustrated Magazine,* Feb., 618–20.

Glave, E. J. 1893. *Six Years of Adventure in Congo-Land.* London: Sampson Low, Marston & Company Limited.

Goffin, Louis. 1907. *Le Chemin de Fer du Congo: (Matadi–Stanley-Pool).* Brussels: M. Weissenbruch.

GoGwilt, Christopher. 1996. "Pramoedya's Fiction and History: An Interview with Indonesian Novelist Pramoedya Ananta Toer." *The Yale Journal of Criticism* 9 (1): 147–64. doi: 10.1353/yale.1996.0005.

GoGwilt, Christopher. 2010. "Joseph Conrad as Guide to Colonial History." In *A Historical Guide to Joseph Conrad,* edited by John G. Peters, 137–61. Oxford: Oxford University Press.

Gondola, Ch. Didier. 2002. *History of Congo.* Westport, CT: Greenwood Press.

Guerard, Albert J. 1958. *Conrad the Novelist.* Cambridge, MA: Harvard University Press.

Hawkins, Hunt. 1979. "Conrad's Critique of Imperialism in *Heart of Darkness.*" *Publications of the Modern Language Association* 94 (2): 286–99.

Hawkins, Hunt. 1981–1982. "Joseph Conrad, Roger Casement, and the Congo Reform Movement." *Journal of Modern Literature* 9 (1): 65–80.

Hay, Eloise Knapp. 1963. *The Political Novels of Joseph Conrad.* Chicago: University of Chicago Press.

Hobson, J. A. 1902. *Imperialism: A Study*. London: James Nisbet.

Hochschild, Adam. 1999. *King Leopold's Ghost: A Story of Greed, Terror, and Heroism in Colonial Africa*. Boston: Mariner Books.

Jean-Aubry, G. 1926. *Joseph Conrad in the Congo*. Boston: Little, Brown.

Jean-Aubry, G. 1927. *Joseph Conrad: Life and Letters*. 2 vols. Garden City, NY: Doubleday, Page.

Jenssen-Tusch, H. 1902–1905. *Skandinaver I Congo: Svenske, Norske og Danske Maends og Kvinders Virksomhed i den uafhaengige Congostat*. Copenhagen: Gyldendalske Boghandel–Nordisk Forlag.

Johnston, Sir Harry. 1908. *George Grenfell and the Congo: A History and Description of the Congo Independent State and Adjoining Districts of Congoland Together with Some Account of the Native Peoples and their Languages, the Fauna and Flora; and Similar Notes on the Cameroons and the Island of Fernando Pô[;] The Whole Founded on the Diaries and Researches of the Late Rev. George Grenfell, B.M.S., F.R.G.S.; on the Records of the British Baptist Missionary Society; and on Additional Information Contributed by the Author, by the Rev. Lawson Forfeitt, Mr. Emil Torday, and Others*. 2 vols. London: Hutchinson.

Kaye, John William. 1853. *The Administration of the East India Company; A History of Indian Progress*. London: Richard Bentley.

Kirkaldy, Adam W. 1914. *British Shipping: Its History, Organisation and Importance*. London: Kegan Paul, Trench, Trübner.

Kirschner, Paul. 1988. "Making You See Geneva: The Sense of Place in *Under Western Eyes*." *L'Époque Conradienne*, 101–27.

Knowles, Owen. 2014. *A Conrad Chronology*. 2nd ed. Houndmills: Palgrave Macmillan.

Knowles, Owen, and Gene M. Moore. 2000. *Oxford Reader's Companion to Conrad*. Oxford: Oxford University Press.

Larabee, Mark D. 2010. "Joseph Conrad and the Maritime Tradition." In *A Historical Guide to Joseph Conrad*, edited by John G. Peters, 47–76. Oxford: Oxford University Press.

Leclerq, Louis. 1970. "Les carnets de campagne de Louis Leclerq. Étude de mentalité d'un colonial belge." Edited by Pierre Salmon. *Revue de l'Université de Bruxelles* Nouvelle Série 3 (Feb.–Apr.): 233–302.

Lefebve de Vivy, Léon. 1955. *Documents d'histoire précoloniale belge (1861–1865): Les idées coloniales de Léopold duc de Brabant*. Brussels: Académie Royale des Sciences Coloniales.

Miller, J. Hillis. 2002. "Should We Read 'Heart of Darkness'?" In *Conrad in Africa: New Essays on "Heart of Darkness,"* edited by Attie de Lange and Gail Fincham, with Wiesław Krajka, 21–40. Boulder, CO: Social Science Monographs.

Morel, Edmund D. 1904. *King Leopold's Rule in Africa*. London: William Heinemann.

Morel, Edmund D. 1968. *E. D. Morel's History of the Congo Reform Movement*. Edited by William Roger Louis and Jean Stengers. Oxford: Clarendon Press.

Morford, Mark P. O., and Robert J. Lenardon. 1999. *Classical Mythology*. 6th ed. New York: Longman.

Najder, Zdzisław, ed. 1964. *Conrad's Polish Background: Letters to and from Polish Friends*. Translated by Halina Carroll. London: Oxford University Press.

Najder, Zdzisław. 2007. *Joseph Conrad: A Life*. Translated by Halina Najder. Rochester: Camden House.

A Naval Encyclopaedia: Comprising A Dictionary of Nautical Words and Phrases; Biographical Notices, and Records of Naval Officers; Special Articles on Naval Art and Science, Written Expressly for this Work By Officers and Others of Recognized Authority in the Branches Treated by Them. Together with Descriptions of the Principal Naval Stations and Seaports of the World. Complete in One Volume. 1881. Philadelphia: L. R. Hamersley.

Newman, James L. 2004. *Imperial Footprints: Henry Morton Stanley's African Journeys*. Washington, D.C.: Potomac Books.

Pakenham, Thomas. 2003. *The Scramble for Africa: White Man's Conquest of the Dark Continent from 1876 to 1912.* New York: Perennial.

Peters, John G. 2006. *The Cambridge Introduction to Joseph Conrad*. Cambridge: Cambridge University Press.

Ritter, Paul. 1936. *Kolonien im deutschen Schrifttum: eine Übersicht über deutsches koloniales Schrifttum unter Berücksichtigung nur volksdeutscher Autoren*. Berlin: Die Brücke zur Heimat.

Sherry, Norman. 1971. *Conrad's Western World.* Cambridge: Cambridge University Press.

Simmons, Allan H. 2002. "The Language of Atrocity: Representing the Congo of Conrad and Casement." In *Conrad in Africa: New Essays on "Heart of Darkness,"* edited by Attie de Lange and Gail Fincham, with Wiesław Krajka, 85–106. Boulder, CO: Social Science Monographs.

Simmons, Allan H. 2007. *Conrad's* Heart of Darkness: *A Reader's Guide*. London: Continuum.

Simmons, Allan H. 2014a. "Africa." In *Joseph Conrad in Context,* edited by Allan H. Simmons, 109–16. Cambridge: Cambridge University Press.

Simmons, Allan H. 2014b. "Nationalism and Empire." In *Conrad in Context,* edited by Allan H. Simmons, 187–94. Cambridge: Cambridge University Press.

Simmons, Allan H. 2015. "Reading *Heart of Darkness*." In *The New Cambridge Companion to Joseph Conrad*, edited by J. H. Stape, 15–28. Cambridge: Cambridge University Press.

Simpson, John, and Jennifer Speake. 2008. *The Oxford Dictionary of Proverbs*. Oxford: Oxford University Press. http://www.oxfordreference.com/view/10.1093/acref/9780199539536.001.0001/acref-9780199539536-e-2111?rskey=yWtZsq&result=1608.

Smyth, Admiral W. H. 1867. *The Sailor's Word Book: An Alphabetical Digest of Nautical Terms, Including Some More Especially Military and Scientific, but Useful to Seamen; As Well as Archaisms of Early Voyagers, Etc.* London: Blackie and Son.

Société de Géographie de Toulouse. 1892. *État Indépendant du Congo*. University of Illinois at Urbana-Champaign Library. https://digital.library.illinois.edu/items/3f387b60-e946-0133-1d3d-0050569601ca-2.

Stanley, Henry M. 1878. *Through the Dark Continent: Or The Sources of the Nile Around the Great Lakes of Equatorial Africa and Down the Livingstone River to the Atlantic Ocean*. London: Sampson Low, Marston, Searle & Rivington.

Stanley, Henry M. 1885. *The Congo and the Founding of Its Free State: A Story of Work and Exploration.* 2 vols. New York: Harper & Brothers.

Stanley, Henry M. 1890. *In Darkest Africa: Or the Quest Rescue and Retreat of Emin; Governor of Equatoria.* 2 vols. London: Sampson Low, Marston, Searle and Rivington.

Stape, J. H. 2004. "'The Dark Places of the Earth': Text and Context in 'Heart of Darkness.'" *The Conradian* 29 (1): 144–61. http://www.jstor.org/stable /20873518.

Stape, J. H. 2010. "Setting Out for Brussels: Conrad and the 'Sepulchral City.'" *The Conradian* 35 (2): 97–116.

Stape, J.H., and Ernest W. Sullivan II. 2002. "The Heinemann Collected Edition of *Lord Jim*: An Unauthoritatative Text." *The Conradian* 27 (1): 72–87. http://www.jstor.org/stable/20874206

Stape, J. H., and Owen Knowles. 2006. "Marlow's Audience in 'Youth' and 'Heart of Darkness': A Historical Note." *The Conradian* 31 (1): 104–16.

Stinglhamber, Gustave, and Paul Dresse. 1945. *Léopold II au Travail.* Brussels: Éditions du Sablon.

Troup, John Rose. 1890. *With Stanley's Rear Column.* 2nd ed. London: Chapman and Hall.

United Kingdom. Admiralty. 1887. *North Sea Pilot. Part IV: Rivers Thames and Medway, and the Shores of the North Sea from Calais to the Skaw.* 4th ed. London: Hydrographic Office.

Verner, S. P. 1903. *Pioneering in Central Africa.* Richmond, VA: Presbyterian Committee of Publication.

Watt, Ian. 1980. *Conrad in the Nineteenth Century.* London: Chatto & Windus.

Watts, Cedric. 1983. "'A Bloody Racist': About Achebe's View of Conrad." *Yearbook of English Studies* 13: 196–209.

White, James P. 1967. "The Sanford Exploring Expedition." *The Journal of African History* 8 (2): 291–302. doi: https://doi.org/10.1017/S0021853700007064.

Williams, George W. 1890a. George W. Williams to Leopold II, Stanley Falls, 18 July. Widener Library, Harvard University. http://nrs.harvard.edu/urn-3 :FHCL:8290213.

Williams, George W. 1890b. *[A Report Upon the Congo-State and Country] to the President of the Republic of the United States of America.* St. Paul de Loanda. http://hdl.handle.net/2027/uc2.ark:/13960/t6rx9539r.

Wissmann, Hermann von. 1891. *My Second Journey through Equatorial Africa: From the Congo to the Zambesi; In the Years 1886 and 1887.* London: Chatto & Windus.

Zuylen, Pierre van. 1959. *L'échiquier congolais ou le secret du roi.* Brussels: Charles Dessart.

Index

Page numbers followed by *f* indicate figures and n indicate footnotes.

Abyssinia, 16
Achebe, Chinua, 32, 36
Affairs of West Africa, 31
Africa: establishment of colonies, 14–23; exploration, 2, 14–19; trade, precolonial, 16
Allen, James Smith, 38
Allen, Jerry, 73n94
Alston, Alfred Henry, 101n136
Amazon River and basin, 14, 40
Angola, 14, 16
Anthon, Charles, 50n32
Anti-Slavery Conference, 22, 136n182
Antislavery Society of Belgium, 114n162
Antwerp, 24–25, 62n67
Apocalypse Now, 11
Arabian Peninsula, 17
Arendt, Hannah, 32, 73n94
Argentina, 16
Arnold, J. A., 101n136
Arthur, Chester A., 20
atrocities, ix–x, 18*f*, 26, 28, 29, 39–40, 41, 73n94, 114n162, 124n171, 137n186

Baerdemaecker, G. C. de, 5, 55n47
Bakongo (tribe), 155
Bakuti (tribe), 18*f*
Banana Point, 62n67, 120n169
Bangala (station), 8, 94n128, 135n180, 138n188

Bangala (tribe), 96n130, 104n143, 105n145
Bannister, Robert C., 63n69
Basoko, 94n128, 125n172
Barttelot, Edmund, 73n94
Bateke (tribe), 67n81
Belgian Limited Company for Trade in the Upper Congo. *See* Société Anonyme Belge pour le Commerce du Haut-Congo
Bentley, W. Holman, 158n18, 160
Berdyczów, 1
beri-beri, 69n86
Berlin Conference (West Africa Conference), 20–21, 32
Blackwood, William, 147
Blackwood's Edinburgh Magazine, 9, 30, 147
Bobrowski, Tadeusz, 3, 6, 59n60, 154
Boer War, 28, 34
Bolenge (Equator Station), 18*f*, 97*f*
Boma: appearance, 66*f*; Casement, Roger in, 154n4; Congo Free State seat of government, 6, 21, 35, 54*f*, 64n74, 65*f*, 75*f*, 154n6; Conrad in (*see* Conrad, Joseph, in Boma); description, 64n74, 65*f*; map, 54*f*, 65*f*, 75*f*; fact vs. fiction, 35, 64n74, 65*f*; suicide at, 67n79
Bontinck, François, 126n174
Booth, William, 49n28

Bordeaux, 6, 57n52, 62n67, 74n96, 76n102, 154n8
Borneo, 7, 9
Boyoma Falls. *See* Stanley Falls
Brantlinger, Patrick, 32, 63n69
Brassey, Thomas, 4
Brazil, 16
Brazzaville, 77n105
British Merchant Service, 3–5, 7
Brourke, G. W., 75n97
Bruce, James, 2
Brussels, 57n53; Anti-Slavery Conference, 22, 136n182; Congo Free State administration, 21; Conrad in (*see* Conrad, Joseph, in Brussels); International African Association headquarters, 18; *Le Mouvement Géographique*, 69n86
Büchler, Max, 24, 71n91
Burton, Richard, 2, 14

cannibalism, 28, 96n130, 104n143, 106n146, 124n171
Cão, Diogo, 14
Caravan route (Matadi to Kinshasa), 8, 26, 54*f*, 68n82, 140n189, 153–162; Bakongo as porters, 155n10; Conrad on (*see* Conrad, Joseph, on caravan route); description, 75n97; map, 54*f*, 75*f*; suicide on, 67n79
cargoes and world trade, 4–5
Carlyle, Thomas, 60n63
Casement, Roger, 31, 34, 73n94, 154; report on the Congo, 31, 36, 73n94, 154n4
cassava, 16, 105n145, 118n165, 157
Century Magazine, 73n94, 124n171
Champel-les-Bains, 7, 140n190
Chandler, Tertius, 45n10
Chapaux, Albert, 65*f*, 117*f*, 118n165, 137n186
Chapman lighthouse, 48
Chernikhiv, 2
chicotte, 26, 26*f*, 28
Christianity, 17, 19, 20, 49n28, 61n65
Classis, 50n33
colonialism, 4–5, 34–35, 41, 49n29–51n36, 53n42, 60n64

Comber, Annie, 159
Comber, Percy E., 159n19
Commission for the Protection of the Natives, 28, 114n162
Committee for Studies of the Upper Congo, 20
Compagnie du Chemin de Fer du Congo. *See* railway
Compagnie du Congo pour le Commerce et l'Industrie, 90n123
Congo (region), 16–17; agriculture, 16, 105n145, 118n165, 157; Bakongo (tribe), 155; Bakuti (tribe), 18*f*; Bangala (tribe), 96n130, 104n143, 105n145; Bateke (tribe), 67n81, Congo Arab control, 109n157; cultures, 17; exploration, 17–19, 90n123; Kingdom of the Kongo, 14; languages, 17; Manyema (tribe), 73n94; religion 17; trade networks, 16
"The Congo Diary," xi, xiii, 153–162; comparison with *Heart of Darkness*, xi, xiii, 37, 153; composition and contents, 8, 67n81, 153, 162n26; publication, 153
Congo Free State, 30–31, 36, 54*f*, 64n74, 77n105; abuses, 25–26, 28–29; administration, 21–23; currency (*mitako*), 25, 56n49, 71n90, 73n94, 105n144; establishment, 5, 21; finances, 21, 24; ivory trade, 24–25, 25*f*; map, 54*f*; rubber trade, 27–28; slave trade, 21–22; trade imbalance, 28, 31–31; transfer to Belgian government, 31*f*, 32, 33*f*. *See also* labor; railway
Congo protest resolution, 31
Congo Reform Association, 30*f*, 31
Congo River, 5, 6, 7, 8, 14, 19, 20, 21, 24, 26, 34, 98*f*, 153; cataracts at Stanley Falls, 118n165; cataracts on the Lower Congo, 6, 14, 22, 23, 26, 54*f*, 68n82; characteristics, 14, 22, 94n128, 107n147, 108n149, 109n156, 117*f*, 118n165; exploration, 14, 15, 19, 53n44; fact vs. fiction, 35, 94n128;

map, 54*f*, 75*f*; river traffic, 94n128; settlements, 94n128; source, 15; trade networks, 16

Conrad, Borys, 8, 9

Conrad, Jessie, 8

Conrad, John, 8

Conrad, Joseph, 1–14, 29–30, 32–41, 44–162; appearance, 10*f* (photo), 11; in Bangala, 8, 94n128, 135n180, 138n188; birth and upbringing, 1–3; in Boma, 6, 62n67, 64n74, 65n76, 65*f*, 140n189; British Merchant Service voyages, 3–5, 7; in Brussels, 5–6, 7, 57n52, 140n190, 140n192, 143n193; on caravan route, 74n96, 76n101, 77n104, 77n105, 81n112, 153–162; citizenship, 3, 4; collaborations, 9; colonialism and imperialism, 11, 29, 34–35, 41, 53n42, 60n64, 148; commercial success, 9; death, 9; education, 2; in Equator Station, 97*f*; examinations (merchant marine), 10; finances, 9; French Merchant Marine voyages, 3; geography, interest in, 2, 41, 53n42; homes in adulthood, 8–9; homes in boyhood, 1, 2; illnesses, 7, 9, 77n105, 138n188, 140n189, 140n190, 158, 162; in Kinshasa, 6–7, 65n75, 73n94, 75*f*, 76n102, 77n105, 78*f*, 78n106, 79*f*, 79n109, 90n123, 93n127, 135n180, 139n189, 140n189, 153, 162n26; languages, 2–3, 11, 33; in Léopoldville, 7, 73n94, 140n189; letters to Marguerite Poradowska, 6, 55n47, 72n92, 80n110, 81n112, 138n188, 139n189, 154; literary prize, 9; in London, 3–5, 6, 7, 57n52, 140n190, 143n193; in Manyanga, 77n105, 81n112, 158–159; marriage and family, 8–9; in Matadi, 6, 7, 8, 31, 65*f*, 65n76, 67n80, 67n81, 72n92, 73n94, 74n96, 75*f*, 77n105, 78*f*, 81n112, 140n189, 143n193, 153–154; race and ethnicity, 10–11, 32–34, 63n69;

reading, 2, 73n94, 124n171; recuperation, 7, 45n1, 140n190; in Stanley Falls, 6–7, 53n42, 78*f*, 90n123, 93n127, 107n147, 117*f*, 125n172, 135n180; at Stanley Pool, 8; writing, 2, 7–11. Ships: *Narcissus*, 4, 8; *Otago*, 4, 5, 52n41, 154n7; other ships, 3–4, 7. *See also Florida*; *Roi des Belges*. Works: *Almayer's Folly*, 7, 8, 11; *Chance*, 9; *The End of the Tether*, 9, 147, 149; "Falk," 106n146; "Geography and Some Explorers," 2, 41, 53n42; *Lord Jim*, 9, 11, 147; *The Nigger of the "Narcissus,"* 8, 147; *Nostromo*, 9, 147; *An Outcast of the Islands*, 8, 11; "An Outpost of Progress," 8, 29, 60n64, 148; *A Personal Record*, 2, 7, 10, 40, 53n42, 140n189; *The Rescue*, 11; *The Secret Agent*, 9; *Tales of Unrest*, 9; *Under Western Eyes*, 10; *Victory*, 10; "Youth," 9, 147–149; *Youth: A Narrative and Two Other Stories*, 30, 147; *Youth and Two Other Stories*, 30, 147. *See also* "The Congo Diary"; *Heart of Darkness*; "Up-river book"

Cooper, James Fenimore, 3

Coppola, Francis Ford, 11

Cornet, René, 68n83

Cornewall-Jones, R. J., 4

Cracow, 2

Crane, Stephen, 9

craniology, 59n60

Cunningham, Valentine, 88n122

Curle, Richard, 147n195, 153

currency, Congo Free State, 25, 56n49, 71n90, 73n94, 105n144

Dahomey, 23, 63n70

Darwin, Charles, 48n27, 63n69, 115n163

Davies, Laurence, 48n27

Davis, Philip, 160

Deal, 76

delayed decoding, 40–41

Delcommune, Alexandre, 87*f*, 90n123, 91n124, 94n128, 129n176, 139n189

Delcommune, Camille, 78n107, 79n108, 80n110, 81n112, 96n131, 138n188, 139n189
Deptford, 47
Dickens, Charles, 2
diseases, 14, 16, 22, 69n86, 70n87, 125n172; beri-beri, 69n86; dysentery, 7, 60n62, 69n86, 72n94, 125n172, 138n188; elephantiasis, 22; fevers, 7, 60n62, 69n86, 77n105, 138n188, 161; Guinea threadworm, 22; malaria, 7, 14, 22, 140n190; river blindness, 22; schistosomiasis, 22; sleeping sickness, 22; smallpox, 69n86; yellow fever, 14, 22
Doyle, Arthur Conan, 32
Drake, Francis, 47
Dresse, Paul, 126n174
Duignan, Peter, 16–17, 22–26, 28, 32, 61n65, 69n84, 69n85, 69n86, 114n162
Dunlop, John, 27
Dutch African Trading Company, 77n105, 120n169, 120n170
dysentery, 7, 60n62, 69n86, 72n94, 125n172, 138n188

Eaglestone, Robert, 38
East India Company, 48
E. D. Morel's History of the Congo Reform Movement, 28, 32, 33*f*
Elder Dempster, 30–31
elephantiasis, 22
Emin Pasha (Eduard Schnitzer), 5, 72n94
Equator Station, 18*f*, 97*f*
Erebus, 47
Erith, 47
État Indépendant du Congo. *See* Congo Free State
Ethiopia, 2, 20
evolution, 63n69, 115n163

Fates, 57n55
fevers, 7, 60n62, 69n86, 77n105, 138n188, 161

fiction, uses of, x, xiii, 11–12, 35–41
Fiji, 16
Firchow, Peter, 32–35, 36, 37, 47n17, 51n36, 56n50, 63n69, 68n82, 73n94, 99n132, 100n133, 124n171
Fleishman, Avrom, 35
Florida, 6, 56n49, 57n52, 65n75, 79n108, 90n123; grounding, 78n106, 160n23, 160n23; salvage, 79n109
Force Publique, 73n94, 76n100; activities 69n84; appearance, 23*f*; creation, 23; discipline, 69n85; officers, 23, 73n94, 84n119; in Stanley Falls, 118n165
Ford, Ford Madox, 9
Ford, Jane, 73n94
Formosa, 16
Fox, Gerald, 45n10
Franklin, John, 47
Freiesleben, Johannes, 6, 56n49, 56n51, 57n52, 79n108
French Merchant Marine, 3
Froud, A. G., 154
Furies, 128n175

Gann, Lewis H., 16–17, 22–26, 28, 32, 61n65, 69n84, 69n85, 69n86, 114n162
Garnett, Edward, 7, 13, 138n188
Geneva, 7, 10, 140n190
Geographical Conference, 17–19
George, Jessie. *See* Conrad, Jessie
German East Africa Company, 73n94
Glave, Edward James, 23, 64n74, 65*f*, 67n81, 75n97, 77n105, 79*f*, 155n10; model for Kurtz, 73n94
Goffin, Louis, 23, 69n86, 70n87
GoGwilt, Christopher, xii, 36, 39
Gold Coast, 23
Golden Hind, 47
Gondola, Ch. Didier, 90n123
Goodyear, Charles, 27
Gordon, Charles George, 72n94
Gosse, Joseph-Louis-Hubert, 72n92, 153–154
Gossens, 96n131

Grand Bassam, 62
Grand Popo, 62n67, 62n68, 63n70
Gravesend, 45, 76
Greenwich, 47
Greenwich Observatory, 9–10, 47n20
Grenfell, George, 134n179, 135*f*
Greshoff, Antoine, 120n170
Griffith, Anselm, 101n136
Guerard, Albert, 36, 73n94
Guinea threadworm, 22

Haiti, 10
Harou, Prosper, 74n96, 76n102,
    77n105, 154–155, 158, 159,
    161–162
Hatton & Cookson, 154
Hausa (tribe), 23, 64n74
Hawkins, Hunt, 32, 36
Hay, Eloise Knapp, 101n136
Heart of Darkness, ix–xiv, 44–149;
    classroom use of, x–xii;
    comparison with "The Congo
    Diary," xi, xiii, 37, 153;
    composition, 8, 9, 29, 73n94,
    138n188, 148–149; as fiction,
    11–12, 32, 35–41, 148–149; as
    history, ix-xii, xiii, 11–12, 13–14,
    32–33, 35–41, 148–149; influence,
    11, 39–40; manuscript, 29, 64n74,
    72n94, 101n136, 126n173,
    136n184; publication, xi, 9, 30, 32,
    147n195; reception and reviews,
    xi-xii, 9, 30, 32, 39–40, 148; study
    resources, xii; themes, ix-x. *See also*
    Conrad, Joseph
Heidegger, Martin, 38
Heyn, Reginald, 77n105, 81n112, 158
Hobson, J. A., 35
Hochschild, Adam, xii, 15–17, 19–22,
    24–30, 36, 64n74, 68n83, 73n94,
    84n119, 114n162, 124n171,
    126n174, 136n182
Hodister, Arthur, 72n94, 114n162,
    120n170, 124n171, 137n186
Holland, 120n169
Hope, G. F. W, 7, 8–9, 45n1, 46n11,
    154
Hugo, Victor, 2

Huntley & Palmers, 88
Huxley, T. H., 63n69

imperialism, 3, 4–5, 11, 29, 34–35, 41,
    49n29–51n36, 53n42
Imperialism: A Study, 35
Ingham, Charles E., 155
International African Association, 18,
    20, 21
International Association of the
    Congo, 20, 21
ivory: Conrad packing, 154;
    Delcommune, Camille, 80n110;
    description and uses, 24; "fossil,"
    24–25, 113n160; Hodister, Arthur,
    72n94; Kinshasa, 77n105, 78*f*;
    Stanley Falls, 117*f*, 118n165,
    129n176; Stokes, Charles Henry,
    73n94, 92n126; trade, 8, 16, 24–25,
    25*f*, 27, 28, 54*f*, 67n81, 71n91,
    77n105, 92n126, 117*f*, 118n165,
    129n176, 154

Jaeger, 77n105, 158
James, Henry, 9
Janssen, Camille, 73n94
Jean-Aubry, G., 13, 37, 72n94,
    77n105, 80n110, 158n17
Jenssen-Tusch, H., 67n79, 134n178
Johnston, Harry, 26*f*, 75*f*, 79*f*, 95*f*,
    96n130, 105n145, 109n156,
    134n179, 157n16
Julius Caesar, 49n29–50n31, 76n98

Kasai River expedition, 139n189
Katanga, 90n123
Katanga Expedition, 90n123
Kaye, John William, 48n23
Kazimierówka, 57n52
Keen, William Brock, 46n14
Keyaerts, Alphonse, 96n131,
    103n140
King Leopold's Rule in Africa, 23*f*,
    30*f*, 31, 32, 40
Kinshasa, 74n95, 77n105; appearance,
    78*f*; brickmaking at, 83n115;
    caravan route, 6, 54*f*, 75*f*, 153;
    Conrad in (*see* Conrad, Joseph, in

Kinshasa); fire at, 82n113; *Florida* at, 65n75, 79n108; Katanga Expedition, 90n123; map, 54*f*, 75*f*, 79*f*; railway, 79*f*; Société Anonyme Belge center, 54*f*, 77n105, 78*f*; steamers at, 68n82, 78n106, 79*f*, 160n23

Kirkaldy, Adam W., 4

Kirschner, Paul, 10

Kisangani. *See* Stanley Falls

Klein, Georges Antoine: death, 7, 138n187, 143n193; illness, 125n172, 138n187; model for Kurtz, 35, 72n94, 109n157, 126n173, 135n181, 140n191–140n192; on the *Roi des Belges*, 7, 138n187

Knowles, Owen, xii, 2–4, 6–10, 45n1, 46n11, 46n14, 55n47, 126n173, 140n190, 154n7

Koch, Ludwig Rasmus, 6, 96n131, 138n188

Kongo, Kingdom of the, 14

Kopernicki, Izydor, 59n60

Korzeniowska, Ewa (née Bobrowka), 2

Korzeniowski, Apollo, 1–2

Korzeniowski, Józef. *See* Conrad, Joseph

Kurtz, models for, 35, 55n48, 72n94, 84n119, 109n157, 114n161, 114n162, 124n171, 126n173, 126n174

labor, 26–28, 68n83, 69n86, 70n87, 70n88, 71n90, 75n97

Larabee, Mark D., 4–5, 101n136

Lavigerie, Charles, 114n162

Leclerq, Louis, 73n94

Le Congo Illustré, 55n48

Lefebve de Vivy, Léon, 17

Le Mouvement Géographique, 55n48, 69n86, 82n113, 83n115, 93n127, 94n128, 109n157, 118n165, 120n169, 137n186

Lenardon, Robert J., 128n175

Leopold II, 5, 15–36, 29*f*, 30*f*, 126n174; Anti-Slavery Conference, 22; Commission for the Protection of the Natives, 28, 114n162; Committee for Studies of the Upper Congo, 20; criticism of, 28–32; establishment of Congo Free State, 21–23; forced labor, 68n83; Geographical Conference, 17–19; interest in colonies, 15–21, 126n174; International African Association, 18, 20, 21; International Association of the Congo, 20, 21; ivory trade, 24–25; model for Kurtz, 73n94, 126n174; rubber trade, 27; Sanford Exploring Expedition, 90n123; slave trade, 17, 19, 21–22; and Stanley, Henry Morton, 17, 19, 60n63, 126n174, 136n182; West Africa Conference, 20–21

Léopoldville: Congo Free State central supply station, 54*f*, 77n105; Conrad in, 7, 73n94, 140n189; map, 54*f*, 75*f*, 79*f*; railway, 54*f*, 75*f*, 79*f*, 153n2; steamers at, 22, 68n82, 77n105, 79*f*

Lesseps, Ferdinand de, 19

Liberia, 20

Little Popo, 62

Liverpool, 24, 30, 154n5

Livingstone, David, 14, 15, 17, 21, 41, 53n42

London: Conrad's departure for the Congo, 6, 57n52; Conrad's hospitalization, 140n190; Conrad's return from the Congo, 7, 143n193; Conrad's voyages, 3–5; ivory trade, 24; population, 45n10; in *The Secret Agent*, 10

Lualaba River, 15

Lublin, 57n52

Lwów, 2

Madagascar, 17

malaria, 7, 14, 22, 140n190

manioc (cassava), 16, 105n145, 118n165, 157

Manyanga, 67n81, 77n105, 81n112, 157, 158, 159

Manyema (tribe), 73n94

Marryat, Frederick, 3
Marseilles, 3, 136n182
Matadi: caravan route, 26, 54*f*, 67n81, 75*f*, 81n112, 153; Casement, Roger in, 31, 73n94; Conrad in (*see* Conrad, Joseph, in Matadi); description, 67n81; Leopold's rights to, 20; map, 54*f*, 75*f*; railway, 23, 26, 31, 54*f*, 68n82, 75*f*, 153n2, 154n4; Société Anonyme Belge station, 54*f*, 67n81, 72n92, 75*f*, 153n2; steamers at, 66n77, 67n80, 67n81, 68n82
medicine, advances in, 22
mentalities, xi, 38
Mickiewicz, Adam, 2
Miller, J. Hillis, 36
missionaries, 49n28; atrocities, publicizing, 28–29; Bentley, W. Holman, 160; Comber, Annie, and Percy E., 159; Congo Free State, 22, 61n65, 94n128; Davis, Philip, 160; Geographical Conference, 18; Ingham, Charles E., 155; Leopold sponsors, 21; Livingstone, David, 14, 15, 17, 21, 41, 53n42; Stokes, Charles Henry, 73n94, 92n126; Tchumbiri mission, 56n49, 72n94, 138n187
mitako (currency), 25, 56n49, 71n90, 73n94, 105n144
Moore, Gene M., xii, 2–4, 8, 9, 10, 55n47, 126n173, 154n7
Morel, Edmund D., 23*f*, 28, 30*f*, 30–32, 33*f*, 36, 40
Morford, Mark P. O., 128n175
Moscow, 2
Mouvement Antiesclavagiste, 124n171
Munich, 3

Najder, Zdzisław, xii, 2–4, 5–7, 11, 21, 29, 35, 36, 45n1, 52n41, 55n47, 57n52, 59n60, 62n67, 64n74, 67n81, 77n105, 78n106, 81n112, 94n128, 135n180, 138n188, 143n193, 153n3, 154n4, 154n7, 158n17, 160n23

Nellie, 7, 9, 45, 46n11
Newman, James L., 126n174
New York Herald, 14, 41, 53n42
Nieuwe Afrikaansche Handels-Vennootschap (Dutch African Trading Company), 77n105, 120n169, 120n170
Niger River, 20
"nigger," 33–34, 56n50
Nile River, 14–15, 16

The Origins of Totalitarianism, 32

Pakenham, Thomas, xii, 18–22, 25*f*, 31, 31*f*, 33*f*, 72n94, 90n123, 92n126
Paraná River, 16
Park, Mungo, 2
Peary, Robert E., 53n43
Persia, 17
Peters, Carl, 73n94
Peters, John G., xii, 3
phrenology, 59n60
Poland, 1–2, 6, 10, 34, 57n52
Poradowska, Marguerite, 55n48; Conrad visits, 6, 7, 57n52, 140n190; Conrad's letters to (*see* Conrad, Joseph, letters to Marguerite Poradowska); model for Marlow's aunt, 7, 55n47, 57n52
Poradowski, Aleksander, 6, 57n52
Pramoedya Ananta Toer, 36
Proceedings of the Royal Geographical Society, 16
Punch, 30*f*, 31*f*, 33*f*
Purdy, Robins, 154
psychiatry, 59n61

race and racism, 10–11, 32–34, 47n17, 59n60, 63n69, 73n94, 99n132, 115n163
railway: Casement, Roger, 31, 154n4; construction, 23, 54*f*, 75*f*, 79*f*; 68n82, 69n86, 70n87; labor, 68n83, 69n86, 70n87; land, 20; map, 54*f*, 75*f*, 79*f*; police, 69n84; surveying, 23
Ravenna, 50
Red Rubber, 31

Ritter, Paul, 73n94

river blindness, 22

Roi des Belges, 6–7, 8, 35, 72n94, 79*f*, 90n123, 94n128, 109n157, 135n180, 138n187, 138n188, 143n193; appearance and description, 87*f*, 108n151; at Bangala, 135n180; Conrad's role, 138n188; crew and passengers, 96n131, 103n140; at Kinshasa, 135n180, 162n26; mission, 93n127, 94n128; at Stanley Falls, 135n180

Rollin, Édouard-François-Léon, 96n131

Rom, Léon, 73n94, 84n119, 124n171

Roman conquest of Britain, 49–51

Roosevelt, Theodore, 31*f*

rubber, 16, 24, 27–28, 40, 67n81

Sanford, Henry Shelton, 90n123, 126n174

Sanford Exploring Expedition, 90n123

The Saturday Review, 73n94, 124n171

schistosomiasis, 22

Schouten, 120n170

Scott, Robert Falcon, 88n122

Seignelay, 63n70

Shagerström, Captain, 79n108

Shakespeare, William, 2

Sherry, Norman, xii, 6, 35, 55n45, 56n49, 56n51, 62n67, 66n77, 67n79, 67n80, 67n81, 68n82, 69n86, 72n94, 74n96, 75n97, 76n102, 78n106, 78n107, 79n108, 79n109, 81n112, 82n113, 83n115, 90n123, 91n124, 93n127, 94n128, 96n130, 96n131, 101n136, 103n140, 104n143, 108n151, 109n157, 114n162, 118n165, 120n169, 120n170, 124n171, 125n172, 126n173, 129n176, 134n178, 135n181, 137n186, 138n187, 140n189, 140n190, 140n191, 140n192, 154n8, 160n23

Sierra Leone, 23, 58n58, 62n67, 68n83

Simmons, Allan H., xii, 11, 34, 36, 39, 40

Simpson, James L., 154

Simpson, John, 84n118

slavery, 18*f*, 114n162, 137n186; Anti-Slavery Conference, societies, and committees, 22, 114n162, 136n182; forced labor as, 26, 28, 69n86; Hodister, Arthur on, 114n162, 137n186; slave trade, 16, 17–19, 19*f*, 21–22, 28, 29, 72n94; Tippu Tip, 25*f*

sleeping sickness, 22

smallpox, 69n86

Smyth, W. H., 45n5, 45n6, 45n7, 45n8, 46n12, 104n142, 112n159, 137n185

snags, 95*f*

Social Darwinism, 48n27, 63n69, 115n163

Société Anonyme Belge pour le Commerce du Haut-Congo, 5, 55n45, 56n49, 57n52, 58n57, 60n62, 72n92, 78*f*, 79n108, 96n131; Brussels headquarters, 57n54; Dutch competition, 120n169; establishment, 5, 21, 90n123; ivory trade, 24 77n105; Kinshasa center, 54*f*, 77n105, 78*f*; Manyanga base, 77n105, 81n112, 158; Matadi station, 54*f*, 67n81, 72n92, 75*f*, 153n2; Stanley Falls factory, 117*f*, 118n165; vessels, 22–23, 66n77, 79*f*, 94n128, 104n143, 160 (*see also Florida*; *Roi des Belges*)

Société Antiesclavagiste de Belgique (Antislavery Society of Belgium), 114n162

Solvyns, Baron, 126n174

Somalia, 23

special creation, 83

Speake, Jennifer, 84n118

The Speaker, 31

Speke, John, 2, 14

Stache, Ernest-Albert-Louis-Adolphe, 160n22

Stanley, 95n129

Stanley, Henry Morton, 61n66, 66*f*, 78*f*, 97*f*, 98*f*, 120n169, 136n182; atrocities, 18*f*; Emin Pasha expedition, 5, 72n94; explorations of Central Africa, 15, 17, 19, 53n44, 60n64, 98*f*, 99n132; Huntley & Palmers biscuits, 88n122; on Leopold and policies, 60n63, 126n174; Livingstone expedition, 14, 41, 53n42; model for Kurtz, 73n94; on natives, 99n132; pictured, 15*f*; publications, 49n28; ship's whistle use, 134n179; slavery, 17, 18*f*

Stanley Falls: Conrad in (*see* Conrad, Joseph, in Stanley Falls); description, 117*f*, 118n165, 129n176; dysentery outbreak, 125n172; Emin Pasha killed near, 73n94; fact vs. fiction, 35, 108n149, 117*f*, 118n165, 129n176, 134n178; ivory trade, 25*f*, 117*f*, 118n165, 129n176; Klein, Georges Antoine in, 72n94, 125n172, 138n187; map, 54*f*, 117*f*; Rom, Léon in, 73n94, 124n171; Société Anonyme Belge station, 54*f*, 117*f*, 118n165, 124n171; Williams, George Washington in, 28

Stanley Pool: caravan route, 26, 75n97, 153; Conrad at, 8; *Florida* at, 78n106; map, 54*f*, 79*f*; native traders at, 67n81; railway, 23, 79*f*; steamers at, 79*f*, 160

Stape, J. H., 45n1, 46n11, 46n14, 49n28, 55n47, 55n48, 57n54, 147n195, 154n7

steam propulsion, 22

Stinglhamber, Gustave, 126n174

Stokes, Charles Henry, 28, 73n94, 92n126

Sudan, 2, 5, 72n94

Suetonius, 59n59

Suez Canal, 4, 5, 19

Sullivan, Ernest W., II, 147n195

Switzerland, 3, 7, 10, 140n190

Tambov, 120

Tanganyika, Lake, 2, 14, 15, 53n42

Tchumbiri, 56n49, 56n51, 72n94, 94n128, 138n187

technology, advances in, 22, 68n82

Terror, 47

Thames, River, 9, 45–48

"three Cs," 17, 20, 21

Thys, Albert, 5, 6, 55n47, 57n52, 58n57

Times (London), 20, 29, 124n171

Tinmouth, Nicholas, 101n136

Tip, Tippu, 25*f*

Tjulin, Axel, 66n77

Towson, John Thomas, 101n136

tribes, Congolese. *See* Congo (region)

Troup, John Rose, 71n90, 95n129

Ukraine, 1, 2, 6, 57n52

"Up-river book," 8, 95n129, 153, 162n26

Uruguay River, 16

Van der Heyden, 96n131

Van Kerckhoven, Guillaume, 73n94

Verner, S. P., 96n130

Victoria, Lake, 2, 14

Vienna, 3

Vietnam War, 11

Ville de Bruxelles, 93n127

Ville de Maceio, 6, 57n52, 58n58, 62n67, 62n68, 68n82, 74n96, 76n102, 154n8

Vologda, 2

Voulet, Paul, 73n94

Waliszewski, Kazimierz, 34, 63n70, 73n94, 114n161

Wallace, Alfred, 63n69

Warsaw, 1, 57n52

Wass, Captain, 67n79

Watt, Ian, 36, 40, 41–41, 72n94

Watts, Cedric, 32

Wauters, Alphonse-Jules-Marie, 55n48

weaponry, advances in, 22

Wells, H. G., 9
West Africa Conference,
　20–21, 32
West African Mail, 31
whistle, ship's, 134n179, 135*f*
White, James P., 90n123
Williams, George Washington, 28,
　70n88, 71n90, 76n100
Winchester, D. F., 103n141

Wissmann, Hermann von, 19*f*,
　134n179, 135*f*

Yanga, 124n171
yellow fever, 14, 22

Zanzibar, 14, 17, 23, 24, 25*f*, 68n83,
　76n100, 155, 161
Zuylen, Pierre van, 126n174

About the Editor

Mark D. Larabee, PhD, is formerly associate professor of English at the U.S. Naval Academy. He is the author of *Front Lines of Modernism: Remapping the Great War in British Fiction* and numerous articles on Joseph Conrad and other authors, including contributions to the books *Conrad and Nature, A Historical Guide to Joseph Conrad, Approaches to Teaching Conrad's "Heart of Darkness" and "The Secret Sharer,"* and *Joseph Conrad: The Short Fiction.* His writing and research have won national awards, including the Bruce Harkness Young Conrad Scholar Award from the Joseph Conrad Society of America and an award from the College English Association. Larabee received the Naval Academy's first-ever Military Professor Teaching Excellence Award. He has served as a regional delegate to the Modern Language Association, is active in the Joseph Conrad Society of America, and is the executive editor of *Joseph Conrad Today,* the official publication of the Joseph Conrad Society of America.

Milton Keynes UK
Ingram Content Group UK Ltd.
UKHW021507011024
449090UK00004B/59